LIBRARY
ST. MARYS SEMINARY JUNIOR COLLEGE

# Why We Behave Like Americans

# Books by Bradford Smith

*Biography*
BRADFORD OF PLYMOUTH
CAPTAIN JOHN SMITH

*Social History*
AMERICANS FROM JAPAN
A DANGEROUS FREEDOM
YANKEES IN PARADISE
WHY WE BEHAVE LIKE AMERICANS

*Novels*
TO THE MOUNTAIN
THIS SOLID FLESH
AMERICAN QUEST
THE ARMS ARE FAIR

*For Young Readers*
WILLIAM BRADFORD—PILGRIM BOY
DANIEL WEBSTER—UNION BOY
STEPHEN DECATUR—GALLANT BOY
ROGERS' RANGERS AND THE FRENCH AND INDIAN WAR
WITH SWORD AND PEN (ADVENTURES OF
CAPTAIN JOHN SMITH)
THE ISLANDS OF HAWAII

*Editor*
A HANDBOOK OF ENGLISH AND AMERICAN LITERATURE
THE STORY OF JESUS

# Why We Behave Like Americans

BRADFORD SMITH

*assisted by*

MARION COLLINS SMITH

J. B. LIPPINCOTT COMPANY
*Philadelphia and New York*

COPYRIGHT © 1957 BY BRADFORD SMITH
SECOND IMPRESSION
PRINTED IN THE UNITED STATES OF AMERICA
LIBRARY OF CONGRESS CATALOG CARD NUMBER 57-11954

# ACKNOWLEDGMENT

Each of the following friends and colleagues has kindly read and criticized a portion of the manuscript: Clyde Brion Davis; Dean Robert D. Leigh and Professors William Mitchell and David Truman of Columbia University; Dean Thomas Brockway and Lucien Hanks, Howard P. Smith and Martin Trow of Bennington College; Horst Mendershausen of the Rand Corporation of Santa Monica; Professor Dominic Rotunda of Mills College and Professor John Vincent of the University of California (Los Angeles). I am deeply indebted to the Huntington Hartford Foundation, Pacific Palisades, California, for a residential fellowship during the course of which the book was written.

# CONTENTS

# Why We Behave Like Americans

# CHAPTER ONE

---

# *The Culture Concept*

Every civilization is an experiment, and survival is its test. The United States of America differs from most civilizations in having been from the very beginning a conscious experiment. The tiny religious communities of Plymouth and Boston, the Continental Congress, the federal government established by the Constitution, Jacksonian democracy, Teddy Roosevelt's Square Deal, Franklin Roosevelt's New Deal, the Marshall Plan, the Truman Doctrine—all were hopefully pragmatic, consciously experimental.

The new conditions Europeans faced when they came to America forced them to try new things. The Pilgrims failed at farming until they learned from their Indian friend Squanto that they must put fish in every hill of corn to fertilize it, and until they let every man produce for himself instead of for the common store. William Bradford, in his fascinating account of the first years at Plymouth, tells of failure after failure while he and his companions were learning the ways of the wilderness. Several English settlements had perished or given up entirely before the men of Jamestown and Plymouth finally learned how to survive.

So Americans * had to learn from the beginning to accept new ideas, to try and fail and try again.

Lincoln, in the noblest of his addresses, and in words that stir every American to the core, expressed the essence of the American idea as an experiment "dedicated to the proposition that all men

---

* At the risk of offending other nationals who are equally entitled to be called Americans, it seems necessary to keep to the usage which, in the English language at least, designates a citizen of the United States as an American and uses the adjective to avoid the inadmissible alternative, United Statesian.

are created equal." The Civil War, he said, was a test to show "whether any nation so conceived and so dedicated can long endure."

Yet Americans have, as a rule, little understanding of the meaning of their own culture, while our friends overseas have even less. Much is known, but little is understood. The surface manifestations of our life are widely recognized—the proliferation of material goods, the strength of our industrial and military establishments, the importance we attach to business and private enterprise, the swank of our women, the dominance of our children. But little is known of the spirit which sustains these things. Those who observe American behavior and institutions often stop with what they see on the surface, praising or condemning without understanding the historic or cultural bass on which the melody is built.

Another stumbling block is to label "American" all the traits observed in an individual. The alleged materialism of Americans, for instance, may simply be a universal middle-class phenomenon, since most Americans are middle-class. The American who strikes a foreign observer as aggressive, noisy, puritanical, cautious and overfed may simply be displaying the traits he gets from his occupation, his family background, his religion, his age and his wealth. Any of these attributes could be observed wherever professional background, religion or prosperity were similar.

Yet there are traits, attitudes, drives, emotions, ambitions, beliefs, loyalties, which are characteristic of Americans, and there are institutions, groups, associations, functions which are characteristic of American society. The key to understanding them is the culture concept.

### What is Culture?

A culture is the way of life of any society, including its artifacts, beliefs, accumulated knowledge, and the system of values by which its members live. Also the arts, family life, child rearing, customs of marriage and courtship, education, occupations, government—in short the total effective legacy of the society which is potentially available to its members.

The culture concept has the advantage of enabling us to look at the whole society, making clear the fact that one cannot understand group behavior except as a part of the culture pattern. Much that has been written about the United States in the past is inadequate because it describes certain "American" traits in isolation, and with an overtone of moral judgment, without really showing their source or fitting them into the total picture. To call any people "materialistic" or "money-loving" or "over-sexed" or "too familiar" is to impose a moral judgment without bothering to understand the background.

The individuals who make up a society are classified and organized in several ways. Each member has a place in the age-sex system, in the prestige series, in the system of specialized occupations, in his family, and in various association groups—alumni, fraternities, secret orders, sports, clubs, boards of trustees. Despite these differences, all members of the society have a number of behavior patterns in common, as well as certain responses belonging to particular social groups within the society.

Culture helps determine personality. It also creates a wide variety of personalities within its boundaries. Within the range of this wide variety, national character can be recognized, since every individual within the culture is influenced by a common heritage. It is legitimate to look for national traits, then, so long as one recognizes that their source is in the culture, and not in some fancied instinct, blood or racial source.

A child born in the United States to American parents, but taken in infancy to France and raised in a French family, would grow up to be French no matter what his technical nationality might be. Similarly, a Chinese youngster raised in an American family would speak, act and think American. He would even look American, for the diet and climate would probably make him huskier, while his facial expressions would imitate those of the family which raised him. Though he would still have the Mongoloid fold and skin color of his parents, he would have the attitudes, habits and aspirations of his foster family.

To understand a people, then, we must look at their physical environment (geography, climate, natural resources, food supply, power resources and industrialization), the human influences (parents, siblings, friends, neighbors, fellow workers, teachers, police and other officials), their institutions (the family, school, church, peer groups, government, occupations), their artistic expressions, their ideology (as expressed in national or local rituals, constitutions, religions, group loyalties, ancestor-worship), and the manner in which they go about achieving the three basic needs—self-preservation, self-reproduction and self-expression.

Every culture is a web, each part woven into the other. The distinctions we make in our minds between economics and government, or between education and recreation (to pick two obvious examples) are more apparent than real. We cannot explain our economy without describing government's role in it—as taxer, regulator of interstate commerce, mediator in labor disputes and all the rest. But because of the limits of our minds, we have to break the human web, the web of culture, into its separate threads. Then we can try to see it as a whole again.

## Crossed Cultures

International exchange has become so quick and easy nowadays that we are able to have more contacts with other cultures than ever before. More than a million and a half Americans go to Europe every year. Even without leaving home we can make such contacts, since we have fifty thousand foreign students and visiting specialists among us.

This crossing of cultures is stimulating and enriching. In fact it is by such cross-breeding that civilization has advanced. Greece was fertilized by what it learned from the ancient empires of the east. Rome was brought out of barbarism by its contact with Greek culture. Northern Europe raised its civilization upon the contact with Roman culture. After the dark ages, contacts with Islam and the rediscovery of the classics brought on a new flowering throughout Europe. The United States is heir, not only to the Judaeo-Greek-Roman-European culture, but to influences from every part of the world—from Africa and Asia, from Spanish America, from the indigenous Indian culture.

Our diet includes dishes from Germany, Mexico, Japan, Italy. The Indians taught us to raise corn and squash, to eat succotash. Chinese restaurants flourish throughout the country, and every supermarket has a shelf of Chinese foods—soy sauce, noodles, chow mein—so that the housewife may serve them at home. Never mind if the result is an Americanized version of the real thing, modification is an essential part of the meeting of cultures.

We take much of our music from Italy and Germany, our painting from France, our ideas of justice from England, our popular music from African rhythms.

While the crossing of cultures is enriching, it also has its dangers. Crossed cultures can also lead to crossed signals, as when the characteristic sidewise headshake of India is taken to mean no when it means yes, or when the Japanese answers a negative question, "Didn't you go?" with "Yes"—meaning "No."

These crossed signals become more serious when they involve what we regard as discourtesies or deception.

In Japan it is thought impolite to say anything which might cause inconvenience or distress. This delicate sense of politeness and consideration often seems dishonest to forthright Americans.

The German respect for authority and rank produces a kind of politeness or deference which is discomforting to Americans who try to treat everyone with equal casualness and to pretend that no ranks exist. It even seems insincere, and therefore irritating.

From crossed signals it is an easy step to cross words and even crossed swords. In the international world we live in today it is more than ever important that we understand what these signals mean. Otherwise, the flood of foreign travel may create more animosity than friendship.

Living and traveling abroad is a delicate business. Those who lack the tools of understanding quickly lose their delight at being in strange places and grow bitterly critical. American tourists are conspicuous examples of this fault, and are well known abroad for complaining that the food, the beds, the trains are not like American food, beds and trains. Of course not! Why did they come traveling, if not to see what was different?

Yet these same Americans at home are highly sensitive to criticism of their own country. They love visitors, they love to entertain them and display the beauties and conveniences of American life. But they resent criticism. In fact there is a routine response to all criticism of America by foreigners:

"Why don't they go back where they came from, then?"

The persistence of this sort of intercultural misunderstanding suggests that one reason why people go abroad is to reassure themselves that home is best. Criticism of the new environment, therefore, is an inevitable part—and perhaps one of the more educational parts—of travel.

Criticism is also the product of homesickness, a sense of having been ripped loose from safe moorings, a fear of failure. It projects the inner feelings of the visitor upon the environment. When he says: "American food is flat and unpalatable," he really means: "I prefer Indian food. Besides, the waitress was not respectful, New Yorkers can't understand English, and if they have trouble understanding my good English accent, will I be able to make the proper impression at the university I'm going to, and pass my courses with high marks?"

As Freud released men from fear and unhappiness by making it possible for them to understand themselves and others as individuals, so the culture concept now makes it possible for men to understand that the differences which divide them into cultural groups are not as important as the underlying humanity which unites them, and that a study of these differences, and allowance made for them, will lead to harmonious international living in a world where men will be visiting distant places ever more frequently.

The life of a nation is more than its history, geography, climate, language, institutions and customs. It is in part a mystery because despite all that the social sciences have achieved, there are questions they cannot answer. Why does one people choose a rigidly class-structured way of life while its neighbor is equalitarian? Why does one people show great energy and drive while another relaxes and takes it easy? Most of the explanations usually given are far too simple to be convincing.

American culture is one of the most difficult to describe because it has so many roots, so many origins, so many contributing streams. It is not a play but a variety show, which is a characteristic form of entertainment with us. We seem to like it this way—a little of everything, thrown together with dash and vigor.

Let us try to look at this civilization as an anthropologist might look at a primitive tribe which he is studying for the first time. What is the meaning of the peculiar rites *homo Americanus* indulges in? Why the ritual dance of young couples in darkened rooms vibrating with brassy music, the mimicry of murder in the games of the young, the fascination with which young and old gape at pictures appearing in the front of a box?

Let us enter this strange land, curious and unafraid.

# CHAPTER TWO

---

## *Forth for to See*

When the sun comes up over the rim of sea, lighting the rocky coast and the offshore islands of Maine, it is still dark in California, where dawn will not come for another three hours. Between the two oceans stretches the great mass of earth, so recently, even by human standards, a wilderness, now the home of men deriving from all parts of the world, yet calling themselves a nation and a people.

Many things divide them—religion, language, skin color, occupation, tradition, climate, folkways. In the village republics of New England they still run their own affairs as they did three hundred years ago, choosing from among themselves those who for little or no pay will carry on the town's business as the voters direct them to do in the annual town meeting. Yet within an hour's drive lie great industrial cities where the influx of workers from many parts of Europe has created a very different sort of community with problems and tensions unknown in the villages.

Those who speak of American life as standardized have done most of their observing from a New York cocktail lounge. There is only one way to know the United States of America, and that is to travel across it—not by train or plane but by car, and at a leisurely pace.

Start in New England, where there are few of the new express highways and where you must slow down every five miles or so to crawl through a town whose streets were never built for the traffic that crowds them. It is unfortunate that you usually see the worst of a town from the highway—the mill houses built like packing boxes, the run-down mansions of an earlier day now serving as cheap rooming houses, the Main Street with shopfronts tacked onto ancient and ugly structures of brick or clapboard. But you are also likely to see a recent housing development. America has been on a housing spree since the end of the war, and it has changed the face of the whole land. These new houses express the temper of the times: they are informal, unpretentious, with wide window areas opening in a friendly manner upon the world. They nudge close to each other along streets that are usually curved instead of being set at cold right angles.

Somewhere near them will be a new shopping area, with its huge supermarket where the housewife picks up a carriage with a space to set the baby, and then roams the long aisles piled high with neatly packaged foods. A clerk will check her out at the cash register and another will carry her package to her car if she needs help. But she waits on herself. Labor has become too expensive a commodity to waste, wherever the customer can take care of himself. Yet there are more Americans engaged in the service trades than ever before.

Crossing from New England into New York, the traveler soon gets onto a parkway which runs through hilly country for nearly a hundred miles without stops or traffic lights or trucks. The traffic flows so smoothly that except on a weekend or at rush hour one can slip through New York City itself and westward onto the New Jersey Turnpike without stops or delays. Then a switch to the connecting Pennsylvania Turnpike will take you all the way to the Ohio border. Planned for speed, these roads are beautifully engineered, and the country they go through is neat, clean, and free of the billboards which disfigure much of the American landscape.

It is not only the turnpikes that make travel easy, though they are a blessing. Every filling station can supply a fistful of excellent maps. It is an easy matter to choose a numbered route and then follow the shields along the highway that repeat the number. If you want advice about routes in advance, you can get it free by dropping a card to an oil company.

Not only the shape of the land, but even the color of the earth changes as the car speeds west. In New Jersey it is yellow and sandy, in Pennsylvania red, then brown in Ohio, rich black in

Illinois. As varied as the earth is what the people do with it and build upon it, from the white barns with their neatly arched and painted green doors in Pennsylvania to the towering grain elevators in the west.

And everywhere the motels. Sprouting along the main highways like toadstools after a rain, they have grown better and better in their competition for tourists. Cheaper and better in the West, they offer everything from wall-to-wall carpets to free television, newspaper, ice cubes, and automatic heat. New furniture, clean and plentiful linen and hot water are taken for granted.

The crowded cities of the East are but a fringe, a coping, an eyelash to the continent beyond. The farther west you move, the smaller they seem, for this is a continent that makes cities insignificant. As the miles roll back under the whirling wheels, the face of the land keeps changing. Even Kansas, by reputation the flattest piece of unimaginative plain, is full of variety. In its black, rich-looking fields the young winter wheat rises bright and spring-green, though the time is fall. Here, beyond the Mississippi, the land spreads out to the lonely horizon, and in the whole circle of earth there are only two or three houses in view. The towns, when you come to them, are often inconspicuous and ugly, with flat-looking store-fronts and boxy houses and grain elevators towering above the spires of the churches.

In New Mexico you learn to spot a river by the clouds of dust blowing out of it. It has seen no water for months. Tumbleweed, whipped into balls, scuds across the road. Tilled fields give way to gray-brown rugged hills spotted with stunted trees. The dry earth near the road supports nothing but sage, and even that looks dead.

Arizona's strewn rocks and cliffs rising like masonry walls, its eroding pillars of stone look like a city in ruins. Now there are no trees at all, not even cactus.

Where the mountains rise or the canyons plunge deep, trees come back. In one small canyon the flora of five of the six world climates are found side by side, and a step will take you from the evergreens of northern climes to the cactus and yucca of the dry, hot desert. This is range country, where the cattle are kept off the highway by steel rails placed close together where the fences stop at the access roads. The cattle will not step on the rails.

This is the country where the skies are not cloudy all day, and the hot sun beats down on the dry earth, and the cattle search among the dried shrubs for anything that is green.

It is also the country of the great spectacles—the Grand Canyon, whose magnificence alone makes the long trip worthwhile; of the isolated Indian pueblos where life is still lived in old patterns. On the streets in town there seem to be more Indians than "Anglos"— the women in bright skirts and blouses, the men occasionally with hair cut in the old fashion and with colored strips of cloth tied around their heads. Filling stations give way to "trading posts" which stress the Indian goods they have for sale—blankets, rugs, jewelry, moccasins—rather than the gasoline.

It is only an illusion that the land is flat, for it has been rising slowly all the way from the Mississippi. In New Mexico and Arizona you are a mile above sea level, and at the Grand Canyon you are better than seven thousand feet high.

Driving even at seventy miles an hour, you wonder whether this long stretch of barren country will ever come to an end. Man has not been able to make much of a mark on this huge tablet. It is easy to drive across the country in eight or ten days if there are two drivers. Anything less is hard work. The trip will consume about two hundred gallons of gas if you add some mileage for sightseeing, several lubrications, one or two changes of oil, and thorough cleaning of the windshield at every stop, to rub off the hundreds of unfortunate insects to whom a seventy-mile-an-hour pane of glass is a trap of death. The car is expected to make the three-thousand-mile trip without faltering or failing. Americans take mechanical perfection for granted.

Where would the American be without a car? It is his horse and armor, for with it he can conquer Arthurian wildernesses and distances. The hum and surge of it are his poetry, and the bright color of its finish and the gleaming chrome are to him as beads and mirrors to a savage. The car expresses his love of the bright and beautiful; it is his badge of prosperity and the bait with which he lures and wins his woman. Its power is his strength and shield, for if boss shouts or wife nags, he has this compensation—the strength of a hundred horses waiting patiently beneath the sole of his right foot, ready to confirm his superiority over wives and bosses by putting him ahead of any stream of traffic and wafting him across great space in brief time.

To travel west, then, is to repeat America, for Americans have always been moving west. To go west is to carry on what our ancestors began.

It is also a lesson in almost every branch of learning. The soils, rivers, plains and varied mountain systems keep thrusting geography and geology before us. It is not difficult to see deer, antelope, buffalo, rabbits, prairie dogs, chipmunks and a host of other animals, each in his own appropriate area. Most of the people of Europe, as well as Mexicans, Indians and Japanese, appear somewhere on the route. Climate itself changes from the uncertain or cloudy skies of the East to the bright clear rainless weather of the West. The river systems, the relation of land resources to people, the placing of industry, the sudden appearance of oil wells on a Kansas plain—these and a thousand other items are instructive.

There are lessons to be learned too from the place names. All the way from Massachusetts to California the Indian culture has left its mark in the beautiful names of rivers—Monongahela, Susquehanna, Missouri, Mississippi, or in the names of the states themselves —Connecticut, Arkansas, Oklahoma. You pass from the English towns of the East—Boston, Hartford, New York—to the names picked out of the classics in western New York—Syracuse, Rome, Carthage, Utica. Ohio and Indiana and Illinois repeat the English names the Yankee settlers brought along with them—Springfield, Salem, and the rest. When we get into Spanish country there are Santa Fe, Albuquerque, Las Vegas, Los Angeles.

The new shapes of the western landscape require new names, too—butte, arroyo, canyon, wash, gulch.

And then, most exciting of all, comes the evidence of what man can do with the desert spaces.

In the northwestern corner of Arizona the road winds through rocky hills thrown this way and that across the landscape. Then suddenly you are plunging down again, and as you round a curve the great bulk of the Hoover Dam lies before you, impounding waters which stretch all the way back to the Grand Canyon. The dam prevents the spring floods that have washed over this dry land. It sends precious water into arid areas and makes them flower. It produces electric current enough to care for the domestic needs of 7,500,000 people. By regulating the flow of water, it makes possible the operation of still other dams downstream, where again more power can be made, and desilting and irrigation achieved.

From Hoover Dam to Las Vegas, Nevada is only twenty-five miles, but in that space you run the gamut of democracy, from the noble concept and performance of a federal project which by cooperating with local governments serves all the people, to a gambling town whose bright lights, milling crowds in the casinos, stage shows and flow of liquor gather together just about all that is tawdry and tasteless, and which then tries to hide the baseness of it in more and more glitter.

From Las Vegas it is but a few miles into California. The bulk of the continent lies behind us now, but we are not yet in the promised land, for eastern California is like Arizona or Nevada—bare, rugged mountains, cactus and sage on gray-brown desert land, and then the stunted juniper trees.

At San Bernardino the desert ends. Palms and orange groves replace the gray-green sage, the crooked arms of the Joshua tree, the deep green of the Juniper. Irrigated lawns take the place of bare earth and nature is green again.

The empty spaces are behind us now, for where nature is lush men crowd in. Traffic grows to four steady streams. One town runs into the next, with an area of orange grove and roadside markets to mark the transition. The mountains still rise rugged and rocky, but the valleys, in biblical phrase, stand so thick with corn that they laugh and sing. This is the mecca of the westward trek, the geographical end of the American adventure.

California is no longer fruit trees and green fields only, nor even the dream factory of Hollywood or the haven of strange religious cults. California is industry now—an industry so expanded that Los Angeles is the largest city (by area) in the country, has more cars than many whole states, and the biggest smog problem in the nation.

To cross this whole land is both monotonous and exciting, a chore and a challenge. There is more to be learned than one can soak up in the quick passage, for a book would not contain all that the eye takes in. But one thing is certain: the dimension of the country is a factor in any calculation about it. Its vastness contains every kind of variety—of landscape, of people, of climate, of occupation, of folkway, of speech and dress, of faith and folly, of government and crime, of magnanimity and depravity, of good and evil.

Traveling from east to west across the middle of the land catches only a little of this variety. It omits the vast inland waterways, which can carry freight from Europe all the way to Chicago through the Great Lakes, or from the Gulf of Mexico two thousand miles upriver to St. Paul, Minnesota. It omits the two-thousand-mile footpath which traverses the wilderness of the Appalachians from Maine to Georgia. It omits the South with its slow, wide rivers, its fine old mansions and crumbling tenant houses, the statued squares of old-worldly Savannah and the flat, semi-tropical peninsula of Florida. It omits the unending vastness of Texas, the moss-hung bayous of Louisiana, the great forests of the Northwest, the shining green lawns of hilly Seattle, the beauty of San Francisco clinging to the slopes that rise from the Golden Gate, its bridges strung with necklaces of lights. Not in a lifetime could a man hope to know this whole land.

The United States has more than three million square miles of land and water within its continental borders. Forty per cent of this land is used for grazing, twenty-eight is in forests, twenty-two in cropland, ten occupied by buildings and roads. The federal government owns thirty per cent of the country, much of it in national forest areas, grazing lands or in parks that preserve some of the most spectacular natural wonders such as the Grand Canyon, the Carlsbad Caverns, or the hot springs and geysers of Yellowstone. Fifty-six million acres—an area almost as large as England, Scotland and Wales—is set aside in Indian reservations.

This rich natural heritage contains the greatest variety of wild animals in the world. The United States produces fantastic quantities of foodstuffs: 3,000,000,000 bushels of corn, 1,000,000,000 bushels of wheat, 355,000,000 bushels of potatoes in 1954. In the same year 25,000,000,000 pounds of meat were produced and consumed.

In the production of coal, petroleum, steel, electric energy, copper, cotton, lumber, and many other products it stands first. Many of these natural treasures it has ruthlessly exploited and wasted in the past, or expended lavishly in helping to defend the world against tyranny or in rehabilitating stricken areas after victory. Yet it still has great riches of soil and mineral and forest, and is much more aware today of the need for properly conserving them.

Visitors usually see the conformity and standardization of American life. Thanks to the movies and radio, thanks to the national marketing of automobiles and clothing, packaged foods and magazines, Americans do look and act pretty much the same. There are many aspects of the culture which they share. But this sharing does not deny them the enjoyment of their differences. Vermont farmer, Southern share-cropper, Mississippi boatman, Kansas storekeeper, Chicago professor, Texas rancher or oilman, Negro industrial worker, restaurant owner of Greek extraction, physician whose parents were born in Poland, Nisei (American of Japanese ancestry) orchardist in the Northwest—all are recognizably American, yet recognizably different.

To preserve variety without falling into chaos, to draw men together in a common culture without forcing them to lose their individuality—is this not one of the higher purposes of human culture? And is it not a test of a culture that it should be able to assimilate many varieties of men, leaving to them the enjoyment of that variety yet adding the power and pleasure of active membership in a community? And is this not what, above all things, has been the achievement of the peoples who have made America?

# CHAPTER THREE

---

# A Teeming Nation of Nations

There had never been anything like it before in human history. From Italy and Ireland, from Germany and Russia, from Greece and the Balkan countries and from Scandinavia they came, leaving the villages where their families had lived time out of mind, and where the comfortable shell of known custom and familiar faces safely ensphered them.

Statistics cannot tell the human story of this uprooting and transplanting, of the discomforts and indignities suffered by people who had never traveled before as they struggled through frontiers and officials to get to the European ports, and as they arrived bewildered and became bait for sharpers in American ports. Yet as early as 1850 the number of immigrants had risen to 370,000 a year, and though it rose and fell according to conditions on both sides of the Atlantic, the course was predominantly upward. By 1905 more than a million a year were coming, until the First World War put an end to the human flood. When it began to rise again after the war, legislation cut it down. It seemed to most Americans that their job now was to assimilate the millions they had taken in. Yet even today the influx, though small for a nation of this size, continues at the rate of about two hundred thousand a year—a number sufficient to people a city the size of Ottawa.

Between 1820 and 1953 about forty million people came to settle in the country—four and a half million from Great Britain, somewhat more from Ireland, two and a half million from Scandinavia, nearly five million from Italy, six and a half million from Germany, and over eight million from those parts of central and eastern Europe which have been so divided and redivided that it is impossible to separate them statistically.

The result: a nation of nations, a land where all the principal tongues of the world are spoken and where you can still find communities as German as Munich, as Spanish as Madrid, as Swiss as Zurich. Hamtramck is a Polish city with its own government, completely surrounded by Detroit. Los Angeles is the second largest Mexican city in the world. San Francisco has one of the largest Chinese communities outside China, complete with its own hospital, post office, theaters, radio station, daily newspapers and a telephone exchange where the operators speak six Chinese dialects and know all the names and numbers of their subscribers by heart. Chicago comes next to Milan in the size of its Italian population, next to Warsaw in the number of Poles. The state of Idaho has the largest Basque colony this side of the Pyrenees. Immigrating Swiss have made Green City, Wisconsin, the Swiss cheese capital of the world.

New Mexico is a bilingual state where official notices must be posted in Spanish as well as English, and where the state constitution itself was ratified in both languages. In New Mexico there are villages deriving from the old Spanish days where no word of English will be heard. Then there is Arizona where the Indians own one-third of the land and continue, many of them, to live in the ways of their fathers.

New York is the most diverse of all our cities. Two hundred papers in languages other than English are published there. Of New York's eight million people, more than half are foreign-born or of foreign parentage. Italians and Russians (about 400,000 of each) are the largest foreign-born groups. The Jews, who come from a number of countries and many of whom have lived in the United States for generations, make up about a fourth of the population. New York is the largest Jewish city in the world. And of course it has large numbers of Negroes, Puerto Ricans, Haitians, Mexicans. Smack in the middle of Harlem lives the largest Finnish community in the United States.

All the nations of Europe and many of the countries of Asia, Africa and the other Americas, have contributed to the making of the American. They *are* the American. For as President Roosevelt once remarked, "We are all immigrants here."

The remark applies even to the Indians, who found their way from Asia across the Bering Straits. About 845,000 are believed to have lived in what is now the United States when the first white settlers arrived. Today they number about 340,000, and their number is increasing.

## Unity in Variety

When the first wave of European immigration began in the seventeenth century, half a dozen nations established their beachheads on the continent Columbus had opened to the European world. The Spaniards moved up into the Southwest and along the California coast. The French, early explorers of the Mississippi, established New Orleans where today their culture is still clearly retained in the old quarter. Along the Louisiana bayous French is still the dominant language.

Delaware was settled first by Swedes and named New Sweden. New York, as everybody knows, was Dutch before it was English. And much of Pennsylvania, though never under the flag of any German state, was heavily settled by Germans (called Pennsylvania Dutch) as early as 1720.

But the dominant settlement from Europe was from the British Isles. England, Scotland, Wales and northern Ireland have given us about half our population, and the basic pattern of American life today is more British than anything else. The language, the law, the family names, the attitude toward government, the literature are unmistakably derived from British culture. How did it happen that this culture was not overwhelmed by all the other influences?

Most important was the fact that the early settlements out of which the nation developed were chiefly English. For 170 years the American colonists were subjects of the king. Their roots, their language, their institutions, even the manner in which they resisted the crown were English. "No taxation without representation" was a right they claimed as freeborn Englishmen rather than as colonists or Americans.

The first permanent English settlement at Jamestown was planned and supported by many of the great men of the realm and of course had a royal charter. Plymouth, the second permanent settlement, was chiefly in the hands of yeomen—small farmers originally from the north of England, proud of their status as free men and determined to hold their lands in fee simple and to worship according to their own interpretations of the Bible rather than as the Anglican Church and the king then required all Englishmen to worship. Plymouth was only the first of these religious communities. At Salem, then at Boston and Providence, at New Haven and inland along the Connecticut the small settlements took root, each independent of the others. Throughout New England the village republics grew and flourished as small, intimate units of government.

All during the colonial period—a span as long as that of our national government since—the immigration was mostly English and Scotch-Irish (Scots who had moved into the north of Ireland). The arrival of two million slaves, important as it was to be in the shaping of American culture, did not challenge the English dominance in laws, government, language.

Though there was great variety in the kinds of Englishmen and Scotsmen who came to America, they tended to have two things in common: dissatisfaction with their circumstances at home and enough means or energy to beat out new paths for themselves. Men of the highest type like William Bradford, John Winthrop, William Penn and Lord Baltimore came with a vision of creating communities where their religious beliefs might be freely expressed. Others were escaping the narrow restrictions of their lives—the lack of adequate land to support their families, harsh landlords, or heavy taxation.

"God sifted a whole nation that he might send choice grain over into this wilderness," wrote William Stoughton. And he was right. The conditions of settlement imposed their own principles of selection.

Immigration was also from the beginning international. With the Pilgrims came people of Walloon and Flemish extraction. Jamestown had Italians, Dutch and Poles. Huguenots from France were early settlers in the colonies, contributing some outstanding Americans—Paul Revere, the Faneuils, the du Ponts. German Protestants, particularly of persecuted sects like the Mennonites and Moravians, poured into Pennsylvania under the friendly cloak of William Penn's tolerance. In every one of the colonies along the Atlantic the English culture was laced with a varied international flavoring.

In 1654 the first Jews reached Manhattan. But as early as 1646 that island had foreshadowed its future destiny as a world melting pot by having twelve nationalities in its tiny community.

The essence of American culture lies in the fact that it is wholly derivative yet unmistakably unique—not a new creation but a blend, the flavor of which is derived from everything that went into it. This result has not been achieved without trials of strength and some shameful injustices. The Dutch drove the Swedes out of Delaware and were in turn driven out by the English. For a hundred years French and British fought for the control of North America, unwilling to share the vast wilderness. They managed also to involve the Indians in their warfare and to add a good deal of cruelty to a conflict which had begun as the byproduct of a struggle for power in Europe.

When the Treaty of Paris (1763) put an end to the threat of attacks from the north, the English colonies were in control of the whole eastern part of the continent, for Spain, having belatedly entered the war on the side of France, was forced to give up Florida. (Returned to her for a brief time in 1783, it was purchased by the United States.) English ideas of government, religion and family life therefore had the advantage. But English ways were enriched by the love of good living of the Dutch, the gallantry of the French, the native wisdom and gentleness, the music and melancholy of the Negro, the thrift and hardihood of the Scot, the patient craftsmanship of the Huguenots.

Englishmen, become Americans, learned to hunt and plant like the Indians. They learned to fight like Indians too—a skill that was almost the only advantage they had over the British when the Revolution came on.

When it came to settling the unbelievably vast areas to the west of the Atlantic fringe, the skill and strength of many people were again called upon. The westward movement began when little Plymouth set up a trading post on the Connecticut and Thomas Hooker led his church through the wilderness to the same river.

When Canada fell into British hands, the west became more attractive than ever. Vermont was settled, the earlier communities of western New York reinforced. When the Revolution was over the Northwest Territory claimed the attention of young men who had fought for independence. Out of New England went members of the Ohio Company of Associates to plant their first settlement at Marietta on the Ohio. Westward from Pennsylvania went Mennonites as well as the tireless Scotch-Irish. Illinois, Wisconsin, Michigan, Indiana began to receive settlements. Then Jefferson's purchase of the vast Louisiana territory opened up another country to be explored. The frontiers leaped westward again.

*Frontierland*

To Americans the word frontier has a meaning quite different from its use in Europe. There the frontier is a stopping place, a place patrolled by guards where one must show his papers before passing through. But the American frontier has meant freedom, opportunity, room to expand in. It is not a stopping place but an open door, not a place where you must identify yourself but a place where you can escape identification if you wish, a place where civilization has not established its rigid pattern, where spaces are wide and men can make their own laws.

The feeling that the frontier was there, to the west, even if a man did not choose to go there has always been a conditioning factor in the American temperament. The frontier, in American thought, was a place beyond civilization where nature took over from man and where the evils concocted by human duplicity were washed away by the great rivers, the wide sky, the brisk, clean air.

Waves of settlement billowed westward—first the trapper and hunter, then the pioneer settler, then the permanent farmer. And eventually, of course, towns and cities in place of isolated homes.

The early westward movement followed one of four main routes: from the South Atlantic States along the Gulf of Mexico; through the southern mountains into Tennessee and the old Southwest; into the valley of the Ohio; or along the passageway afforded by the Great Lakes. From these main routes the trails branched off into any likely-looking piece of country.

When the trek all the way west to the Pacific began in the 1840's, geography again decreed certain routes across the plains and through the mountain passes. Not until much later did the plains states themselves begin to fill up.

Many of the farmers who replaced the pioneers as they moved

west were recent immigrants. In the 1820's and 1830's they took the evacuated lands in western New York, Pennsylvania and Ohio. In the forties they moved into Missouri and Illinois and southern Wisconsin. In the fifties and sixties they were in eastern Iowa and Minnesota, and by the seventies they were in the prairie states.

It has long since become a truism that the frontier played a vital part in shaping American character. In presenting this thesis, Frederick Jackson Turner stressed the independence, the self-reliance, the individualism it fostered.

Although the first westward movements were individual, when it came to settling permanent towns the indispensable instrument was the voluntary association—the emigrant company or the emigrating society. Sometimes these groups drew up written constitutions, using phrases reminiscent of the Mayflower Compact. Sometimes the group was small enough and intimate enough to need no written rules. Whether it was the Western Emigration Society crossing the plains on its way to California, or the Oregon Emigration Society of Iowa Territory, safe and successful pioneering called for organization. Some of the companies formed to reach California during the gold rush had elaborate constitutions, uniforms, and professional staffs including doctors, geologists, ministers, mineralogists and mechanics.

The tone of the early American community is to be heard, not in the boasts of rugged individuals, but in the countless activities people shared together—the barn raisings, quilting parties, apple parings, bear hunts, road building, corn huskings. This pattern of mutual aid made fun out of hard work and a social occasion out of what would otherwise have been drudgery.*

Coming from the continent of Europe immigrants often settled together in one area, establishing churches, social groups, newspapers and cultural activities by the same method of voluntary association. This habit of group cooperation or voluntary aid, found in rural communities throughout the world, was already familiar to the vast majority of immigrants who had been peasants at home, who had helped one another in the fields, and whose few pleasures came from shared activity.

* For a much fuller treatment of the importance of voluntary association in the founding and settling of the United States, see my *A Dangerous Freedom*.

Until 1882 most of the immigrants came from Germany, Scandinavia and the British Isles. Many of the English went into the Mississippi Valley where they helped to maintain English culture in an area that had been growing Germanic. After 1896 the immigration from southern and eastern Europe outstripped that from the north, until in the last ten years before World War I it became a flood. Many immigrants came to escape the hated military conscription, a factor in American isolationism.

## The Immigrant Community

Arrival in America must have been a fearsome thing to people fresh from small European villages. They could speak no English. The crowding and the lack of privacy in the steerage had touched their self-respect. Once cleared by immigration authorities, they faced a bewildering world. Merchants, themselves perhaps recent immigrants, waited at the dock to buy their mattresses, their old clothes. Others pressed them to buy fruit or bread, or shouted offers for housemaids or laborers. Banners offering farms for sale were waved in their faces, while agents for boarding houses and railroads shouted for attention.

The earlier immigrants from Germany and Scandinavia often settled communities of their own where they could reproduce many aspects of the life they had left behind—not only simple rural communities, but towns graced with the comforts and culture of civilized life. Fifty-six newspapers were being published in German in 1856. In Cincinnati during the 1860's a German theater gave nightly performances of the classics. A dozen churches held services in German. A parochial school offered an education in German. Recitals, lectures, athletic contests and musical competitions kept people busy in the evenings. In the summer they could sit in beer gardens enjoying their favorite food and drink and listening to an orchestra play familiar, nostalgic tunes.

To a greater or less degree, every immigrant group managed to recreate the culture of the homeland. Musical clubs, insurance groups, cooperatives, Welsh eisteddfods, Polish falcons and Bohemian sokols flourished throughout the land.

The churches were bulwarks, not only of the home culture and conservatism, but of a Puritanism which matched that of the early

English settlers. The ministers who were willing to emigrate tended to be the more zealous ones, and therefore more strict with their people. Removing into the wilderness merely emphasized the obligation to hold onto the mother culture. So strong was this need that not even the Catholic Church could unite Catholics of Polish, German and Italian ancestry. Each group wanted its own church, and still does. The church, with its appeal to divine sanctions, was an effective weapon in the fight for cultural survival. The immigrant lost so much in his uprooting that a strong stabilizing force was essential. As a peasant he had possessed definite status, no matter how precarious his living. But as an immigrant laborer he had none. His peasant upbringing had taught him to maintain his status but not thrust himself ahead or rebel against his station. In America it was the brash, shrewd fellow who succeeded.

Having nothing to contribute but his labor, the immigrant had to take what work he could get. Often he joined a gang of compatriots whose boss or padrone contracted for the whole group. By the end of the nineteenth century, immigrant labor supplied not only the gangs to build the railroads and other construction work, but also a large part of the labor force in the mines and factories, helping to convert industry from craft to mechanized methods. Immigrant labor made possible the rapid conversion from an agricultural to an industrial economy.

Often the leaders in the immigrant communities were political refugees, men of good education who had escaped to America and who operated independence movements from this side of the Atlantic, awaiting a favorable time to return. Their presence fostered nationalistic feelings and to that extent delayed Americanization. But they also performed useful services as editors and teachers and community leaders. Politically conscious, they were frequently sensitive to the need for reconciling the conflicts between the immigrant group and the surrounding community.

Often the immigrants longed for the familiar sights and activities of the old country. Those who lived lives of toil, whose world was a dark and noisy factory and a crowded, ugly tenement, were no doubt disillusioned with America. Some returned home. But the majority stayed. The young, and those who were temperamentally able to take advantage of the opportunities, found America exhilarating.

"Here it is not asked, what or who was your father, but the question is, what are you?" wrote a young Norwegian in 1849. "Freedom is here an element which is drawn in, as it were, with mother milk, and seems as essential to every citizen of the United States as the air he breathes."

While the immigrants did on the whole feel welcome here, since their labor was bid for and their custom invited, and though they were free to go their own way and not compelled to conform, yet they became conscious too that they would never entirely belong. Alienated from their own culture by their own choice, they were aliens too in the new. This sense of rootlessness has had profound effects on American culture.

The immigrant felt pulled in both directions. He missed the warmth of village life, yet recognized when faced with reality that he had passed beyond it. He felt his old values being attacked and for that very reason he had to defend them. If he tried to adopt American ways and move into a better residential area, he might be rebuffed for pushing in where he wasn't wanted.

*Acculturation*

So his hope came to rest in his children. Yet here too he was up against a dilemma. They were essentially American. They resented his attempt to teach them the old country culture, to impose old country discipline. At school they found that the English origins and culture were most honored. On the playground they heard their home culture evaluated in such words as dago, canuck, mick.

Like all the young, they wanted desperately to belong. Their parents had clung to the old ways while ceasing to honor them, having no other standards. The second generation performed the act of rejection. The third was to find that rejection—using a better education to surpass the economic and social status of the parents—had become a part of the American way.

Often the American children turned nationalistic in hope of being accepted, and this is an important source of the nationalism observers find in the current scene. Sometimes youngsters desiring to raise themselves above their despised origins formed gangs to protect themselves against those who discriminated against them. Gangs easily developed into rackets. Youngsters without any other advantage but their brawn, and goaded by the American demand for success, found their way into the fringes of politics where muscle men came in handy. Or more legitimately, they began their climb up the ladder in sports, to such an extent that jokes about the unpronounceable Polish names on football teams became standard. Many with good minds took advantage of the educational system to get into the professions and win respect in that way.

Rejecting the foreignness of parents, these young people were eager for marriage because it allowed them to cast off family ties and set up a household of their own, an American household. Love became a symbol of emancipation, a final Americanizing step. And thus another urgency was added to the characteristic American emphasis on romantic love, on the loving couple as the basis of the family rather than the extended family group.

The break between the generations, pathetic enough in any case, was doubly so for the foreign-born and their children. Some could not take it: pauperism, intemperance, gambling, crime, insanity are a part of the picture, too. Yet for every failure there were a dozen successes. On the whole, the immigrant became remarkably Americanized. To realize this one has merely to compare those of German descent in Brazil or New South Wales with those in the United States. In Brazil they still speak, think and vote German. Those in New South Wales remained more German than those in Missouri, though surrounded by a far more English society. Why?

Consider the story of John Deferrari who began to peddle fruit in the streets of Boston when he was nine years old. His father, an immigrant from Italy, had eight children to provide for, and young John was the oldest. The boy knew that many of Boston's financial houses were located in the State Street area, and he decided that where there was the most money he would find his best market. When he had emptied his basket he would return home and turn the money over to his father.

He left school after the eighth grade, but he continued to study. He knew that his customers in State Street made great sums of money through investments. To learn how they went about it, he got out books from the public library, but he continued to peddle fruit. At sixteen he was able to buy a horse and wagon. Three years later he opened a wholesale fruit business near Faneuil Hall. Still too young to make legal contracts, he put his father's name over the door and soon had a thriving business. In 1890 he opened a large store on Boylston Street near the public library. At night he would borrow books that dealt with subjects he was interested in—fruit, investment, real estate, law, the lives of successful business men. He decided that he could make more money by importing fancy fruits and selling them to hotels, restaurants, ships, and well-to-do homes.

By the time he had money to invest, his years of reading had led him to some basic conclusions. One was that the only business worth investing in was one run by men who had worked their way up from the bottom. "If the man is sound," he reasoned, "the business must be sound." Another conclusion was that the safest investment of all was in land and real estate. He began to buy small houses, remodelling them himself and renting rooms.

By the time he was eighty, John Deferrari was worth four million dollars. Realizing that he could not last forever, he began to consider what he should do with this fortune. Again he went to the library to learn what other men had done, but nothing he read satisfied him. He wanted to do something for the young men of Boston—lads who, like himself, had ambition and drive. He began to ask cautious questions in the many banks among which he had divided his cash holdings. No one knew that the plain, little old man was a millionaire.

At last he found a trust officer who appealed to him and to whom he explained his wishes. "Boston gave me what I have," he said. "I want to do something for the poor boys of Boston. I want to encourage human beings to make good use of their time."

To the library which had helped him, John Deferrari gave a million dollars. When the fund by reinvestment reaches two million, half may be spent on building a John Deferrari wing. When the fund again grows to two million, the income may be used as the trustees see fit.

Having made his gift, the self-made son of an immigrant returned to a plain room in one of the many houses he owns, at an address he would not divulge.

The limitations of John Deferrari's life are as instructive as the financial success which to him meant proving one's Americanism. John could not renounce the cautious scrimping of his forebears. He never spent an unnecessary nickel—would not even take a streetcar if he could possibly walk, did all the repairs on his property, kept his own books, had no telephone, would not even write a letter but conducted all his affairs in person. He did his own cooking, allowed himself no comforts. He never married.

The American success formula was a product of great natural resources and commercial opportunity, only the very struggle to succeed robbed a man of the desire or ability to spend what he had worked so hard to gain. It would take another generation, removed from the immigrant fear of layoff and depression, to add conspicuous spending to the formula of success.

## Assimilation

After World War I it seemed to many Americans that the time had come to halt or slow down the influx from Europe. One-eighth of the total population was foreign born. Three-fourths of them were living in cities, many in crowded slums where their children could easily fall into delinquency or crime.

Concerned by the social problems, caught up in a post-war mood of nationalism and disenchanted with the results of the crusade to make the world safe for democracy, then faced with a depression, the American people decided to place strong restraints on immigration. In 1921 and again in 1924 Congress restricted the influx. In 1929 the national origins provision went into effect, imposing quotas which favored the British Isles and northern Europe. Although the total annual quota was only a little over 150,000, the actual influx was much greater because of such non-quota groups as children of immigrants already here.

By this time the country had achieved a complicated pattern of ethnic variety. To New England, a great manufacturing area, most of the immigrations supplied workers. The old settlers might grumble that the Irish, the French Canadians, the Poles or the Italians were taking over, but they employed them readily enough, and often in the jobs no one else wanted. Even today one out of every five persons in Massachusetts is foreign born. Seventy-five per cent of the people of Rhode Island are of foreign birth or parentage. Though the children intermingle at school, marriages still tend to run along ethnic lines.

The Middle Atlantic states, located between the ocean and the grainland of the West, excelled in commerce. Waterways to the west made it possible to transport bulky products all the way from Michigan and Minnesota to New York. Though it had fine dairy and fruit farms, still it too was primarily urban. It too could absorb great numbers of workers, so its ethnic stock is richly varied.

Wisconsin, first populated by New Englanders, received Germans as early as 1848. They brought with them craft industries which still play an important part in the state's economy. Milwaukee, of course, is famous for its breweries. Norwegians, Poles, Finns and Danes also settled in the state.

The North Central Plains area, a land of lakes and fertile flat farmland, producing grain, motor cars, agricultural machinery, and iron ore, attracted Europeans who had followed the Yankee migration westward—Irish, German, Polish, Czech, Italian and most of all Scandinavian. Names like Stassen, Steinway, Wurlitzer, Eisenhower, Rockefeller, Weyerhauser, Chrysler, Heinz and Merck testify to the important part played in American life today by the sons and grandsons of Germanic immigrants.

The really open country is in the Great Central Plains beyond the world's longest river, the Mississippi (including its main branch, the Missouri). Much of this land is good only for grazing, so that a man may need as much as two thousand acres to make a living. Sparsely settled, therefore, it is a remnant of the old frontier, a land of floods, blizzards, drought. There are ores and oil here too. Here the latter-day immigrants have come less numerously, yet Nebraska is eleven per cent Czech, and has more people of German extraction than any state but Wisconsin. Czech is spoken as much as English in some counties.

South Dakota, with a population of about 650,000, has 140,000 of German extraction, 90,000 from the Scandinavian countries. North Dakota is even more striking—forty per cent Scandinavian in origin (largely Norwegian), thirty per cent German and "Volga" German, which means basically Russian. Montana is forty-six per cent foreign born or of foreign-born or mixed parentage—Swedes, Poles, Italians,

Jugoslavs, Cornishmen, Finns, Irish. In the mines of Butte forty different ethnic stocks are represented.

The South is different. Though it has become increasingly industrial, with a whole cluster of new industries benefiting from the power generated by the Tennessee Valley Authority, it was agricultural during the great immigrations. Since its own tenant farmers were already subsisting on marginal farms, there was no inducement to immigrants to move in. Its cotton, sugar, tobacco and rice could be raised pretty much as they always had been, by workers already there. The South has remained predominantly British and Negro, with special exceptions like the Greek sponge fishermen in Florida. In Texas there are, in addition to the Mexican neighborhoods, places that still seem as German as Bavaria. It was from one of these communities that Admiral Chester Nimitz came.

The West Coast, fast becoming an industrial as well as an agricultural area, has Italians, Japanese, Chinese, Filipinos, Mexicans, Indians. To Southern California has come many an intellectual refugee from European totalitarianism or from inclement weather anywhere.

The richness and variety of the regional texture, each section with its own ethnic combination, constitutes one of the strengths of the United States. The consciousness of this extent and variety gives a kind of continental confidence, perhaps even a brashness and boastfulness to the American character.

In 1790 ninety-two per cent of the population was from the British Isles. Aside from this group (which included 1.6% from Ireland) only the Germans (5.6%) and the Dutch (2%) were numerous enough to note. By 1920 the picture stood this way: Great Britain (with Northern Ireland), forty-one per cent; Eire, eleven per cent; Germany, sixteen per cent; Poland, four per cent; Italy, slightly under four per cent; Sweden and the Netherlands, two per cent each; and France, Czechoslovakia, Russia, Norway, and Switzerland, between one and two per cent each. Other stocks supplied less than one per cent each to the ethnic potpourri.

As in the past, the most recent arrivals have had to face the most serious problems of integration, as for instance those from Mexico in the West and Southwest, or the Puerto Ricans (who are, of course, American citizens) in New York. Low income, poor health, lack of facility in English, and hence lack of education, prevent a rise in status. Yet these groups, like those before them, are taking the first painful steps up the ladder. A few years ago a Mexican-American social worker, Edward Roybal, ran for city councilman in Los Angeles. He was badly defeated. Realizing that his people lacked political awareness, he got twenty other veterans and their wives together and formed a community service organization. Within a year eight hundred people were working together to improve their community, devoting their spare time to many needed projects. When Roybal ran again, thousands of Mexicans who had never voted before went to the polls and many "Anglos" who had watched Roybal's work as a community leader voted for him. He was swept into office.

Efforts are likewise being made in New York to ease the integration process for Puerto Ricans—with "big brothers" to help school children, special classes in English and American community life, adult evening classes, and organizations fostering inter-group relations. Assimilation of these more recent groups is eased by a better public understanding nowadays of the fact that cultural patterns differ and that assimilation takes time.

### Immigration and American Culture

An early effect of immigration on American culture was a chauvinistic support of old world causes. But the second generation, rejecting any entanglements with its ancestral lands though resisting war against them, was an important source of isolationism. Still the long-term result now appears to be a feeling of moral commitment in the world's affairs, fortified by the knowledge that men and women from most of the areas now struggling for higher living standards or for freedom from imperialistic control have helped to build America's present strength.

Immigration provided the manpower needed to build the railroads and cities and highways, and to convert a simple agricultural economy to a highly industrialized one. In farming, immigrants took over lands that had been ruthlessly worked and made them fertile again.

Not only in supplying the raw foodstuffs, but in giving variety to American cooking, the new Americans have contributed. Spaghetti, goulash, veal cutlet (Wienerschnitzel), chow mein, curry, shishkabob, scallopini, pizza, bouillabaise, chili con carne, and a hundred other dishes are now widely known and enjoyed.

The immigrant has contributed immeasurably to the arts. Many of our early writers combined English with other ancestry—Melville, Whitman, Thoreau, Freneau. The Negro contribution to American music, in the spirituals and work songs as well as in jazz and in staged music such as *Porgy and Bess,* is fundamental. Some of our finest singers, and many good writers, are Negroes. Germans and Italians brought with them their love of music, providing both an audience for it and many of the singers and performers in our symphony orchestras and opera companies today.

The Jewish contribution stretches all the way from control of the garment trades and influence in the mass media to scientific and artistic achievements. As business people, they spread out through the cities and towns, opening clothing stores, hardware stores, laundries, and other retail shops. The Strausses, Gimbels, Guggenheims, Frohmans and Rosenwalds all trace their ancestry to pack-peddlers who built up their fortunes from nothing. Among the thousands of Jews who have enriched American life are Supreme Court Justices, Nobel prize winners, theater people, musicians of top rank, writers of popular music, playwrights, leaders in the movie field, government officials, industrial leaders.

Colorful variety is one of the more attractive consequences of our immigrant origins. There are still small towns in New England and in the southern mountain country where the people are mostly of old British stock, but these communities have themselves become picturesque because they are so rare. Like the Hispano-American communities of New Mexico, the Chinatowns and little Tokyos and little Italys, they are exceptional. The typical American scene is one which blends a dozen backgrounds.

Look at the Main Street of a small town—Bennington, Vermont, for instance. The market that handles fancy fruits, confections and baked goods is Greek. So are the two excellent restaurants and the tailor just around the corner on North Street. An Italian family runs the shoe repair shop. The cigar shop is Sicilian. Jewish enterprises include a hardware store, a pharmacy, several clothing shops.

Yankee names appear in all these categories too. One of the best markets is run by a Syrian. French Canadians are active in various small enterprises such as grocery stores and filling stations. A printing establishment is in the hands of an American of Dutch ancestry. Among the lawyers you find such names as Agostini, Levin and Morrissey along with Barber and Holden. Many of these families have lived in Vermont for generations, others are recent arrivals. In America people who have quarreled and fought for centuries in their homelands have managed to live peaceably together. That is no small accomplishment.

In our efforts to bring this about, we have not been sure whether to encourage folk festivals, ethnic group organizations, language schools and separate churches, or whether to press for a common culture. Does America gain most by fostering old-world folkways or by throwing them overboard?

It is perhaps characteristic of the pluralistic, pragmatic American approach that we have done both. When the tulip festivals are over in the Dutch communities of Holland, Michigan and Pella, Iowa, the people go back to being plain Americans. At Tarpon Springs, Florida, the Greek community has its festival of blessing the waters, but after the cross has been retrieved from the ocean, life returns to its round of movie shows, TV and Rotary. The Italo-American and Polish-American societies tend to disappear as the second and third generation become members of the city council or take their places on the various civic boards. Only in that most traditional and symbolic area of life, religion, do the distinctions continue even after the linguistic or theological differences have disappeared. But this is the case with old-stock Americans too.

Although the new immigrant has always had to fight his way up against odds and against prejudice, it may be that the challenge is what has stimulated him to achieve distinction. The long list of eminent Americans who were either immigrants or the children of immigrants suggests that this is so.

The story of Julius Lehmann sums it up as well as any. He came from Bavaria as a young man, landed in New York, studied while he worked, married, saw three generations grow up. He did not grow rich, but he did well. When he died at ninety-two he left a will with only two major bequests: $1,000 for the care of his parents' graves in Germany, and the balance, about $60,000, to the United States government, "to which my wife and I are so much indebted for the blessings we have received as citizens."

## CHAPTER FOUR

---

# *Language*

Not since the days of Shakespeare had the English language been
so lively as it became during the early years of the American
republic.

When the first English settlers stepped ashore at Jamestown in
1607, they found that they had to adopt Indian words for animals,
plants and foods that were new to them. Captain John Smith introduced "opossum" (which he spelled "opasum") in his *True Relation* published in 1608, and "raccoon" (which he spelled
"raugroughcum"). Englishmen were soon using words like "moose,"
"skunk," "hickory," and "squash," so frequently as to forget that
they were Indian. "Canoe," "hominy," "moccasin," "sachem,"
"tomahawk" and "squaw" became equally familiar.

Facing the new conditions of the wilderness, men who had the
strength and the ingenuity to adapt themselves in order to conquer
the new environment also had the capacity to adapt their language
to the frontier. What could be more expressive, to a man who had
struggled to clear a field and get rid of the tremendous roots of
virgin forest, than the word "stumped"?

Out of the exuberant reaction to the lavishness of nature and the
magnitude of the tasks the pioneers had to tackle, came many such
words as bullfrog, garter snake, turkey gobbler, hog wallow, light-
ning bug. New conditions or contact with other languages gave
bottom land, foothill, clearing, rapids, pioneering, backwoodsman.
Words of praise and disgust, in a frontier community where a man
was quickly judged by his actions, sprang into life: no-account,

one-horse, squatter, to whitewash, take to the woods, face the music, go on the warpath, fly off the handle.

England, having forgotten the exuberance with which she had coined words herself in the age of Elizabeth, was scandalized by the liberties Americans took with the language. The readiness to make verbs like oppose, progress, obligate, immigrate, and locate aroused cries of horror across the water, but England herself has adopted many of these words once thought barbarous. Words like influential and reliable evoked such protests in England that one would have thought the monarch himself had been called dirty names. But Americans went right on vitalizing (another horrid Americanism) the language by borrowing from other tongues, shifting parts of speech, dropping inflections, and by the exercise of a humorous imagination.

Raciness is the quality that stands forth most clearly—a love of wrenching words out of their customary places and functions so that in their new meanings they will blow across a conversation with a fresh wind of novelty, satisfying the hankering for what is picturable or ridiculous—muttonhead, egghead, hoosegow. Crisp, short forms are also favored: phone, gas, co-ed, gym, movie, plane, auto, diner.

Americans love action, devising short, crisp verb forms such as jell, commute, orate, contact. They hop a cab (take a taxi), grab a drink or a few winks, snatch a bite, have a snort (a drink), date a girl, scan a newspaper (which they call merely a paper), catch a train, and then spend the evening in front of the television set watching other people dash through expensively produced comic marathons, much of the humor of which is based on word play.

Inventiveness in language is so prized that highest admiration and top salaries are paid to men like Winchell who make a profession of it, while no teen-ager could hope to survive without knowing the latest smart talk made current by television and especially by jazz fans, the most fertile inventors of new phrases.

The American language loves quick, humorous characterizations such as rubberneck, roughhouse, lameduck, bonehead, lowbrow, goofed . . . the list is endless.

The country's most widely circulated magazine, *The Reader's Digest*, runs several pages each month devoted to word play: "Much adieu about nothing"—two women saying good-by; artist's model—a girl unsuited to her work; education—what's left over after you've forgotten the facts. Sometimes these experiments with words (for Americans are pragmatists in language too) take the form of a shrewd comment on contemporary life. "What I like about a trailer," said the comedian Herb Shriner, "is that you have some place to live while you're looking for a place to park."

Much of the simplifying and much of the color have come from the streams of immigrants who spoke at first in an English stripped of niceties, and who contributed words from their own languages. First Indian, then Dutch, French, German and Irish influences have battered at the language. Before these attacks could be beaten off or assimilated came new waves from Italy, Poland and the rest of eastern Europe. Sauerkraut, noodle, hamburger and kindergarten from German; camouflage, rendezvous, employee, bureau and prairie from the French; spaghetti, padrone and chianti from Italian; cuspidor from Portuguese; kosher and kibitzing from Yiddish; presidio, mosquito and alligator from Spanish; Nisei and suki-yaki from Japanese—these are but a few of the thousands of words that come crowding into the language with every wave of immigrants.

To the traditionalist, the language is too mobile, too impatient of rules. But no one would deny that it is lively, gay, good-humored with a touch of self-mockery which makes fun of the very mega-lomania and enthusiasm and exaggeration which Americans recognize in themselves.

"When we Americans are through with the English language," said Mr. Dooley, "it will look as if it had been run over by a musical comedy."

"Hiya," or plain "Hi" is a sufficient greeting when friends meet. At the Hoover Dam—vast, dignified and awe-inspiring symbol of what democratic government can achieve—the official guide begins his talk something like this: "Now, folks, you're standing 728 feet above the bottom of the dam. We're going to take this elevator down to the bottom. There's nothing to get worried about; it's only failed to stop three or four times that I can recall."

American is a levelling language, the language of a people who believe in equality. There are no grammatical forms with which to denote class difference, whether up or down, no levels of politeness as in Japanese, no clinging to honorary titles. Even the highest officer of the land is plain Mr. President—or, more often, just plain Ike.

No verbal deference exists between the waiter and the served, the clerk and the customer, except in swank spots depending on snob appeal. Overseas visitors often mistake this familiarity for rudeness, but it is just another case of democratic levelling. We like it. What American would not prefer a cheery "What's yours, Mac?" when he stops in at his grocer's to anything more formal? To be recognized, known and liked—these are the things an American yearns for. To be deferred to and showered with honorifics makes him uneasy.

Much of the informality of his talk comes from the sports he loves. A hit is as much desired on Broadway as on the baseball diamond from which it derives. A man is admired if he's got something on the ball, but a foul ball is a man nobody likes. A man who has lost a customer or a job is thrown for a loss as in football. A good worker is one who can carry the ball.

Greatly admired in addition to sports talk is the wise crack, bon mot or aphorism. The magazines are full of brisk retorts, characteristically "taking down" someone who assumes an attitude of superiority. When Governor Talmadge of Georgia was asked to comment on the fact that many Georgians were leaving the state for balmy, sunny Florida, he replied: "I think it raises the level of intelligence in both states." A bus driver, faced with the old problem of crowding at the front, shouted: "Push each other to the rear of the bus, please."

## Speak English—Talk American

Educated Americans and Englishmen speak virtually the same language. But among the less educated, spoken American, as H. L. Mencken has pointed out in his pioneering study of the language, has a vocabulary of its own, a syntax of its own, even a grammar of its own. Though by any academic standard it is atrocious, it has a kind of rude force in its double negatives, while its brutal flouting of the rules belongs to a people who hacked their communities out of virgin forest, took their chances against Indians, and often made their own laws—complete with hangings when necessary—in rude frontier communities where government had not yet caught up with the westward thrust of settlement. It is easy to find members of the school board in small towns who speak this language at the board meetings which manage the affairs of schools teaching youngsters to speak standard English. Such members apparently see nothing incongruous in this, or are, perhaps, unconscious of it. Their children speak the standard brand at school, and at home the kind of English they hear from their parents. Thus democracy is satisfied: free education for all, and likewise the freedom to be untouched by it! Will the television habit succeed in replacing the folk speech with standard English where the schools have failed? Maybe, though Americans have been going to sound movies for thirty years, and listening to the radio for an even longer time without much effect on their grammar. But with TV invading the bar and the living room, providing patterns of life the viewer is supposed to yearn for, is it not likely that its linguistic standards will come to be adopted? Most observers agree that the level has risen markedly in the past fifty years.

Americans have always enjoyed a linguistic solidarity unique in the world, especially considering the size of the country and the diversity of its ethnic stock. The man from Portland, Maine, has no difficulty understanding the man from Portland, Oregon. (In fact, they might be relatives, since New Englanders settled Oregon, as well as most of the country between the two Portlands in the northern section of the continent.) The Georgian's soft voice and broad vowels may seem as strange to the Dakotan as the Dakotan's flat, nasal tones seem to him. But they will understand each other.

Three major dialects, however, are recognized—Eastern (New England and a strip of New York), Southern (south of Pennsylvania and the Ohio River), and Western or General American. There are plenty of minor dialects, as in the Ozarks or the remoter hill towns of New England. New York City itself has many variants, and an expert can usually spot which borough a New Yorker comes from, while the Brooklyn accent is a national joke. About three-quarters of the population speaks General American, though within this dialect are many local variations. Flattened vowels and a prolonged or clearly pronounced *r* are characteristic, and in general a clarity of speech which gives full value to all the syllables of a word.

Southern speech, on the other hand, omits the final *r* and sub-stitutes an *ah* sound for *i:* I like bright skies becomes something like Ah lahk braht skahs. There is a pleasant softness, roundness, and slow rhythm to the voice, somewhat more range in tones, from a low, rather fuzzy pitch to rather sudden rises, and (to those not accustomed to it) a slight whine.

New England, east of the Connecticut River at least, has the broad *a* (ahnt for aunt), a tendency to drop the *r* sound (Hahvahd, fathah), and sometimes, perversely, to put *r*'s where they don't belong as in idear.

Sometimes you can tell more about a man's origin from his choice of words than from his pronunciation. Does he call that paper con-venience a bag, sack or poke? Does he like to eat, along with a cup of coffee, a doughnut, cruller, fried cake or fat cake? Does he use you-all to indicate a plural? Does he call a stream a branch, brook, wash, creek or kill? Americans will argue that this word or that is the "right" one, but the difference is merely regional.

On the whole American pronunciation is clearer than the English, and in many instances it retains an earlier clarity which the British have given up. It was Doctor Johnson who led an attack, for in-stance, on what he considered the "snarling sound" of the English *r*. So Englishmen came to say "sawd of the Lawd" instead of "sword of the Lord." Americans (except in parts of the East and South) have preserved the *r*.

They have preserved all the syllables of words like dictionary, extraordinary, secretary and military, where the British lop off one or even two. Though this preciseness may sound harsh to British ears, it does show a kind of respect for the language, a liking for what is clear and workmanlike and unambiguous, and possibly a feeling that in a nation formed of many peoples there must be no gap between the words as written and as pronounced.

As Sir Winston Churchill remarked, the United States and Great Britain are two great nations divided by a common language. Still, though an American in England is occasionally shocked by hearing a very proper lady say that she had stayed up late last night and was knocked up—in the United States a vulgar expression for becoming pregnant—he does manage to get around without difficulty. He may think it quaint that an elevator is called a lift, a bathrobe a dressing gown, or kerosene paraffin. It may trouble him a little that both a cracker and a cookie are a biscuit, and a biscuit a bun. Differences in rhythm and intonation prove even greater than those in diction or grammar. But he gets along.

For international purposes, at least, Britons and Americans can fortunately consider their language as one. The British Commonwealth of Nations together with the United States and its associated territories, to say nothing of the lands where English is the lingua franca of commerce and international relations, constitute the world's greatest language community. This is one of the reasons why Americans have been such poor linguists: there has been very little need for them to learn. Yet paradoxically we have a greater number of people speaking a foreign language in their homes than any other country. We have assumed, however, that it was their business to learn English, and not ours to learn their languages.

Despite the difficulties of English—the impossible spelling which includes at least sixty-six different ways to spell the eight long vowel sounds and the use of *ough* to indicate at least half a dozen pronunciations, or the gigantic vocabulary of over half a million words which still allows some words to have opposite meanings, or the inexplicable idioms—still the language has fewer inflections, less grammar, shorter words than any other tongue. Though mastering it can take a lifetime, a working knowledge can be gained in short order.

## Language as a Tool

There is a lively interest in the language, popular as well as academic. Speech departments have sprung into being in the universities. Reaching wide, they have embraced a number of fields—drama and dramatic arts such as movies and television, the other mass communications media, public speaking, debating, advertising, the study of speech variations, the art of persuasion, and human relations. Quite an order!

Speech is taught as a major in many colleges, and the emphasis is on how to use language as a weapon or a tool—how to sell, persuade, organize.

Translated to the field of advertising, this produces the shenanigans by which the customer is first brought to recognize his need for a new car, cigarette or eye lotion, and is then led inevitably to the conclusion that he cannot live happily or successfully (the two are synonymous in American culture) without this particular car, cigarette or eye lotion.

As in so many other departments of American life, technique is exalted at the expense of content, or at least it has been in the past. The professors are trying to emphasize content now. But that has not prevented the ad-men, the Madison Avenue word-merchants, from capitalizing on the method—and some "educationists" too.

"An American cannot converse, but he can discuss," wrote de Tocqueville. In American life the prizes go to the man who can persuade. The country is spilling over with persuasion. It gushes out of radio and television sets, floods across full pages of news-papers, in the form of billboards blots out the landscape, and pro-vides the staple for magazines which use just enough text to fill the space not paid for by advertisers. The verb to sell has become a standard expression for activities not only commercial but cultural.

A successful professor must "sell" his subject to the students, who assume the posture of potential customers. That is, they come to lectures prepared to be bored, defying the professor to arouse them. If he fails, they regard it as a kind of triumph on their part, though with something of the reluctance that a girl might feel in having successfully defended her virtue. They have wasted a term, to be sure, but their "sales resistance" has proved superior to his sales ability. If, on the other hand, the professor is energetic enough to arouse their interest, they become his admiring disciples, for he is that paragon of society, a man who can sell his product despite continued resistance.

In a democracy, where public opinion is an essential support to public policy, the art of persuasion and discussion is of course in-dispensable. This is the other side of the "selling game." The De-partment of State, Congress, the President himself are powerless to act on major issues (and on many minor ones) until they can sense the public feeling and know that it will support them. Much of the irritating delay in government action comes from this need for public discussion and the arrival at a consensus. Again the arts of persuasion are at a premium.

Perhaps this is why everyone seems agreed that Americans are poor conversationalists. With us the goal of speech is action, and hence something outside the sphere of discourse itself. There is a good deal of professional fun-making and a huge audience for it. There is also a love of colorful talk, especially humorous talk. But the parry and thrust of ideas, the flashing of experienced blades— that is a rare phenomenon, as no doubt it is in any culture.

Yet there is plenty of good talk in America if not much excellent conversation. A friendly interest in people is in it, a healthy curiosity, a readiness to swap experiences in a land where occupations and regions offer great variety and where mobility can easily bring much knowing into one room. A run-of-the-mill after-dinner conversation may easily include modern pottery and methods of firing; methods of preventing juvenile delinquency; the progress of the current fund-raising campaign (there is always at least one going on in an American community); a glance at several new books and movies; discussion of the latest international crisis; what to do about the neighborhood's overcrowded school; and of course a scattering of remarks on business, children, housekeeping, and acquaintances not present. The talk will be informal, without pretensions, and unless a political argument makes up, it will be friendly. Even a political argument will soon simmer down, because Americans are not ideologically divided in politics; they merely belong to the team that is either carrying the ball or tackling, and they look at politics that way.

As to friendliness, total strangers when introduced talk to each other as if they were old friends. They make use of such devices as first names, "kidding," or a search for mutual acquaintances and similar hobbies to hasten the process. If two strangers find that they have lived in the same city somewhere in the past, even if they were not there at the same time, it is enough to clinch the relationship.

So the spoken language, diverging from English, has been shaped to meet the needs of a pioneering people, an ethnically varied people, a people who love to persuade and be persuaded, act and be acted upon, love and be loved.

In its written form, too, the language has gone toward informality, crispness, speed, bright colors rather than subtle shades. You will not believe this if you look into the *Congressional Record,* but it is the newspapers and popular magazines that give the true picture—the telegraphic headlines, the clipped style of *Time,* the news story that crams all the essential facts into the first paragraph and then develops the details below. Journalism is the characteristic mood of American writing (more about this later), as most of our novels readily prove.

In other fields, too, writing has grown informal and chatty. The old-fashioned business letter with its "Yours of the 16th inst. received and contents noted" is about as extinct as the dinosaur. Now the letter will probably begin: "Dear Jack— Thanks a lot for your letter of the sixteenth. We're mighty happy to hear from you so promptly and can promise you fast service on your order." As a footnote, it might be added that a good deal of business is conducted these days by long-distance telephone, a further influence towards informality and the conversational tone.

Almost the last citadels of writing overburdened with words and short on ideas are the college textbook and the government document, and even they are changing. Grammar school and high school textbooks have long been using attractive presswork in four colors, with texts whose vocabulary is carefully calculated for each age level and planned to convey information rather than to obscure it. An expert in the art of plain English now excises many of the empty phrases once ground out by government word mills.

Perhaps enough has been said to indicate that American is an ever-changing language, dedicated to simplicity and color, and well suited to the larger aims and drives of the culture.

But enough. At our shoulder we can hear, in plain American idiom, the admonition:

"Cut off the motor, Charlie; you're wasting gas."

CHAPTER FIVE

---

# Family Life

One of the notable things about the American family is that it is a small unit—father, mother and children. In many parts of the world the family is a much larger affair, including under one roof the grandparents, their sons and the families of those sons. But in the United States, as of course in much of the western world, the marriage bond is the nucleus, and each marriage creates a new family. A person begins life in the family of his parents of which he remains a member even after marrying and establishing his own unit. He also, by marriage, joins the family of his wife, and is connected less intimately with the families established by his or her siblings, or those into which these siblings marry. So the American belongs to many families. Once married, however, the family he establishes is the most important—that is, his strongest obligations are to it. But he usually continues to be strongly attached to that of his parents.

The parents, however, are careful not to interfere with the new family. If one of them dies, the other usually continues to live alone, or moves in with a sister or perhaps goes to a home for old people. American life is planned for youth and mobility, and it is rather unusual for a couple with children to have any of their parents living with them. Relationships with parents, brothers, and sisters may however remain very intimate, and it is a common thing for members of the family to visit back and forth, staying for periods of a week or more, if they live far enough apart to warrant it.

Most families feel a proprietary pride in the members of the larger family—not only brothers and "in-laws" but cousins, uncles, and even relations of cousins with whom there is no blood connection. Especially strong is the feeling between brothers and sisters, and between grandparents and grandchildren. Counting grandchildren is one of the permitted forms of boasting; it confers a kind of patriarchal dignity. Especially at Thanksgiving the family feeling grows strong, when children and grandchildren make long trips to gather at the "family" home for a feast and a reforging of bonds.

But which family? The American system is impartial. Because the name comes through the husband, his family has a sort of priority. But courtesy demands special deference to the woman and therefore to the wife's family. The grandparents on both sides feel that the grandchildren are equally theirs. So the effort is made to balance courtesies. If you go to one family for Thanksgiving, you go to the other for Christmas. If you name one child for his paternal grandparent, you name another for the other side. (More likely nowadays, though, parents simply pick a name they like the sound of.)

When the United States was primarily agricultural, the family was a producing unit, and at least one son stayed home to take over the farm. But families nowadays are merely consuming units. Thus the rationale for keeping the extended family under one roof has disappeared. The lot of unmarried elders, or of the widowed, is something else again, and we have not done too well at solving it.

Some observers assume that the American family is a weak institution because of its habit of splitting off into small biological units, or because other institutions such as the school, the courts, or youth organizations have deprived it of some of its functions. But this is a mistake.

In a business society, the family has proved itself to be a much more persistent and long-lived institution than business itself. A larger number of families survive for long periods than do businesses.

It is the family, of course, that provides the first education, that protects and nourishes the helpless infant, determines his religion, teaches him the attitudes and correct behavior of the culture, and provides the first lessons in recreation and interpersonal relations.

Through the family the child gets his status in the community, though he may as an adult rise or fall from it. Children very quickly acquire a sense of status from the parents and carry it to school with them, where they get still further lessons. The standing of the family in the community is based on an intricate and unmentioned formula which includes the father's job and income, family background, place of residence, activity in civic affairs, religion, length of residence in the community, ethnic origin.

Then there are the objects of the household—the house itself, (56% of our families own their own homes) the things the parents take pride in, such as their car, the household appliances, the heirlooms that tie the family to its past. And there are the intangibles— the stories the parents tell of their own youth, or about family "characters" like the aunt who lived to ninety-five and wondered why all her friends had died off so young. But strongest of all is the knowledge that they are what they are—a unique biological unit, irrevocably joined together so that what one does affects all the rest.

One firm reason for the solidarity of the American family is the very thing which foreign observers often regard as a weakness— the equality of its members. To be sure, there are families where the father demands unquestioning obedience, where wives have little to say about how the money will be spent, where children are slapped for minor infractions or only because the mother is tired and irritable. But on the average, and when compared with other cultures, American families practice equality.

This equality begins with the marriage, which both members nowadays enter as a partnership. Often the wife works until the first child comes, and sometimes she goes back to work when the children are old enough to take care of themselves. In any case she does more than a full day's work at home, for only the rich have servants and even with mechanical aids and frozen foods, running a household for five or six people and meeting one's civic obligations make a full working day.

The American male would say that there is economic equality of another sort: he makes the money; his wife spends it. The women's magazines and the daytime radio and television programs, built as they are around advertising and based upon what they think the American woman likes, are all tailored to catch her attention.

To get a new car, or some other shiny product of American industry, a wife may go back to work for a while. The very possibility that she may do this, or has done it in the past, increases the feeling of equality in the marriage.

It is true that the husband still retains a formal position as head of the house. But while the male's leadership is symbolic, that of the female is real. Property—house or car—is often held in both names. The checking account is usually a joint one and women often pay the monthly bills and compute the income tax.

The nature of the American marriage leads inevitably toward this equality. The married couple, forming a separate family, look to each other for the satisfaction of their emotional needs. They want an intimate relationship which they share as lovers, as parents, as playmates, as a working team, as consumers, as partners in a life-time adventure. One of the problems of the American marriage is that so much is demanded of it. Marriage is expected to satisfy the three basic needs of man—biological, social, psychic—with relatively little help from outside.

*Marriage Rites and Rights*

Because of the importance of marriage, society has attempted to assure its permanence by legal devices, religious sanctions and social tabus. Most states require blood tests to make sure that venereal disease is absent. A waiting period after applying for a license is aimed at preventing hasty marriages. While civil marriages are permitted, most young couples want a religious service—not only for the social prestige and the esthetic advantages, but because of a feeling that something momentous is involved which demands the dignity and the mystery of the church to match or enhance it, and the blessing of God to insure its happiness and permanence.

It is taken for granted that the bride will enjoy the wedding while the groom will suffer. Once he has asked the girl to marry him and has been accepted, he has little control over the events that follow. Here if anywhere rigid convention rules. There must be an announcement party, a bridal party, a sending-out of engraved invitations, a methodical listing, acknowledgement and display of presents, a gathering of the clans, introductions between the members of the two families, often unacquainted before, arrangements for the decoration of the church, the lining up and outfitting of bridesmaids and ushers, the choosing and purchase of rings, planning the honeymoon, renting a house or apartment and furnishing it.

It is therefore with the force of an effective symbolism that the groom confronts a sea of faces in church as he waits for his bride to walk down the aisle on her father's arm. If the aisle seems long, the wait interminable and the situation embarrassing, all these things emphasize the value of the prize. If he feels like fleeing from the church but knows that he is caught, this too symbolizes the fact that he has put the freedom of bachelorhood behind him and taken on obligations from which he cannot turn back.

If the ceremony emphasizes the spirituality of the partnership, the events which follow emphasize its sexuality. Even as the couple comes out the church door they are showered with rice as a symbol of fertility. At the reception wine flows, unless the families are teetotallers, and every male in the place is allowed to kiss the bride —vestige of the feudal custom which gave the lord of the manor a right to every maiden before her bridal night, or perhaps merely a symbolic leave-taking of the young lady who from now on is to have but one suitor and lover. The couple hold a knife together and make a slit in the wedding cake—obvious symbol of deflowering. Before going away the bride throws her bouquet into the crowd. So strong is the aura of the bride's success at having found a mate, that the girl who catches the bouquet is supposed to be the next to marry.

Then comes the getaway, carefully planned by groom and best man to speed the couple off on their honeymoon, and equally well planned by the self-appointed pranksters in the crowd to intercept and embarrass the fleeing couple. Various deployments of automobiles figure in the strategy, but in the end the young couple usually fails to get away unnoticed and a mad chase develops which symbolizes the desirability of the female, the reluctance of her family or friends or former suitors to part with her, the obligation of the groom to prove his right to her by superior strength or strategy.

## How Children are Trained

The equality with which they enter the partnership will be carried over to the children as they arrive. While it is obvious that parents must guide and rule their little ones, still the American idea is to make them independent and self-reliant at the earliest possible moment. Toilet-training comes early as compared with some cultures (though later than it used to), and praise is given to the child who learns to care for himself. Mothers compare their children with others, encouraging them to walk, talk, and mature, if possible, a little faster than the neighbor's child. The Gesell studies, however, have influenced educated mothers not to push their children too fast.

Other factors in child rearing emphasize the individual's separateness, freedom and equality. The bottle feeding so common with us tends to set off the infant as a separate personality. So, too, does the separate room he often has to himself, his own highchair and toys. If there are several children in the household, each one customarily has his own possessions. The warm house which makes swaddling clothes unnecessary has contributed to the freedom from restraint which the youngster enjoys, helping him to know and to demand freedom. His parents are likely to be young, and his arrival was probably not a biological accident, but carefully planned. The number of children in the family will often be limited in order to assure them a good education, good clothes, medical care and recreational facilities.

Parents are expected to treat all their children impartially and without favoritism, though children may not think they do. Children as a rule share equally in the parents' estates.

From an early age they are encouraged to think for themselves, sharing in the household's decisions. They are given the chance to make choices, and if they are asked to do something (particularly something they don't like), it is generally felt that they are entitled to an explanation instead of being expected to obey peremptory commands. In a word, the American family at its best is a democratic community in which every member has rights and duties, with father as the legislator, mother as the administrator, and the children as voting members. Indeed it is one of the marks of American culture that the familial, the political, the economic, and the religious aspects should be so interwoven as to be inseparable, and therefore difficult to describe. Children quickly learn to apply at home what they learn at school about the freedom of the individual and the principles of democracy, just as they expect in school a parental regard for their problems and interests.

One of the leading ideas that school and parents try to implant in the young, and which children soon begin to teach one another, is fair play. This concept comes into our lives so early that we take it for granted as if it were coeval with the law of gravity.

Fair play demands consideration for the weak, not letting your team down, abiding by the rules, taking no unfair advantage ("Don't hit him when he's down"), putting your maximum effort into the game, being "a good sport," which means mostly that you lose gracefully—and win gracefully too. At the end of a football game, each team sets up a cheer for the other, and this spirit is carried into our political campaigns, where the loser congratulates the winner and asks his own followers to back the new man.

If a small child tries to grab a toy away from a playmate, his mother is likely to say, "Don't do that; he had it first." Prior possession and ownership must be honored. But if the child holds onto the toy too long, he may be told: "You've had it long enough; now let Johnny play with it." An owner or possessor must be willing to share. So, early in life, our children have to learn the subtle distinction between possession and sharing, between competition and cooperation. There are signs throughout the culture—and some of these (such as labor relations) will be referred to later—that we are becoming less blatantly competitive and more willingly cooperative, seeking to balance the advantages of both attitudes.

The concept of fair play involves another cherished symbol: team work. To work together towards a shared goal in a voluntary association and under rules accepted by both sides is an important pattern of culture. The training begins in games, but it ends in the teams which more and more account for our advance in business, science, civic progress, and in the mass media where the individual creator has been replaced by teams pooling the many required skills.

There is a strong moral bent to child training. Home, school, church and youth organizations work together to enforce it. Boys who enter scouting are required to learn by heart that "A Scout is trustworthy, loyal, helpful, friendly, courteous, kind, obedient, cheerful, thrifty, brave, clean and reverent." The fact that one can write this off without pause after a lapse of thirty-five years indicates some kind of lasting influence. The parables of the Bible and the Beatitudes are other important influences which keep echoing in the mind of a traditionally-raised child, throughout his life.

Concepts of right and wrong are implanted very early, and if he flouts them it is with the knowledge that he may be found out and punished. Somewhere along the line a cynic will teach him the Eleventh Commandment: Don't get caught. But except for the deviates, the habit of obedience will already be too strong to let him defy the laws.

Child training is a thing American parents take very seriously. In their eagerness to do the job right, they read magazines and bulletins, listen to lectures, and swap ideas with other parents. They would like to go about it scientifically, but as the scientists change their notions about proper upbringing every season, this turns out to be difficult. Said one disillusioned mother: "I've given up reading those child psychology books. Anything that makes you unsure of yourself, always questioning, is bad." Yet the fact that the young mother is often on her own, supplied only with her memories of her own upbringing and often far away from her own parents, forces her back upon the experts.

In the nuclear family, the mother's role is a large one. Until the age of five or six the youngster is almost exclusively under her influence for much of the day, is both dependent on her for his needs and pleasures and subject to her discipline. Even if grandparents are nearby, the parents do not welcome too much interference, because so mobile and changeable is American society that the traditions of one generation seem old-fashioned and, often times, even harmful to the next.

There is some pathos in the fact that American parents train their children to an independence which will lead inevitably to separation from them. Could it be that the knowledge of this coming independence tempers the attitude of parent toward child, creating a deference for him as an individual who will some day be on his own?

In any case, many pressures in American life weaken the parent-child relationship. The school takes over education and a good deal of recreation. It checks the child's teeth, eyes, and general health, recommends immunization shots, and will arrange for glasses or dental work if the parents cannot afford them. Those needing special care are referred to clinics which take care of everything from malformation to remedial reading and psychiatric aid. Boy Scouts, Girl Scouts and church groups provide recreation and social opportunities. Summer camps whisk away the child who might otherwise see something of his home during the school vacation. Chances to earn money in part-time jobs further weaken his dependence on home, but strengthen reliance upon himself.

The shift in our economic pattern from scarcity to abundance has indeed affected the child-parent relationship. When work was scarce and workers were subservient to the boss, fathers imposed at home the same kind of authority that was imposed on them at work, training the children to be subservient in order to survive. But an economy of abundance offers work looking for workers. Submissiveness is therefore no longer necessary and does not need to be taught.

Foreign observers are apt to think that we have gone altogether too far, that we have a child-centered culture with resulting child-like attitudes, that we "spoil" our children by letting them talk when they should be silent, argue when they should follow orders, speak insolently to grownups when they should defer to them as superiors. In urban areas particularly the father's lack of authority in a fluid society where the wife is also a wage earner often leaves the growing child without any solid law to lean on, and sometimes leads him into delinquency.

Even if we plead guilty, we can only answer that culture is a web, and that our children are taught independence because we believe in it and because it will be required of them in a competitive society. But there is another reason, one which runs deep in our way of life: our love of youth. Everything points to and reinforces this orientation. Fiction is usually about young love. Women will not tell their true ages. Grandmothers strive for a trim figure, dress like young women, and keep themselves busy with social or civic activity.

Men, knowing that industry may be shy of employing them even after forty, do their best to keep fit and look young.

Why do we value youth so?

The reasons are subtle and numerous. No doubt the settlement of America called for hardy young men. The Pilgrim "fathers" were young men in their twenties and thirties. Captain John Smith was twenty-seven when he reached America. Among the founding "fathers" who signed the Declaration of Independence, Jefferson was thirty-three, Hancock thirty-nine, Thomas Lynch, Jr., only twenty-seven. The country was built with the muscles of young men, and its strenuous industrial pace continues to call for men who are strong and quick on the trigger.

We are oriented toward the future, toward that better time and place which only the young will reach. And youth therefore becomes for us an ideal symbol of our national life with its accent on progress, perfectibility, forward drive, lively competition, agile young athletes, shapely girls in bathing suits, and the tonics, brassieres, cathartics and dresses which the advertisers keep assuring us will never let us grow old.

The national sport, baseball, stresses young agility, speed, quick responses, an ability as much mental as physical to keep one's eye on the ball. The national music, jazz, is spectacularly the language of the young with its frenzy, its beat, its repetitiveness, but above all its verve. Even in religion it is not a patriarchal god but a virile, earthbound young son, or even infant, who attracts our devotion. We are drawn to the hopeful figure of the Christ child rather than to the tragic figure on the cross.

## The Teens

Yet with all our accent on youth, we have not done a very good job of integrating the adolescent into our culture. We lack the *rites du passage* by which simpler societies recognize the change from childhood to adulthood. The coming-out party and the fraternity initiation are about the only vestiges of this sort of thing, and they have no meaning to America at large. Even the change from short to long pants has disappeared, and the use of lipstick and falsies has plunged to such early ages that one can no longer tell the nursery from the boudoir.

Our boys and girls consequently do not know when they are supposed to act grown up, or precisely what "grown up" is. The accent on youth which they find all about them suggests that they already possess, without effort, a prized quality. Yet something more is required. The child, to be grown up, must reject the authority of his parents. He must assert his own individuality, his right to decide for himself.

Hence the adolescent revolt, with all its painful cross-currents and puzzling, contrary demands. Both parents and child recognize the necessity of this rebirth. Both desire it, yet resent and resist it. The child wants to assert his ability to stand on his own feet as he has been taught to do, yet the loneliness of it frightens him. The parents want to encourage him, yet they are sure that he must be too young—surely he can wait a little longer. But when?

This struggle is all the more serious for the American child because, as the member of a small family, all his emotions are bound in with the family. He is dependent for love and sympathy upon the very parents from whom he must revolt. He has no intimate relationship with a grandparent or perhaps not even with an older brother to fall back on. There will probably be one of those intense friendships with one of his own sex such as mature life can never duplicate. Though this helps, it cannot substitute for the lost mother or father—the permissive, protective parent of infancy.

No aspect of growing up is quite so painful as that which has to do with sexual behavior. The traditional institutions demand strict chastity until marriage. But almost every other social influence flaunts the delights of sex in the faces of the hypersensitive young and hints that one will not be truly grown up until he has tasted them.

The girl has biological as well as social reasons for behaving cautiously. But everything challenges the young male to prove his masculinity by conquest. One who fails—or at least fails to try—is queer. If he succeeds once, he finds that the number of conquests is to be the real test.

American society throws boys and girls together—in school, in young people's organizations operated by the churches, at dances arranged by the school. Boys are expected to "date" girls—to take them to movies, games, dances. The age for dating seems to get younger year by year and has now reached the preadolescent stage. This constant intermixing of the sexes is good insofar as it gets them accustomed to each other, and preadolescent dating probably eases the tensions once generated by the first date. All this is a necessary part of a social system which leaves the choice of mates to the young people themselves.

But young people have a hard time knowing how far they should go in intimacy. The older they are, and the nearer to serious courtship and the age of marriage, the more intimate they are likely to become. But if the man attempts to have intercourse with the girl he is courting, the vagueness of the ethical code confronts them both with a dilemma. He may insist that she give him this ultimate proof of her devotion, yet if she gives in he may feel that she has given in before. Though he demands sexual freedom for himself, he is likely to want his wife to be a virgin. The girl can thus never know whether complete surrender is the way to win or to lose her man. Yet she feels that she must know him as intimately as possible before committing herself to him for life.

"Going steady" is a compromise the young have worked out for themselves. This is a sort of trial marriage (though usually without the sexual sanctions) by which the young seek a suitable mate. The modern youngster is horrified to learn that his parents when they were young had dates with many different partners and, when they went to dances, considered themselves failures if they did not dance with every friend of the opposite sex in the hall.

The modern youngster has gone monogamous. From high school (perhaps even earlier) on up, a young couple after they have "dated" four or five times are considered to be going steady. This means that they will have all their social engagements with each other. If they go to a dance, they will dance only with each other. They study together, are constantly back and forth between each other's houses, or on the telephone. No young man would think of attempting to date a girl who is already going steady. The relationship may last for weeks or years; it is thought frivolous to change too often. A number of these trials may be made before the right mate is found.

Early marriages, before the man can support the girl, are frequent. More children come of the marriages. It appears that the young have solved one of the deep problems of our society—how to bring about congenial mating where the idea of romantic love prevents made marriages. Going steady is an excellent example of the pragmatic approach so characteristic of Americans. It is also a fascinating illustration of the way individuals seek and find security in an unsettled world, and of the growing antipathy towards competition as a way of solving problems.*

The Kinsey reports claim that half the women and more than eighty per cent of the men in the country have had sexual relations before marriage, though often only with the partner they ultimately marry.

Nowhere else is there such a flood of books designed to teach young people how to make a good marriage. These texts handle everything from specific description of the techniques of sexual intercourse to hints on homemaking and how to avoid quarrels.

One underlying assumption unites them all: psychological and sexual gratification for both partners is essential to a sound marriage. The union does not exist primarily for economic ends, or even to produce babies, but to establish a life partnership, a sharing of joys and responsibilities, a relationship that will enhance the personality of each partner.

This accent tends to throw the emphasis on techniques—an American weakness. It tends to ignore the real sources of conflict—the husband's fear of losing his job or of failing to climb the ladder of success as fast as his competitors, the wife's suspicion that he married her only as an incident in his career or to gratify his physical needs. Yet the emphasis on techniques means something else too. It reiterates that optimism which runs through American life. "Everything's O.K." All we need to do is find the right method. That is all we have ever had to do, in order to convert raw resources into wealth, to win the wars other people start, to turn juvenile delinquents into good citizens, to make a marriage successful.

Lives there an American with soul so dead that he has never devised a scheme to make a product more cheaply, clean up a corrupt city government, or provide the sure road to success? Americans are suckers for the latest technique. Is it a book on how to stop

* See Charles W. Cole's interesting article, "American Youth Goes Monogamous" in *Harper's*, March, 1957.

smoking? Thousands of them go out and buy a copy, light a ciga-rette, and sit down to read it. A new plan for world peace? They send in their contributions. Where but in the United States would one expect to find an adult education course for expectant fathers?

If all these schemes and plans fail to bring the millennium, the American does not despair. He invents more schemes and plans. Somewhere, in some fertile brain, must be the plan that will really turn the trick.

## The Role of Women

A girl nowadays can earn her own living until she finds a hus-band, or can leave her husband and support herself if necessary. The threat of this possibility in itself breeds respect. Half of the women working today are married. The wife has thus become an economic asset as in the days of the family farm. As a result, the husband helps more with the housework, and thus the roles of the sexes are more and more equalized. Authority is divided, and the dominant personality can take the lead regardless of sex, or there can be an equal sharing.

Women have the edge over men in many important ways. They have 2,400,000 more votes. They live longer. The life expectancy of a girl born in 1952 is seventy-three years, of a boy, sixty-seven. They are less subject to ulcer, heart disease, and many other ail-ments. The law, which once discriminated against them, now gives them equal property rights with men and some advantages which men do not have. They are eligible for public office, and in recent years have held such important posts as ambassadorships and posi-tions of cabinet rank. They hold a slight majority (51.6%) of in-vestments.

They still receive the deference of the male: they pass through doors first, are seated first at table and served first. They are the family's social arbiters, deciding whom to entertain (though with the husband's approval), where to live, whether a gift is called for.

They can go to the same universities men attend and enter the same careers. They can go to bars which once admitted only men, take part in strenuous sports, choose their own husbands, decide how many babies they will have. Nowadays they can even wear trousers, or coverings as brief as shorts and halter. They direct much of the civic activity through the organizations and committees they serve—sixty-five per cent of them belong to at least one service organization—and through clubs, lectures, concerts and private reading they are the dominant factor in the cultural life.

Overseas observers think they dominate the society. But women are likely to answer that they do not yet hold any sizable number of the top jobs in industry, government or education; that men get practically all of the best-paid jobs while women are paid less even when they do the same work; that when they work outside the home they are still expected to do the housework; and that no one has yet invented a way for men to have the babies.

A wife is expected to be cook, mother, nursemaid, cleaning woman, social secretary, purchasing agent, chauffeur (youngsters are always being shunted around from school to music lesson to scout meeting), gardener, social worker, clubwoman, good neighbor—as well as companion, adviser and sexual mate to her husband.

The pattern for womanhood is changing rapidly, and many women find themselves somewhat adrift as they search their new freedoms and ponder their new responsibilities. Many grow restless and try to lose themselves in feverish activity. But with a strength based upon the pioneer past, when women settled the wilderness and even hoed and fought by the side of their men, the modern wife is adjusting herself to her new role.

Men are still primarily the wage earners, women the homemakers. But the roles overlap more and more, and as they do, equality is advanced. If there is any principle of organic development in American life, this drive toward equality is it, whether between sexes, generations, classes, boss and worker, teacher and student, waiter and customer. Sometimes it is so noticeable that strangers mistake a waiter's familiarity for rudeness, a taxi driver's chattiness as intrusive. But to us they are merely signals which say, in the familiar folk phrase: "I'm as good as you, and maybe a damn sight better."

Traditionalists like to argue that this equality in marriage is to blame for our high divorce rate—twenty per cent of all marriages. Others blame the "lack of responsibility" which is saying nothing, or the lack of religion—though church attendance is at an all-time high.

Divorce is more frequent among working people with low incomes than among those with middle incomes and in the professions. It is higher in cities than in small communities, higher in the West and Southwest than in the South and the Northeast, higher among the uneducated than the educated.

It is certain in any case that men and women are no longer willing to endure a marriage they find unsatisfactory. No longer will they live out their lives in misery rather than submit to the social stigma of divorce. The very frequency of divorce has in fact removed some of the stigma, thus making it easier. Yet with all the aids of psychology, all the guaranteed plans for making a success of marriage, why does the rate not come down?

The law does its best to make both marriage and divorce difficult. Reversing its usual rule where contracts are concerned, it says that if both partners are guilty of behavior (adultery, for instance) which would permit divorce if only one were guilty, no divorce shall be granted. Thirty-two states specify that divorce may not be granted purely on the testimony or confession of the partners. Nevada is the exception rather than the rule—which of course is why so many go to Reno.

Divorces are now most likely to occur in the third year of marriage, and about two-thirds of them are sought by couples without children. Thus, though they dissolve marriages, they do not break up families. Moreover, seventy per cent of those who get divorces marry again with good chances of success. In view of the random method by which mates are selected, this record does not appear surprising. More serious are the divorces which involve children.

*Delinquency—Juvenile or Adult?*

Children from "broken homes" are more likely to be in doubt about social standards, or in revolt against them, than those whose security has not been disturbed. Still more difficult is life for those who have been discriminated against for ethnic reasons and who have grown up in slums. These children clearly perceive the preferential treatment given to others in school and in society. Their defense maybe to withdraw, to combine, to assault the institutions which have discriminated against them. Having heard personal liberty praised as patriotic, they may seek attention and satisfaction in

revolt. The most serious areas of delinquency are those where ethnic groups, driven by poverty, ignorance, and discrimination, seek
to right the social balance in the only way they see open to them.

The prevalence of juvenile delinquency is one of the most conspicuous failures of American society. Its causes are much more
complicated than those just named. War and the aftermath of war,
poor housing, working parents, constant moving about without
striking down roots, the desire for a "thrill" to compensate for a
poor or quarrelsome home, the urge to be admired by the group or
gang, and the rapid shifting of standards which leaves a youngster
confused about the mores—these are a few of the causes. To regard
delinquency merely as a personal aberration to be controlled by
punishment is an error. The causes of delinquency are in society.
The more discrimination, segregation, poverty and ignorance are
brought under control, the less delinquency there will be. The citizen who votes against slum clearance or improvement in housing
and recreational areas or who practises discrimination is the real
delinquent. Such people use the presence of delinquency as an argument for discriminating against the underprivileged, instead of
recognizing that the cure is to end discrimination and inequality.

Serious as the problem is, Americans can confidently predict from
their long history of assimilating immigrant groups that current
problems will be surmounted too. The general rise in the standard
of living is on the side of improvement. So, too, is the understanding of delinquency problems provided by the social sciences and
used by professionally trained workers. The juvenile court movement, aimed at treating errant youngsters sympathetically instead
of as criminals, and providing needed psychiatric counselling, is
another step.

The country is full of plans to cope with delinquency. In Pennsylvania a judge concerned about delinquency persuaded his Rotary
Club to establish a non-profit probation association, raise a fund
and hire a probation officer. Then he suggested a committee of
volunteer helpers whom the probation officer could call on for
assistance. One of the aims of the program was to help the public
understand that juvenile problems are community problems, and
that prevention rather than punishment is the only sensible approach. It is characteristic of American life that a judge should

have turned, not to government but to a voluntary organization for help. Government agencies can provide professional aid, but they cannot arouse the community as well as an organization which, by tackling such a job, involves first its own members and then everyone else with an intelligent concern for the common welfare.

One case the probation officer had to deal with was that of Frank, a boy who kept running away from home and school and who had a record of several small thefts. The officer discovered that Frank had mathematical ability, and got him an after-school job where he could put it to use. He found that Frank was crazy about working on old cars. When a volunteer donor supplied a 1940 model another important step was taken. Frank now had positive interests to replace his negative defiance of the social order. Energies and resentments which might have led him to serious crime have now been directed into clear channels.

Teen agers, more than anything else, need the security of feeling that they are wanted and that they can play useful roles in the adult world. Many successful programs, some started by teen agers themselves, have sprung up throughout the country to meet this need for useful, rewarding work in the community. A group in Pascack, New Jersey, organized to raise funds for a badly needed hospital and did everything from putting on dances to delivering directories and selling tickets to a model house exhibit. With a little guidance, the energy of the adolescent can be harnessed for useful ends while at the same time the youngster learns how to grow into a mature life in the community.

*Senior Citizens*

The juvenile problem is balanced by a problem of old age, and in both cases the root of the matter is neglect. A rapid, mobile, strenuous industrial society has not yet found adequate ways to use the energies and abilities of the young and the old. As youngsters fail to find responsibilities to harness their energies to, so the old find themselves deprived of their functions. Men are expected to retire at sixty-five, or even at sixty.

Recently the rising number of older people has led to a new branch of medicine—geriatrics—and to community programs for "senior citizens." Clubrooms are being prepared for them by volunteer organizations, and they are being encouraged to plan the kind of program they want—hobbies, games, dances, crafts, reading, or just the chance to sit and talk.

Said one woman who had watched the effect of such a program on her father: "He has so many new interests, he's like a different person."

"I think it's wonderful," said one of the elders. "Heaven on earth this is, believe me."

Social security with its payments to the retired has made a vast difference to people who once dreaded being dependent in their old age. Although the payments are small, a couple can live simply on them if they have a home of their own, or a widow or widower can pay his way if he goes to live with a son or daughter. Others, if they need nursing care, go into privately operated nursing homes —a recent but now common phenomenon. Here, for forty dollars and upwards a week, those with infirmities can get professional care. Perhaps the most pathetic of all old people are those who live in rented rooms in large cities and who seem to spend their days alone, mumbling to themselves as they eat a meager meal in a restaurant or, in search of some contact with the living, feed crumbs to the pigeons in the park. Increasingly, however, for those who want companionship, facilities are being provided.

The retired business or professional man can, if he wishes, lead a full life by turning his abilities to the service of the community. Every town is full of volunteer groups organized to improve the health, the mind, or the spirit of its citizens. All of these organizations need volunteer workers. Community life is greatly enriched by the work senior citizens do as volunteers.

Social scientists tend to stress the idea that the older generation has less prestige and influence than formerly, and to a certain extent this is true. Yet as adviser to his sons and as playmate to his grandchildren, the grandfather still plays an important role in the family. A visit to or from the grandparents is a cherished treat for American children. Grandmother's skill with needle or oven, her lore of the past are still admired. The old have time for the young; they are drawn to each other by their sense of being on the fringes of the meteor-paced life around them. Age has a kind of mystery to children; it is history and the unseen past personified. It is a guarantee of the security and permanence and ongoingness of the family upon which the child is so dependent. The very fact that grandparents survive into their seventies and eighties conveys a kind of dignity and strength and status to the family. These things still remain.

Although the family has lost many of its functions to other institutions, it is still the center of the emotional life of its members, the focus of their deepest loyalties, the source of their first and therefore strongest attitudes, the training ground of democracy. Because of ignorance and frustration, many a harmful attitude is implanted there by parents who know no better. Yet faulty as it may be, it opens the way to that give-and-take which every individual must learn. And when it does its job well, it raises up citizens prepared to transfer the love they have found there to their dealings with all mankind.

# CHAPTER SIX

---

## *The American Character*

When visitors from abroad undertake to describe the American character, the results are frequently puzzling to Americans.

"All Americans are Puritans; that's what's wrong with them," says one.

"They're always thinking about enjoying themselves," says another.

"They spend too much time at work," a distinguished visitor tells us. "They don't know how to play."

"Americans don't know what work is," retorts another. "Their machines do it all."

"American women are shameless sirens."— "No, they're prudes."

"The children here are wonderful—outgoing and natural."— "Natural as little beasts. They have no manners, no respect for their elders."

There is, of course, no single pattern of American character any more than there is a single English or Turkish or Chinese character. Personality in America is further complicated by our diverse racial and cultural origins, by successive waves of immigration from all parts of the world, by our regional diversities. It is complicated by several hundred varieties of religious belief with their varying impact on the believers. It is further diversified by the generation to which the person belongs—first generation immigrant, second generation child of immigrants, and on down the line.

The temptation is strong to lump all Americans together. Yet those who look a little deeper are puzzled by the seeming contradictions in American life. It is true that Americans as a whole work hard. But they also play hard. They spend more time and money in traveling, camping, hunting, watching sports, drinking, smoking, going to movies, watching television and reading newspapers and magazines than any other people in the world. Yet they also spend more money on churches, social services, hospitals and all kinds of charities. They are always in a hurry, yet they spend more time relaxing. They are at the same time sensitive to the rights of the individual and habitual conformists. They worship bigness yet idealize the little man, whether he be the small business man as opposed to the big one or the plain citizen as opposed to the big wheel.

*Success as a Goal*

One thing almost everyone is agreed on, including Americans, is that they place a very high valuation upon success. Success does not necessarily mean material rewards, but recognition of some sort —preferably measurable. If the boy turns out to be a preacher instead of a business man, that's all right. But the bigger his church and congregation, the more successful he is judged to be.

A good many things contributed to this accent on success. There was the Puritan belief in the virtue of work, both for its own sake and because the rewards it brought were regarded as signs of God's love. There was the richness of opportunity in a land waiting to be settled. There was the lack of a settled society with fixed ranks and classes, so that a man was certain to rise through achievement.

There was the determination of the immigrant to gain in the new world what had been denied to him in the old, and on the part of his children an urge to throw off the immigrant onus by still more success and still more rise in a fluid, classless society. Brothers did not compete within the family for the favor of the parents as in Europe, but strove for success in the outer world, along paths of their own choosing.

The English anthropologist, Geoffrey Gorer, sees the whole situation in Freudian terms. Europe is the father rejected by every immigrant who turned his back on his own culture in order to make a new life in America. The immigrant's struggle for success never ends, because there is no limit to the possible goal. The second generation child, in turn, rejects the alien parents because they cannot measure up to American standards. The only way he can soften the blow is to achieve a still greater success. All over America the lawyers, doctors, professors and politicians with Italian, Irish, German or Polish names testify to the urgency of this drive.

Not to strive, not to take advantage of the opportunities in such a world, not to succeed where success was so available—these things naturally became a sort of crime against the state. To develop the resources of a new country required energetic people, bent upon using their energies—not only for the rewards that would result to themselves, but even more important, to the community. So material success in the United States is not looked upon as selfish. Its results are seen to have communal value.

Ford, Carnegie, Rockefeller built great fortunes for themselves. But they also built an economy which has brought a great deal of material well-being, higher health standards and better educational opportunities to millions of Americans. This is how it looks to us, anyway, from inside.

A society which values competition so highly is inevitably an aggressive one, even though the laws carefully limit the forms aggression may take. It has a toughness about it which is good for the muscle tone of the economy but hard on some individuals. In our pioneering days this aggressiveness was essential to survival. Now it can be a menace to society. The factory worker who reaches a dead end and sees himself stuck in the same job year after year may take out his aggressive feelings in race hatred or fighting management, or he may even turn it against himself by way of alcoholism, proneness to accident, or neurotic behavior.

Since a high regard is felt for success, the rewards are high. Money is rarely cherished for itself in America; it is rather a symbol and a tool. As a man's status rises, the demands upon him also increase. He is expected to give liberally to the hundreds of voluntary associations (see Chapter Seven) which nourish and minister to the community. Look at the *Who's Who* entry for any prominent business man, and you are likely to find him involved in an amazing number of committees and associations organized for the public good.

This striving for success and prestige, according to psychologists, is a way of overcoming fears and a sense of inner emptiness. In a mobile society an energetic person can hardly help matching himself against others and seeing how far he can go.

Such a system is fine for those who have it in them to succeed. It is not so good for the mediocre. The fear of failure, the fear of competitors, the loss of self esteem—these arouse tensions that some people cannot handle. In their turn they produce an excessive craving for love. So love and success are linked. Gorer believes that most Americans by the time they are adolescents have confused two ideas: to be successful is to be loved, and to be loved is to be successful. Mothers help to impose the pattern by showing affection and admiration when their children do well at school and by withholding affection when they fail.

Since there are no limits of class, inherited occupation or education to hold a child back, there are, in theory, no limits to what he can achieve. Consequently there is no point at which he can say: "There, I've done it. From now on all I have to do is to hold on." Since any boy can, in theory, become President, striving is a moral obligation. Achievement, not class, is the standard by which men are judged. There is little or no glory attached to being born wealthy or privileged; the real test is how far you climb from where you started.

Americans love work. It is meat and drink to them. In recent years they have learned how to play, but they make work of that too. If it's skiing, they throw themselves at it with an effort that would kill a horse. If it's a vacation, they travel five or six hundred miles a day, take in the sights at sixty miles an hour, pause only long enough to snap pictures, and then discover what it was they went to see when they get home and look at the photographs.

Until very recently there has always been a great deal of work to do in this country, a great deal that needed doing. At the beginning men of all sorts and conditions had to pitch in. The preacher had to fell trees and plough fields. The teacher, the doctor and the magistrate had to shoulder guns for the common defense. The farmer made his own tools, harness, household equipment. He was blacksmith, carpenter, tinsmith, brewer and veterinary all rolled into one, as his wife was spinster, weaver and doctor.

Americans still like to be handy at all things. College professors go in for making furniture or remodelling an old house in the country. Bankers don aprons and become expert barbecue chefs. Nearly everyone knows how to use tools, make simple repairs to plumbing or electrical fixtures, refinish furniture or paint a wall. Far from being thought a disgrace if he performs these "menial" tasks, a man is thought ridiculous if he does not know how to perform them.

Along with this urge to be jack-of-all-trades goes a willingness to change from one occupation to another. It surprises no one in America when the banker's son becomes a farmer or vice versa. Or when a college professor shifts into industry, or a young man who starts out with a truck purchased on credit ends up running an enterprise with fleets of trucks spanning several states. President Truman was a farmer, an operator of a haberdashery and an army officer before he turned to law and politics. James Bryant Conant, first a chemist, then President of Harvard University, resigned this highest post in the academic world to become High Commissioner and then Ambassador to Germany.

"For a European," writes Andre Maurois,* "life is a career; for an American, it is a succession of hazards."

A single individual can be at once an intellectual, a Boy Scout leader, a business man, a sportsman, a dabbler in music or painting, a nature-lover, and one who does many of his own household chores. An employer, he may go hunting with his own or someone else's employees. A shopkeeper, he may run for local office and be on familiar terms with professional men and government officials. He will live on several levels which in other countries might be separated by class distinctions.

The emphasis on success and achievement, coupled as it is with a desire to be loved and admired, leads to a critical dilemma of personality. To succeed one must be aggressive; to be liked, one must be easy-going and friendly.

One way out of the difficulty is to acquire groups of friends—lodge brothers, members of the same church, a veteran's organization—towards whom you are pledged in friendship. Having thus acquired assured friends, you can practice your aggression on those who don't belong. This pattern explains to some extent the suspicion or hostility towards those of other races or religions.

* *La Table Ronde*, Sept. 1956, p. 29.

*Materialism*

The men and women who staked everything on America were for the most part poor. They struggled hard, went without, and saved in order to build up a business or buy a farm of their own. The freedom to own rather than the freedom to vote was the magnet that drew the majority of them across oceans. Naturally enough they put a high value upon the land or the business they acquired through their own efforts.

In contrast with this natural acquisitiveness of the new arrivals, the American attitude toward money is quite different. As the German psychologist Hugo Munsterberg observed, the American "prizes the gold he gets primarily as an indication of his ability. . . . It is, therefore, fundamentally false to stigmatize the American as a materialist, and to deny his idealism. . . . The American merchant works for money in exactly the sense that a great painter works for money—" as a mark of appreciation for his work.*

The *acquisition* of money is important as the clearest proof of success, though there are other acceptable proofs—prominence, public notice, good works, fame. But the *retention* of money is not important at all. Indeed, it may be frowned upon if it keeps the owner from living well, subscribing generously to a long list of charities, and providing for members of the family who may have been less fortunate.

So the materialism that strikes a visitor to America is not that of loving and hoarding wealth; it is a love of making and consuming wealth. It is probably a middle-class rather than a distinctively American phenomenon, for most Americans are middle-class.

America has been blessed with a rich supply of raw materials. It learned during the depression that even a rich country can become impoverished if it fails to use its wealth to benefit the majority. And it does not propose to make that error again. A sizable portion of what it produces goes overseas, including agricultural and industrial machinery sent with the hope that standards of production and consumption can be raised in other parts of the world too.

There is no denying the fact that the high level of production does lead to a high level of material comfort, and that Americans

* *America in Perspective*, p. 168.

are mighty fond of having things that are new, shiny, softly padded, conveniently arranged, efficient, and so far as may be, effortless. The bread comes already sliced so that the housewife need not exert herself to slice it. It used to be that when she put the bread in the toaster, she had to turn it once to toast both sides. Then came the toaster which did both sides at once, then the toaster which popped the toast out when it was done, so that she did not have to turn a handle to raise it. Soon, no doubt, there will be a toaster which butters the toast, cuts it in quarters, and puts it on a plate. Perhaps there is one even now.

Food comes ready-cooked and frozen, vegetables already washed. Floor wax must be self-polishing, pens write for years without having to be filled. Storm windows change to summer screens at a touch. Heat is thoroughly automatic, and air conditioning keeps the house equally comfortable in summer. Automation now promises to put a final end to all drudgery, even to building in the controls which will keep the machines from making mistakes.

Why is it that, having created a world in which he could live without raising a hand or taking a step, the American habitually seeks ways of letting off steam? His towns are full of bowling alleys, golf clubs, tennis courts, clubs, lodges, churches and associations into which he pours energy both physical and mental. The labor-saving gadgets, the love of comfort turn out to be ways of saving his time and energy for something else.

## The Ideal of Service

There is an implication of selfishness in the words materialism and comfort—a suggestion of self-pampering at the expense of others. Yet, vulnerable as Americans are to criticism on other points, even their critics have not denied them generosity and a concern to help those who have not been so richly blessed with material goods. The Christian command, "Do unto others as you would have them do unto you," is frequently invoked. A disaster, whether at home or abroad, invariably brings forth a flood of voluntary contributions. The necessity for mutual aid in the first settlements and on the frontier may have passed, but the response is still there.

Magazines are full of stories like the one about Mike Katsanevas who had come to America from Greece in 1909 at the age of nineteen. He fought in World War I, married, but lost his wife and baby. When his mother became ill in Greece he returned to help her, married there, and had nine children. The Second World War reduced him and his family to poverty. Mike fought the Nazi parachutists, was penned up in a prison camp for three years. After the war, he returned home to find his family living skeletons.

An American citizen, he took advantage of the State Department offer to return him to the United States, along with three of the older children. But it was hard to save enough money to pay the passage for the rest of his family. Mike was now sixty-five. When his story got into the papers, the $2,600 needed to bring them over was quickly raised. The welfare director at the Naval Supply Depot where Mike worked helped with all the official red tape and located a modest home Mike could afford to buy. Painters donated their services, furniture stores gave furnishings, and the ladies of the Greek church supplied linens and kitchenware. And Mike got his family. "Only in America could such things happen," he said.

Service as an ideal has spread out into many branches of American life. More and more the institutions of a community are expected to anticipate the needs of the citizen, and to make possible a healthier, happier, richer life. (More of this in the next chapter.) Meanwhile service as a commercial activity has leaped ahead. Since 1870 the experienced labor force engaged in production of services has risen from twenty-five per cent to fifty-three per cent. Whether you want a daily diaper service for the new infant, a carwash (many of them mechanized so as to be completed in ten or fifteen minutes) or a clipping for your poodle, you are sure to find it. The yellow pages in the back of every telephone book list hundreds of such offerings.

While the supermarkets have been moving in the direction of self-service in exchange for lower prices, smaller enterprises have sprung up to supply home service to those who want it, especially to the many people who now live in rural or suburban areas. Our country district is visited regularly by a grocer, a greengrocer, several bakers, a dispenser of frozen foods and three ice cream men, not to mention the occasional salesman of brushes, vacuum cleaners, insurance, magazines or cars, and that absolutely indispensable country institution, the rural letter carrier.

The accent on service suggests an attempt to blend the two conflicting forces in the national character—the hard-headed drive for business success and the soft, religiously inspired urge to serve others. As the recipients of such services we in turn find ourselves wanting to patronize them all, for if they are taking the trouble to serve us it seems only fair that they should be helped to succeed.

The modern mother tries to teach her children such ideals as service to others, considerateness for the weak and for women, fair play and all the other desirable moral traits. Psychologists believe that since it is practically universal in America for the mother to rear her own children, Americans think of good behavior as feminine. But most Americans will confess that father, as the final arbiter and dispenser of punishment, sticks in their minds as the avenger of the moral law, and that goodness consequently bears a strongly masculine imprint—even one that is physiologically locatable.

Gorer, who says that no other society gives so important a role to the mothers of grown sons, sees the mother symbol in the Goddess of Liberty as the moral force which keeps aggressiveness in check. Americans, he feels, have two standards of conduct, one for business, the other for human relations. They are symbolized by Uncle Sam, the shrewd, demanding father, and by the Goddess of Liberty, the encapsulated mother speaking moral imperatives. The contradiction between male and female worlds comes to the fore in arguments over political and welfare projects. Thus resistance to the New Deal was partly an objection to introducing social legislation into the domain of masculine affairs, and confusion in foreign policy often arises because we want to be hard-headed as well as generous and likable.

Although there is some truth in his observation about conflicting impulses, the current trend is for business to absorb the social consciousness into its own orbit, as we shall see in Chapter Eleven.

## A Nation of Conformists?

One aspect of American life most visitors agree on is its conformity. Because they had to establish traditions, because they had to absorb millions of people from diverse cultures, Americans tended to insist upon conformity in fundamentals. Yet the conformity visitors see here is outward, and even then not inclusive. American business men are much freer to dress as they like than their counterparts in England. Women appear at the supermarket in everything from fur coats to Bermuda shorts. If the cities look alike, with their neon signs aglow in the night, they have their separate personalities when one comes to know them. Though the movie theaters throughout the land are offering the same fare, every town has its amateur music makers, its camera clubs and painting classes. In a nation of 170,000,000 people, there is a wide variety of temperaments and tastes.

New religions pop up, schools of human relations and popular psychology open their doors, new fads in diet are introduced, and all find avid followers. Love of the new and different seems to be a built-in feature.

Yet no society can flourish without some unifying principle—something which makes its members want to act in the way they must act if the society is to achieve its goals. David Riesman's theory of the other-directed personality gives us a helpful understanding of how this happens in the United States. Riesman believes that the other-directed personality, especially in the cities, is replacing the inner-directed type which has been typical of America during its period of frontier exploration and industrial development. While the inner-directed channeled his efforts into production, the other-directed puts his drive and energy into consumption, for in our present economy of abundance the main problem is not how to conserve but how to create enough consumption to keep everyone at work and the economy rolling.

The other-directed man seeks approval rather than power. He wants to be "in the know," to wear the "right" thing, approve the "right" tunes, books, or music, and to have peace of mind rather than great wealth, happiness rather than a place conspicuously above the rest of the crowd.

Seeking approval, he learns like a chameleon to conform his tastes and actions to those about him, changing from day to day or from moment to moment. He learns to manipulate himself in order to manipulate others; this is the whole basis of the technique of "winning friends and influencing people." Oriented toward people rather than toward things, he is not as materialistic as other character types. It is influence, approval, acceptance and security that he seeks rather than exhilarating risk with  the chance of great rewards and fame. The income tax has done its share in producing this point of view. What a man wants nowadays is not a bank account but an expense account, which does not have to be saved or worked for and which is not taxable.

All this suggests that the old pattern of rugged individualism has changed and is changing. We no longer admire the man who gets to the top by climbing over the bodies of his competitors. Rather, we like a man who gets along well with his competitors as well as with his employees and colleagues, and one whose traits of character conform to our ideal of the warm, friendly, adaptable, cooperative personality. In the place of Teddy Roosevelt with his love of throwing bombs and poking hornet's nests we like to see Ike with his friendly, equalitarian manner and his winning smile. If anyone can manage people, we feel, he can. And because we place such a high valuation on manipulation, he has our confidence.

While accent on the traditional American trait of individualism has been weakened by an economy of abundance with its diminished need for competitiveness, our traditional accent on equality has gained ground. Not so long ago the rich man of the town or the public figure in the national eye preserved a distance and dignity in dress, manner and speech, and was expected to do so. But today a Charles Evans Hughes would be an impossibility. Now the high appear equal with the low, and vice versa, in dress, manners, education.

Whether in his relations with his children, his barber, his employees, his fellow workers or the stranger in the next seat on the plane, the American wants to be known as a good guy. It is important to him to be well regarded, and one of the reasons why he forms so many clubs and fraternities is so that he may be sure of being surrounded by a comfortable group whose mutual membership pledges them above all things to like each other.

Because the average American respects work and is quite willing to work with his own hands, he really feels no barrier of class between himself and the waitress who serves him or the boss who gives him his orders. Overseas visitors are constantly surprised to find employees and employers calling each other by their first names, and some of them do not like it. They think it shows lack of respect. But Americans do not want respect; they want to be liked. Liking does not readily climb the walls of class or caste, so the walls come down.

## Mobility

Equality does not mean a uniform position on a common level; the variety in human capabilities and the specialized division of labor would make this impossible even if it were desirable. Rather, the ideal—and to a remarkable extent the reality—is universal opportunity to move through the whole gamut of statuses, from day laborer to corporation president, from immigrant son to college professor. To find such stories it is not necessary to turn to the fictions of Horatio Alger, but merely to the biographies of the successful.

There was a time when no American could hope to become President unless he could claim to have born in a log cabin. One of Mr. Eisenhower's advantages over Mr. Stevenson was that he had been born a poor boy, while Stevenson was born rich. Sociologists like to point out that the road from laborer or clerk to corporation president is not as open as it once was. Yet Harlow Curtice, once a bookkeeper, is the head of General Motors, and the former messenger boy David Sarnoff is head of RCA. Today, moreover, the son of the laborer is far more likely to go to college, from which he can step more quickly up the ladder, while at the same time the gulf between the captain of industry and his employees has been narrowed by the constantly rising standard of living. When the workingman has his car and his television set, and his wife her electric refrigerator, washing machine and vacuum cleaner, when the children go through high school and often to college, and when the boss has all the worries while the worker has only to do his thirty-five or forty hours a week, the high posts lose a good deal of their attractiveness for all but the most ambitious.

The greatest of Marx's many errors was failing to take social mobility into account. Our visitors from overseas often wonder why no political parties have developed here along the lines of class conflict. The answer is simple: we do not have classes in the

European sense, because each generation is on the move. To fight an "upper class" would be to tear down the very goal towards which the ambitious worker is moving. High wages, short hours and the guaranteed annual wage make the employee's lot look enviable to many an entrepreneur or professional man. Social status itself is changing when the plumber can afford to spend a month in Florida while the lawyer cannot afford to lose a case by being away from home.

Nor is it possible any longer to look at the industrialist as a crass materialist. More and more he wants to use his money for some cultural end. Alistair Cooke * tells of the Chicago meat packer who happened to visit a museum, became interested in painting, and is now one of the world's best informed collectors of French moderns. Or there is Huntington Hartford, who has used his fortune to advance the arts in many ways—as a movie producer, as founder of a place where creative artists can work undisturbed, as a collector of paintings, builder of a New York art gallery and founder of a legitimate theater in Hollywood.

Americans hunger for a harmonious home, for love, success and companionship like people everywhere. But it is as wanderers that many of them find where they belong, and to whom. They meet the girl (or the man) they are looking for in a plane, at a dance, or at an office party. They find a career by experimenting with courses in many fields at college, and then by moving from one company to another until they find the right job. Advancement often comes more quickly by switching to a competitive company than by staying in the one where they started, and so mobility is rewarded while stability is penalized.

Then as they work up the ladder, they keep moving into a better neighborhood, or into bigger houses to accommodate more children. They are not afraid of moving; they love it. To pioneer is in their bones, and though their westering may no longer be geographical it is spiritual and instinctive. Americans believe, as their basic statement of faith asserts, that happiness is something to be pursued, not waited for. They are dedicated to the quest, and even to the vague unrest that goes with it.

Where all is shifting and changing, there is need for some kind

* *One Man's America*, p. 242.

of measuring stick. Hence (and also because of our pragmatic bias) the prevalence of numerical standards—the marking system in school, the dollar valuation of jobs or works of art, the love of what is highest, biggest, hottest, coldest, firstest.

Americans accept change, not only as something that happens to them but as something they do to the environment. As Clyde Kluckhohn has observed, men meet a crisis by changing either the environment or themselves. The East has generally chosen the latter course, the West the former. Americans seem to take particular delight in such changes—in removing a mountain to make a road straight, diverting rivers so as to change desert into farmland, replacing hand labor with automatic machinery, and then creating an industry out of recreation itself in order to give new outlets for increased leisure and to employ those who would otherwise be idled by automation.

## The Influence of the Frontier

The special quality of American culture arises from what the American land and climate did to men who brought with them the glories and the burdens of European culture. Released from the feudal restraints which still clung to ownership even in the seventeenth century, they were driven by long hunger to possess land of their own. The hazards of settling that land—taking it from the Indian by treaty or battle, struggling through trackless forests to find it, hewing out homes and raising crops with nothing but a few simple tools, dying sometimes in battle or from weather or hunger—these hazards quickly changed into Americans the Europeans who survived. It was struggle that shaped the American spirit.

This frontier experience, so strong in its impact, so harsh a teacher, brought new traits to the fore. The hard conditions of the daily life made for crudeness in manners. The competition for favorable land (or later for gold), the need to kill in order to stay alive, the absence of law and order made men tough, brutal sometimes, and quick to resort to brute strength. This violence has continued in such aspects of our life as gangsterism, race riots, corrupt politics, union racketeering and the violent political attack.

Hard as the life was, it also offered great riches, sometimes for a small return. Hence the "get rich quick" philosophy—the belief that hard work and a little luck would turn all things into gold. Traders got rich furs from the Indians for mere trinkets. Out of the earth came gold, silver, oil—richer than the shower of gold Zeus rained down upon Danae. Then came the robber barons to make vast fortunes by manipulating railroads, and finally the gambling in stocks which affected everyone until the Wall Street collapse in 1929.

But the frontier fostered positive traits too. It encouraged energetic activity and dignified labor with the hands. It made of the independent, self-reliant farmer a symbol which still influences our national life. It produced a resourceful, inquisitive, practical-minded type, able to turn his hand to any sort of work, preferring to govern himself in small, easily manageable communities, inventive, quickly adaptable to a new environment, relatively free of class distinctions, full of optimism and faith in the country which had rewarded him so well.

All these traits live on, one way or another, in the contemporary American. The frontier has not disappeared with the spanning of the continent, or the end of homesteading. As a matter of fact, the government still has lands for homesteading which it disposes of at the rate of forty thousand to fifty thousand acres a year. More important, the pioneer spirit is deeply embedded in the American's concept of himself.

A nation hacked out of wilderness by men constantly on the move, constantly regrouping and forming new personal associations, is bound to alter its concept of friendship. Men must learn to size each other up quickly, to judge by deeds rather than by reputation or family background. A man coming into a new community must have a friendly manner if he wants to make friends, and he needs friends in order to get along.

This quick friendliness, often regarded as insincere by foreigners, remains a spontaneous habit. All relationships, we feel, should have something of love or friendship in them. We do not make a strong distinction, common in some countries, between a few close friends and the rest of mankind. The more friends we have, the more people we call by first name on the street or greet at board meetings, at church or at the movies, the more comfortably immersed we feel in our environment.

The phrase, "He's a friend of mine," is not confined to two or three intimate companions. It includes neighbors, members of the clubs and organizations one belongs to, fellow workers, the man who fills the car with gasoline, former teachers, the minister, the storekeeper. Where other cultures regard friendship as so precious that it must be restricted to a few, we regard it as so precious that it must be shared with all. As our economy teaches us that the more we consume, the more we have, so our psychic economy leads us to believe that the more friendship we expend, the more we have. We have learned, from our agricultural surpluses and from our errors after the First World War, that hoarding does not enrich; it impoverishes.

The search for friends is not limited to private persons; it has become intercontinental. The good neighbor policy for the Americas, aid to underdeveloped areas, food surpluses to the hungry, private organizations such as World Neighbors—these cannot be fully understood as moves of political expediency. They are rooted in the urge to love and be loved, and in the conviction (which led Roosevelt into error in his dealings with Stalin) that if only you will like people enough, they will like you in return and everything will be lovely. If this is naive, it is at least an attempt to replace force with suasion, the mailed fist with the arm around the shoulder.

## The American Creed

What then are the ideas or beliefs that shape American character?

Says George Santayana: "This national faith and morality are vague in idea, but inexorable in spirit; they are the gospel of work and the belief in progress." *

Clyde Kluckhohn finds implicit in the American creed a faith in the rational, a need for moralistic rationalization, an optimistic conviction that rational effort counts, faith in the individual and his rights, the cult of the common man (not only as to his rights, but as to his massed political wisdom), the high valuation put on change and progress, and on pleasure consciously pursued as a good.†

* *Character and Opinion in the United States,* p. 211.
† *Mirror for Man,* p. 232.

Equally strong is the American's faith in his institutions. The Declaration of Independence and the Constitution lay down the fundamental principles of self-government with such clarity and finality that we are prone to regard them as an American invention, or at any rate as principles and rights which are peculiarly ours. These hallowed documents provide us with basic principles which, thanks to their deistic background, are presented as coeval with creation and incapable of being questioned or upset. Therefore we do not have to agonize over basic principles; they are given us, once for all.

The lack of reflectiveness which observers find in us arises partly from this conviction that our goals are set and do not need to be debated; we have only to work hard in order to reach them. To create, to build—to clear a new field, sink a new mine, start a new civic organization, develop a new business—this is what Americans admire. This is what they dream of. Like all creators, they are suspicious of critics.

For this reason, and because they are active participants rather than passive observers, they feel obliged to defend the country against any outside censures, no matter how bitterly they attack its shortcomings themselves. De Tocqueville, much as he admired the United States, found this patriotism irritating. If you stop praising them, he complains, the Americans fall to praising themselves. What he observed, of course, was part of the love and be loved pattern which in spite of its naïveté has obvious advantages over the hate and be hated regimen which has determined so much of human history.

If many of the items in this American credo were the product of pioneering, some were an inheritance from the Puritans whose ideas their descendants carried west with them. Respect for the individual as a creature of God, made in his own image, was one of these. The idea of government by compact and consent went back to the Pilgrims, the authority of reason to the grand and intricate arguments of the seventeenth century theologians. Allegiance to principles rather than persons, and a conviction that religious faith was the only firm foundation for the governing of men, were the heartwood of the Puritan idea.

So Americans played out the drama of redemption on a stage

whose boards were nailed down by Calvinist morality. If they broke its stern laws, they expected to be punished, and if the crime was not found out, sometimes they punished themselves. The temptations of the flesh they resisted by working harder, and thus work came to have a double value. Even today, despite the relaxing influences of Freud, most Americans have a somewhat ambivalent attitude toward the pleasures of the senses, and no one feels quite at ease unless he is doing his share of work.

No story is more typical of this religious attitude towards work than that of Colonel Abraham Davenport when, on a day in 1780, it was thought that the day of judgment was at hand. As the sky darkened, Davenport rose in the Connecticut House of Representatives to oppose the suggestion that the session adjourn.

"The Day of Judgment is either approaching or it is not," he said. "If it is not, there is no cause for adjournment. If it is, I choose to be found doing my duty. I wish, therefore, that candles may be brought."

*Humor*

The sense of humor is often the most revealing aspect of a culture. Surely humor has never been valued more highly in any civilization than in this one. Will Rogers is venerated as a national hero for his pungent, earthy comment on the American scene—for his gift of making Americans see what is ridiculous in themselves. Mark Twain, in many ways our most representative writer, is admired not so much because of his skill at picturing American life as for his humor. It is part of the optimism of our outlook that we prefer comedy to tragedy, and that the funny men get top billing and top salaries on television.

Humor is the great reliever of tension, the counterbalance to the dash and roar of our fast-paced industrialized life with its whirring machines, traffic snarls and frayed tempers. Humor shows these very things to us in such a way that we can laugh about them.

Nothing is too sacred for the comic transformation; in fact, the more sacred the topic, the stronger the impact. Jokes about the minister are legion. Says the parishioner to the minister who explains that while shaving he was thinking about his sermon and cut his chin: "You should have been thinking about your chin and cut the sermon."

The most frequent subject in all media, from the comic pages to television, from *The Reader's Digest* to the word of mouth joke, is the relation between men and women. Says the pretty girl at the perfume counter: "Give me something to bring out the mink in a man without stirring up the wolf." That men are out to get all they can from a woman without marrying her is an equally prevalent theme.

("She has the kind of figure that gets the once over twice.")

Once caught, however, the male is subject to his wife's whims. "Husbands are a sorry lot," says Dagwood in *Blondie,* one of the most popular comic strips. He knows he is "being took," yet he likes it, because his admiration for Blondie is increased by her cleverness. Her skill at manipulating him is the major theme of the strip—which reveals more about American family life than a pile of learned monographs.

That tensions exist in the home life, however, the humorist loves to point out. No joke has the changes rung on it more frequently than that of the woman driver who is usually pictured sitting in the midst of a wrecked car. ("Didn't you see me signal that I'd changed my mind?") Men probably wreck far more cars than women, but it satisfies the male ego to think that women have not yet mastered the machine.

The shop which advertised that it would "Oil sewing machines and adjust tension in the home for $1" had already relieved the tension through humor once the unintentional *double-entendre* was recognized.

A popular variant of the dominant female is the mother-in-law. Year after year the jokes about her continue—evidence not so much of any serious tension as of the Freudian implications—projection of marital friction onto an associated but less immediate object, seeing in the wife's mother the inevitable approach of the mate's old age and hence one's own.

Humor reveals our attitude toward children—our love of their innocently wise comments on life, our delight in the evidences they give of being fully formed individuals with rights and spunk of their own, even to the point of talking back to their parents. (Says

the little girl at the table, urged by her mother to eat up her broc-
coli: "I say it's spinach, and I say the hell with it.")

Can psychiatry help to overcome the frustrations of life? "There's
nothing wrong with the average person that a good psychiatrist
can't exaggerate," says the comedian, thus confirming our suspicions
and making it a little easier for us to put up with ourselves.

The thirst for humor drives advertisers to resort to it, in the hope
of catching an audience long since jaded by all the other appeals.
"You die—we do the rest," an undertaker advertises. What welcome
relief from the usual unctuousness of his kind!

American humor, in short, confirms the importance of mating
and the family, the high status of women and children, the pace
and tension of life, and perhaps above all the love of humor itself
as an approach to life more to be prized than riches, a gift to be
cherished and applauded. The minister uses it in his sermons, the
doctor in his healing, the lawyer in his pleading, the teacher in his
teaching. About the worst thing we can say of a man is that he
has no sense of humor. For humor is regarded as an essential part of
"the American way."

It helps to equalize, and we believe in equality. It is often a symbol of freedom, for it permits the common man to speak freely of
his leaders; it helps him cut them down to size. It deflates stuffed
shirts. It allows us to look at ourselves in perspective, for when we
laugh at ourselves we have surmounted our shortcomings. And in
a land where new contacts are always being made, humor provides
a quickly available emotional unity—not subtle or regional but
universal, one which lets us feel immediately at home anywhere.
It is the grammar of confidence, the rhetoric of optimism, the music
of brotherhood.

## What is an American?

"I can't make you out," Henry James has Mrs. Tristram say to
the American, "whether you are very simple or very deep." This
is a dilemma which has often confronted Europeans. Usually they
conclude that Americans are childish. But one cannot accurately
call one society mature, another immature. Each has its own logic.

What is it then that makes Americans recognizable wherever they
go? It is not, we hope, the noisy, boasting, critical, money-scattering

impression made by one class of tourists. The only thing to be said in their defense is that, released from the social restraints which would make them act very differently at home, they are bent on making the most of this freedom.

Americans carry with them an appearance which is more a result of attitude than of clothing. This attitude combines a lack of class consciousness, a somewhat jaunty optimism and an inquisitiveness which in combination look to the European like naïveté. Also a liking for facts and figures, an alertness more muscular and ocular than intellectual, and above all a desire to be friendly. (Let us, for the moment, leave out of the picture such stigmata as gum chewing, too much smoking, and an urge to compare everything with Kansas City or Keokuk.)

To boil it down to the briefest summary, American characteristics are the product of response to an unusually competitive situation combined with unusual opportunity.

Americans are a peculiar people. They work like mad, then give away much of what they earn. They play until they are exhausted, and call this a vacation. They love to think of themselves as tough-minded business men, yet they are push-overs for any hard luck story. They have the biggest of nearly everything including government, motor cars and debts, yet they are afraid of bigness. They are always trying to chip away at big government, big business, big unions, big influence. They like to think of themselves as little people, average men, and they would like to cut everything down to their own size. Yet they boast of their tall buildings, high mountains, long rivers, big meals. Theirs is the best family, the best neighborhood, the best state, the best country, the best world, the best heaven. They also have the most traffic deaths, the most waste, the most racketeering.

When they meet, they are always telling each other, "Take it easy," then they rush off like crazy in opposite directions. They play games as if they were fighting a war, and fight wars as if playing a game. They marry more, go broke more often, and make more money than any other people. They love children, animals, gadgets, mother, work, excitement, noise, nature, television shows, comedy, installment buying, fast motion, spectator sports, the underdog, the flag, Christmas, jazz, shapely women and muscular men, classical recordings, crowds, comics, cigarettes, warm houses in winter and cool ones in summer, thick beefsteaks, coffee, ice cream, informal dress, plenty of running water, do-it-yourself, and a working week trimmed to forty hours or less.

They crowd their highways with cars while complaining about the traffic, flock to movies and television while griping about the quality and the commercials, go to church but don't care much for sermons, and drink too much in the hope of relaxing—only to find themselves stimulated to even bigger dreams.

There is, of course, no typical American. But if you added them all together and then divided by 170,000,000, they would look something like what this chapter has tried to portray.

## CHAPTER SEVEN

---

# *The Community*

G iven the character traits and family life we have described, what kind of community do Americans make for themselves?

It is easier to look at a small community first. More Americans live in small communities than a casual look at the statistics would imply. The Bureau of the Census classifies as "urban" all concentrations of more than 2,500. But towns of 2,500 are usually more rural than citified, and anyone living in a town as large as twenty-five thousand or perhaps even fifty thousand feels identified with it as a unit—feels that he knows it well. Thirty-seven per cent of our people live in the country (political units of 1,000 or less) another twenty-two per cent in towns and small cities up to twenty-five thousand, and forty-one per cent in larger cities. The majority of Americans are still by instinct provincial and small town, often even when cosmopolitanism is forced upon them. Since the war they have been fleeing to suburban communities as fast as houses can be built. Fond of running their own affairs, they resist the oversized community because it makes self-management so difficult, and whenever possible they break it up by one means or another into smaller units.

Almost the first evidence that you are entering a town is symbolic—the service club signs of Rotary, Kiwanis, Lions. The stated purpose of these clubs is to perform useful service to the community—building a park or needed recreational facility, tackling the problem of juvenile delinquency, supporting the Boy Scouts, supplying free eye care to those who cannot pay for it, buying uniforms for the high school band.

Strung out along the highway as you head into town will be the motels and filling stations and drive-in theater which mark our civilization as one built upon the motor car. No matter how small the town, its parking facilities and its streets never seem able to keep up with the growing population of cars, trucks, buses, trailers. The trucks grow larger year by year until they approach the size of freight cars. The house trailers, stream-lined and gleaming in their aluminum coats, have grown so long that it now takes a truck to haul one. Every sizable town has its trailer park where these homes on wheels may roll in and settle down, like migrating birds.

The approaches to the average town are not conspicuously attractive. The stigmata of a commercial civilization are all too clear in the huge, ugly billboards with their garish colors and insulting commands, the auto graveyards with dead and rusting carcasses grotesquely sprawled and heaped as if they had fought and died in machinal conflict, the drab labyrinths of ancient factories with their cluster of drabber tenements for workers.

Slowly or in some places with unbelievable rapidity the face of America is being rejuvenated with modern factories, all windows and stainless steel, and with homes at once gracious and simple, but the old still outnumber the new. There will be a slum area where the poor live in rotting houses with the paint peeling off. Usually the main approaches bypass the best residential districts with their shade trees, wide green lawns, and friendly houses open to the street rather than hidden behind walls. To wall oneself in is not quite "American." Only the rich do it, and not too many of them.

Any town is by nature a commercial center, and American Main Streets make no effort to hide this. From the store fronts signs jut out in every aspect likely to attract attention, enlivened at night by the bright and eerie glow of fluorescent tubing in red, green and blue. Concentrated within a few blocks are the services and institutions which are both dependent on the town and which the town depends on—the banks, post office, telephone exchange, electric company, fire and police stations, courthouse, town offices, railroad and bus stations, movie houses, and retail stores. Clothing, hardware and food seem to dominate, but electrical appliances and dry cleaning are prominent too. Then there is that American institution, the drug store, which supplies ice cream in all the variety of concoc-

LIBRARY
ST. MARYS SEMINARY JUNIOR COLLEGE

tions the American sweet tooth demands, as well as snacks, candy, toilet articles, books and magazines, household appliances, cigars and cigarettes, toys—and even drugs!

Upstairs over the shops are other services on which the town depends—the doctors, lawyers, photographers, dentists, hairdressers, architects, insurance and real estate agents.

Close to Main Street, and often dominating it, are the churches, the free public library and the Y.M.C.A.—symbolic of the roles religion and equal access to education and recreation play in the town's life.

Tucked in among all these—in upstairs rooms and old mansions surrounded by the commercial tide—are the clubs and lodges. No primitive people ever appropriated more totem animals than the American, with his lodges of Elks, Eagles, Moose, and Owls. In a society that is increasingly fragmented and mobile, they help to preserve the sense of the small, tightly-knit social group. Though their overt purposes are fraternal and include benefits for the sick or disabled, they also serve as a haven for the man who wants to get out of the house. By giving him a fortress into which women do not intrude, they compensate the male for the encroachments of the female on his ancient prerogatives. They also promote the friendships out of which business or political deals may develop.

## The Individual in the Community

The small town (or small city) resident is tied and stitched into his community in a hundred ways. Take, as a representative example, a middle class married couple living in a New England town of ten thousand. John, a divisional supervisor in an electrical parts factory, belongs with his wife Mary to a bridge club which meets at the country club to which they also belong. Each of these social groups extends its relationships across a fairly wide segment of the modestly well-off. They not only attend church, but also go to the meetings of its Young Couples Club.

John's boss belongs to Rotary, but he himself belongs to Lions. Even among service clubs there is a pecking order, though the preference will vary from town to town. As a member of the school board, John finds membership in the Lions useful. He can talk to the school superintendent there. He can also find out what others are thinking about the schools, or try to arouse an interest in some of the board's problems.

Other activities or memberships include: his college alumni association, his college fraternity, the high school alumni association (not very active), a square dance group which he and Mary joined because about the only way they could seem to have some evenings together was by joining something else; the Rod and Gun Club (attends meetings occasionally), the church choir, a national association of plant managers, and the Republican Party.

Mary's life is, if anything, even busier. Like the vast majority of wives, she does her own housekeeping, including the laundry (for which she has an electric washer, drier, mangle and iron). She plans her day like a general planning an attack, and then fits her cooking and cleaning, her sewing and gardening around her other obligations.

On her desk is a pile of campaign material for one of the many fund-raising campaigns she gets involved in. This time it's the big one, the Community Chest, which makes an appeal once a year to get funds for the voluntary services on which the life of the town depends—Y.M.C.A. (and Y.W.C.A. if the town is large enough), Boy and Girl Scouts, mental health center, family service, hospital, aid to dependent children and half a dozen more. At other times of the year she may be called on to visit her neighbors on behalf of the Red Cross, Crippled Children, the blind, the Heart Fund, or the March of Dimes, to mention only a few. Many of these organizations, operating from a state headquarters, have not been assimilated into the Community Chest. Then from time to time there will be special appeals, such as a drive to improve the school cafeteria. It might be argued that this is the responsibility of the school board—in fact Mary may tell her husband so. But the board has a tight budget. So the women will raise the money—by food sales, auctions, "white elephant" sales, bridge parties, dances. The community is always raising money for something.

Why not let government take care of all these services, and raise taxes to meet the costs? Because Americans have been conditioned by their history to shy away from a monolithic, all-powerful government, because they prefer to keep the reins in their own hands so far as possible, and because if government had to do all the things now done by the voluntary efforts of citizens, the cost would be more than they could pay. Even the fire department, in most small towns, is manned by volunteers who leave their jobs and dash off in their cars whenever the siren blows. Opposed to "socialized medicine," Americans join voluntary health insurance plans; 110 million people now have this protection.

In addition to her regular jobs, Mary is always being called on for special contributions—a cake for somebody's food sale, used clothing in good condition to be sent overseas by the church women's association to which she belongs, books for the high school library, driving a group of teen agers to a play contest in a neighboring town, making posters for an auction and placing them in store windows, phoning mothers whose pre-school children should turn out for a well-baby clinic.

The civic activities of such a middle-class couple do not describe the whole picture. They are tied into their community in countless ways and take it all for granted. If all these activities encroach upon their time and limit their leisure, they also extend the ego out beyond its narrow confines and give a sense of growth and enlargement through a merging of the self with the community. The individual who is organically related to his community through such group activities loses the sense of isolation and apartness and comes to think of himself as integrated into the whole society with which he has so many overlapping points of contact. "Service above self" is the Rotary slogan. "Love thy neighbor as thyself," says the church. It is a simple philosophy, one John and his wife can understand because they experience it, day by day, in the community.

Mutual, voluntary service is the means by which the active citizen realizes his position in society, satisfies his need for achievement, and develops a sense of security and mutual respect. Such people have none of the feeling of isolation and insecurity so frequently stressed by social scientists as a mark of our civilization.

The serious flaw in the system is that too many people fail to get involved, especially among the low income groups. While they benefit from services, they often do not support them—partly for lack of free time, partly because those who do the community's work call on the people they know and trust. The low income groups lack the know-how, the confidence and the motivation to raise funds or attend board meetings. The only solution to this problem is to raise standards of education until such differences are wiped out.

## Voluntary Association

The observer who wants to understand the United States must look at the small community first, and at its voluntary associations.

The voluntary association is the perfect instrument for men who want to remain private citizens and free individuals, yet socially bound to the community and exerting their influence upon it. It is, as Jacques Barzun points out, moral philosophy in action. "We don't let God carry the burdens or the blame, we take them on." *

These associations also are channels by which men and women of different social, economic, religious and ethnic backgrounds get to know one another. Eating together at service club lunches, church suppers or campaign dinners, exchanging money and services for social ends at bazaars and auctions, they are drawn more closely together and democracy is advanced. Contributing time and money also becomes a way of advancing one's status. The participants feel that they are helping to create the environment in which they live, instead of being mastered by it. (Of course the forces leading one to associational activity were also in the environment.) Thus they come to believe that they are what they are by choice— a comforting faith for Americans, with their emphasis on action rather than reflection, results rather than ideas.

No one has observed better than de Tocqueville the central importance of voluntary associations. "The free institutions which the inhabitants of the United States possess, and the political rights of which they make so much use, remind every citizen, and in a thousand ways, . . . that it is the duty, as well as the interest of men, to make themselves useful to their fellow-creatures. . . . Men attend to the interests of the public, first by necessity, afterwards by choice: what was intentional becomes an instinct; and by dint of working for the good of one's fellow citizens, the habit and the taste for serving them is at length acquired." (P. 197.)

It is this habit of voluntary association, proliferated throughout the society, which makes the nation invulnerable to dictatorships

* *God's Country and Mine*, p. 15.

and which provides a kind of chain-mail defense against any tyrannical group. The individual by himself is powerless. But as the member of an association he is strong. The associations are so numerous and so varied in their aims that they balance and regulate each other. For every ridiculous or potentially dangerous one like the Ku Klux Klan there are a hundred, a thousand, devoted to some constructive purpose.

There are functional groups like labor unions, occupational groups like the medical societies and farmers' organizations, philanthropic or reformist like the associations to stamp out disease or improve education, religious groups, nationality groups which depend on the Old World ties of immigrants, groups which perpetuate shared experiences such as the Daughters of the American Revolution, college alumni or war veterans, symbolic groups like the totem lodges or the Masons, and recreational, political and feminist organizations.

Associations proliferate like guinea pigs. Around the church, for example, will form groups for various ages or to serve certain needs of the church—such as the committee of wardens or the altar guild. When the number of civic groups grows so large that they begin to get in each other's way, they combine to form one more association —a community council.

Every possible interest, hobby, ailment, sport, occupation or crotchet has its association, from the Anti-Profanity League and the Horseshoe Pitchers to the Society for the Preservation of Barber Shop Quartet Singing. In one American city that was carefully studied, forty-one per cent of the population was found to be members of one or more associations—from seventy-two per cent of the top socio-economic group down to twenty-two per cent in the lowest. One man, as we have seen, may play many different roles, so that the combined roles of all the active individuals make an extremely complicated network.

Those who get caught up in the firestorm of community activity complain that there are too many organizations and too much going on, and no doubt they are right. But it is really beside the point to complain that some associations are useless or harmful. For if you have freedom of association, you are bound to have associations of goats as well as sheep. It may even do some good for such organizations to learn, in the process of competing for public favor, that a good many people are opposed to what they stand for. Our society, in short, is competitive in its social and civic groupings as in its economy. We do not know any other way to guarantee that where the majority rules (at least in elections), every minority should have its chance.

When it comes to organizing useful community associations, women are really ahead of the men, for in addition to doing much of the hard work in outfits like Community Chest and social services, they have a whole set of organizations of their own. There is no League of Men Voters, but the League of Women Voters does a wonderful job, both locally and nationally, in digging out the facts on current issues and making them available to the public. The General Federation of Women's Clubs (15,000 of them, with 11,000,000 members) has played an important part in establishing free libraries, juvenile courts, conservation of resources, adult education and other reforms. Then there are the Home Demonstration Groups which operate in rural areas with help from the Department of Agriculture. A young Frenchwoman who visited one of these was astounded to find middle-aged farm wives discussing such problems as nutrition, foreign affairs and national policy.

## Origins of Voluntarism

The presence of all this voluntary activity is as obvious as it is important. Where did it come from?

When the men and women we know as the Pilgrims left England for Holland in 1607, they had already bound themselves in what they called "a covenant with the Lord." They believed a true church must be a voluntary association of like-minded people—this at a time when the English were required to profess the same faith as their king and to attend service regularly or face serious punishment.

When they decided to leave the Netherlands for America, and when they found themselves off the coast of New England with no government and no officers, they turned again to the device of association. The Mayflower Compact, signed aboard the ship which had brought them across the Atlantic, committed them to abide by such laws as they should devise for themselves. They elected a governor, and other officers as need arose. Three thousand miles from the nation to which they owed allegiance, they ruled themselves with remarkably good success. Though far from a modern democracy, for they carefully restricted the franchise to those they approved, they managed themselves and their affairs with wisdom and skill.

Thus from the earliest days the New England settlers ran their own local affairs. Government itself was, on the local level, a voluntary association. It was only natural, therefore, that as the needs of the people grew more complex, other associations arose to satisfy them. First came the churches, for often the emigrant group was a church group, like that of the famous Thomas Hooker which moved from Massachusetts to the Connecticut.

Such a colony, established by Vermonters in Vermontville, Michigan, was troubled by the visits of a bear who usually managed to carry a pig away with him. All the men, dogs and guns that could be collected formed an association for the liquidation of the bear. They encircled the territory where they knew he was hiding, chased him out and killed him. But death did not end the uses of the bear for purposes of association. His meat was divided to all the families of the village (including, it is hoped, the dogs), while his hide was sold and the proceeds used "to replenish the Sabbath School library"!

The Protestant insistence on the autonomous local body combined with the hazards of the frontier which forced men to band together in order to survive and prosper—these fostered the voluntary association and gave it the central position in American life which it still occupies. Key to much that is American, voluntary association lies at the bottom of our suspicion of bigness, our easy mobility and ready formation of new relationships.

The small town in New England, or built on the New England model, is still more like a voluntary association than a formal government. There are no plums to be picked from the political tree. Men take their turn in office, and get more criticism than thanks for doing the town's business, mostly without pay. Merchants or farmers, they are political amateurs who accept public office from a sense of duty or a desire of raising their status.

Government began on the local level; this is a central fact that must never be forgotten since it explains many of the puzzles of American behavior.

At every crisis in American history, voluntary association has been a decisive factor. When Britain attempted to apply the Stamp Act in 1765, groups calling themselves the Sons of Liberty sprang up throughout the colonies to combat what they regarded as unjust taxation without representation. They burned prominent officials in effigy, erected liberty poles or dedicated liberty trees, made bonfires of the stamps, and prevented stamp masters from taking office. Their committees of correspondence, by which they united the movement throughout the colonies, provided valuable experience for similar committees on the eve of the Revolution—committees which John Adams said "embodied the whole Revolution." For ten years the Sons skillfully rallied public opinion to the cause of liberty, talking the language which was to appear in the Declaration of Independence and supplying the emotional culture without which the movement for independence could not have occurred.*

"The American Revolution broke out, and the doctrine of the sovereignty of the people came out of the townships, and took possession of the State," says de Tocqueville (page 56). European revolutions, he might have added, are city-made, but in America the roots were in the small, self-governing community.

The other great crisis, over the freeing of the slaves, was handled by the same means. Abolition societies demanded action; the Underground Railroad, one of the most romantic and remarkable of associations, acted. By secret and extra-legal means it led thousands of escaped slaves to freedom long before the Civil War broke out.

It was by voluntary association, too, that women fought the long fight for legal and voting rights, and for temperance. By the same means came the remarkable program of adult education known as the Lyceum movement, and out of it came the improvement of the whole public school system. In the same way came the labor movement and the fight of the farmers for a fair share in the nation's prosperity.

All of these testings, political or communal, strengthened the instrument of voluntary association, and each extension of its use

* For this, and the rest of the story of voluntary association in American history and contemporary life, see Bradford Smith: *A Dangerous Freedom*.

made it that much more adaptable to the increasing complexities of an industrializing civilization.

Its ethical-religious basis remained an important factor. When ladies fought for equal rights, or to conquer the demon rum or to make better homes and gardens, they were conscious of a moral imperative. Farmers and laborers felt that they had a moral right to a greater share in the nation's wealth.

Since it was an American habit to identify Christianity with the accepted code of ethics, government itself was looked upon as a by-product, so to speak, of religion. All men, said the Declaration, were endowed by their creator with certain inalienable rights. Since God was the source of their rights, it was natural for Americans to think it a religious as well as a political duty to defend them. Within the brief course of their own history, moreover, Americans could see that religious and political liberties had been interfused, since in order to follow their own forms of worship they had set up independent settlements which required some form of self-government.

Freedom to worship meant freedom to govern, and vice versa. The man who would not bear his share of civic responsibility was shirking a moral duty. By contrast, the man who bore his share was well regarded. Involvement in the community's affairs was, and is, a test of moral worth.

In America, as de Tocqueville astutely observed, the spirit of religion and the spirit of liberty have combined with each other, instead of working in opposition. Democratic church organizations, such as those of the Congregationalists, the Baptists and the Quakers, were training grounds in democratic methods long before we became a nation. By stressing each individual's approach to God, moreover, they have fostered a sense of personal responsibility which further merges the moral with the political, the ethical with the communal.

Yet by a strange paradox, the interfusion of religion with politics is paralleled by a fierce determination to keep church and state separate. We want our leaders to be religious-minded—that is, to acknowledge faith in a God who has created men equal and whose moral law rules the universe—but we want them to keep the affairs of church and state in separate pockets. Here is the origin of our habit of compartmentalization—for each function or need, a separate association. When we face a new problem (infantile paralysis, waste of natural resources, how to bring good music to a community), we form a new association. Each one of us is a complex of memberships, committeemen, fund raisers. Thus, in a terribly complicated world, we try by membership in many associations of manageable size and face-to-face contacts to maintain the sense and spirit of community.

## Religion

Nowhere else in the world has religion shown so fecund and spontaneous a nature, and in no other modern state has it played so active a role. There are more than 250 denominations and cults, some of them having millions of members, some only a handful. Some, like the Unitarians, are intellectual while others go in for shouting and body jerking as evidences of faith.

Church membership in all faiths is close to one hundred million. Throughout our history, the proportion of church members in the population has been rising, and of late it has been rising faster than ever. Between 1950 and 1954 church attendance rose by nine million. White collar families are more regular in attendance than workers, college people than those who did not get to college.

Some of the strongest faiths, like the Mormons (Church of Jesus Christ of Latter Day Saints) and the Christian Scientists are purely indigenous. Others, like the Baptists and Congregationalists, had their characteristic development here. Still others, such as the Roman Catholic, the Lutheran, the Episcopalian and the Jewish, came ready-formed but to a greater or less degree, depending upon their definition of authority, have adjusted themselves to the prevailing pattern of voluntary association.

The rich variety of religious beliefs and practices gives color to the community life, while it breeds a tolerance of all creeds. Strangely, the theological or ritual differences become less important where the variety is so great. There is a whole literature of jokes which makes fun of the special marks of each religion (the total immersion of the Baptist, the fish-eating Friday of the Catholic, Jewish circumcision), so that the differences are dissipated in humor. Where tensions do arise, they develop not out of theological differences but out of a fear that a religious group may attempt to gain political control.

There are seventy million Americans, more or less, who belong to no church. Between them and the members there is no sharp division as there tends to be in Europe. Many of them have probably been members at one time but have drifted away. Many live in large cities where the lack of a community of manageable size tends to impersonalize human relations. Some are opposed to the teachings, the ritual, or what they regard as the hypocrisy of the churches. Others believe that religion cannot be squared with science—a position disputed by many scientists. Some take the view that where there are so many roads to salvation they do not know how to choose the right one. Some carry the cult of individualism to the point of not joining anything—a sad misinterpretation of American democracy. Most are simply indifferent—neither hostile nor thoughtful, preferring not to get involved.

Because it has been important to us not to let religion interfere with our national unity, we have stressed the unifying nature of faith rather than the disuniting effect of many faiths. "The brotherhood of man and the fatherhood of God" has become the slogan to which all faiths subscribe. We prefer a broad statement on which all will unite to a disputation over points of theology which would end by atomizing us. This, as a result of our history (first thirteen separate colonies, then a nation torn by Civil War), is our general tendency—to ignore the quibbles and seek a general consensus.

As a result, visitors often feel that we lack ideas and intellectuality. The fact is that our constant effort to accommodate and include all ideas, all religions, all cultures has made us impatient of small quarrels and eager for large affirmations and harmonies. Which is more important, whether wine becomes blood in the communion service, or whether all men are brothers under God? At worst, church attendance becomes mere religiosity—conforming to social pressures or pursuing social advantages rather than seeking true religious inspiration.

As in all things, so in religion, too, the American wants to see results. If religion makes men better, if it leads them to good works, good thoughts and good conduct, then it deserves to be supported.

Religion has to deliver the goods. It has to contribute to morality, peace and order, even to individual success. And it does.

Surveys have shown that married couples who attend church have a better chance of living harmoniously together. Three times as many marital failures occur among people without religious affiliation.

Out of the churches came the impulse for social reform. It was the social gospel which brought on the settlement house, the social survey, and the professionalization of social work, though other factors were involved too. The casual observer might not see anything religious about great health centers like that in East Harlem, New York, which supplies to over one hundred thousand people a program of education, diagnosis, prevention and care of health problems, coordinating the work of twenty-three agencies. But the human results, in suffering prevented and healthy lives saved for society, have moral value. In the United States, where the attitude towards religion is pragmatic, its test will be on moral or ethical grounds rather than in the realm of theology.

A doctrine of action assumes that man can improve his own condition and that it is immoral not to do so. The influence of religion is thus to reinforce American optimism and perfectionism. Despite the nominally somber Calvinist point of view and the efforts of theologians like Reinhold Niebuhr to accent the sinfulness and tragedy of the human condition, the churches continue to stress action programs of social and individual welfare based upon a faith in man's perfectibility.

## Are There Classes in the United States?

Inevitably men are ranked by their peers according to their possessions and their performance. Possessions (wealth, occupation, source of income, type and location of home), personal qualities (including ethnic origin), achievement, authority (such as that held by a minister or judge by virtue of office) and power (to affect others by withholding or exerting influence) are universal criteria of rank. In the United States those criteria dependent upon inheritance are less important than in many older societies, partly because of the rapidity with which men can rise in the social system. And one of the means of rising is to engage in voluntary activity for the good of the community.

The American value system emphasizes personal qualities, for in theory, at least, success depends upon individual merit. Those with inherited wealth or position start off with an initial advantage (an advantage which often turns out to be a handicap by weakening their urge to compete), but men without these advantages succeed so frequently as to minimize the importance of the "old family." Achievement, measured either by wealth or by professional and community standing, is the important criterion.

Clearly, individuals are ranked by the community *as* individuals. Are they also members of a class?

Every sociologist seems to have his own way of answering this question. Margaret Mead says that it is possible to describe the American system without mentioning class, since there is no real class system. Lloyd Warner and Paul Lunt in their elaborate study of Yankee City derived six classes—from upper-upper to lower-lower, and eighty-nine positions based upon a combination of seven structures—family, clique, association, economic status, school, church, and political affiliations. Each class merges into those above and below, however. There are no sharp lines and there is much movement up and down the scale. It might therefore be more accurate to think of American society as having a number of strata which are nothing more than positions on a spiral staircase, with men and women constantly intercommunicating and moving up and down.

The upper middle group provides the hard core of solid citizens and active community leaders. Above them are a few people of wealth or inherited position who give money or lend their names to good causes, but do not mix and mingle much. Below them the gradations reach down to a group which takes little part in community life, is often out of work, in trouble with the law, poorly housed, ignorant and often unstable as to family life. All these disabilities irritate each other and cause discrimination which further isolates the group. Groups higher in the scale resent intrusion from beneath, even in church and school where equality nominally prevails. Underprivileged youngsters in school soon learn that their families are stigmatized and that they share the stigma. Their reaction to this state of affairs is often the cause of juvenile delinquency.

The outstanding fact about the social system is that equality and status are both necessary to the functioning of democracy, but are antithetical in nature. Our ideals are embodied in all the equalizing mechanisms. Yet rank and status provide the driving force which makes men strive to excel. The American dream harmonizes the two principles by giving us a Lincoln who though humbly born rose to the highest post in the nation.

To those in positions of power, the maintenance of status is often more important than the ideals of liberty and equality to which they give lip service. So it is possible for them, from their positions of power, to give special privileges to their own group and to discriminate against the lowly. The judge who "fixes" a ticket for a friend but lays a heavy fine on a low-class offender, the teacher who bears down on a poor child but pampers the rich, the minister who must defer to the wealthy parishioner—all help to reinforce distinctions of status.

Partly to offset privilege the ward system grew up, with its ward-heeler who tends to the needs of the poor in order to get their votes for the machine. He, too, can fix tickets, make things right for a boy who is in trouble with the police, find relief money for the indigent or a hand-out for an emergency.

Where accumulated wealth is so great, the marvel is that the American people have kept distinctions of rank down to a minimum. The diversity of ethnic origins and religions has helped. So has geography. The country is too big, too varied in its colonial origins to permit one system of social ranks.

While most marriages are made between people of equal rank, there are enough outside unions to maintain social mobility. In one study, for example, small business men were found to have married into upper income families in a little over half the cases, but forty per cent had married the daughters of wage earners. Since young people move around a good deal, the families of an engaged couple may have no reliable way of ranking each other.

Here are a few other influences which minimize or erase class differences:

Low occupational rank may be compensated by an important role in civic or social activities.

Large cities and constant mobility make any accurate positioning impossible.

The huge salaries paid to baseball players, labor leaders, prize fighters and entertainers make it clear that the society does not restrict its rewards to the well born and the well educated.

Manners, clothing, speech and amusements tend to be universalized.

Equal rights do exist in many important areas—in public education and recreational facilities, the vote, military service, jury duty, the right to run for public office, police protection and the law.

For all these reasons, the class struggle as conceived by Marx is practically non-existent. Workers may feel resentment against managers and bosses; they may feel frustration in their jobs if no channels of advancement are open. Bitterness in the face of poverty, unemployment, unpleasant work or unstable family life are a part of the social picture, and there are wide differences in privilege and opportunity. But rigid class structure is absent.

American society has failed gravely, however, in assuring equal opportunity to Negroes. The story of the mistreatment of this people, from the time when they were sold into slavery in Africa by members of their own race until the rise of Jim Crowism in the South with its aftermath of second-class citizenship, is well known throughout the world. Hardly noticed, however, is the phenomenal improvement of recent years. For instance:

Illiteracy was reduced from over ninety-seven per cent in 1860 to less than ten per cent in 1952.

There are more Negroes (128,000) in college in the United States than all the Germans in German universities.

More Negroes own automobiles in the United States than all 216,000,000 Russians and all the 193,000,000 Negroes in Africa.

Full integration has taken place in the armed forces.

Since 1940 Negro wages have risen four hundred per cent as against two hundred fifty per cent for whites.

Since 1930 there has been a twenty-five hundred per cent increase in enrollment of Negroes in colleges. Since 1900 the rate has increased six times faster than that of white students.

Complete integration of public schools and an end to separate seating in public conveyances have been ordered by the Supreme Court.

About two hundred thousand Negroes own farms averaging seventy-eight acres in size.

In 1900 only one per cent of Negro workers were in industry. Now the figure is over thirty per cent—1,500,000 workers. About 1,250,000 of the nation's 16,000,000 union members are Negroes.

Ninety-three tax-supported city commissions and 345 semi-official agencies are working to improve race relations.

Negroes have been elected with the help of white votes to places on city councils in the South. They sit in legislatures and in Congress. Ralph Bunche serves as Undersecretary of the United Nations. Department stores, the telephone company, the federal government and many other employers hire Negroes without discrimination. Artists and entertainers like Marian Anderson and Louis Armstrong contribute much to the nation's life and are known throughout the world. No national political party can stay in power if it ignores the Negro vote.

A department store in Savannah, Georgia, had two drinking fountains. Over one, carved in marble, was the word White; over the other, Colored. A quiet letter campaign of complaint was waged. The signs were removed. Ministers in some Southern churches have told their congregations that Christianity knows no distinctions of color, and that if Negroes wish to come, they will be welcome.

Prejudice is a disease which exists everywhere, and its roots go back to primitive times when men felt that strangers carried contamination with them and were a dangerous threat to the community. It has been quite an achievement to bind together all the strangers who make America, and it is regrettably all too easy to seize upon the most obvious difference as an object for the repressed hostility that builds up in some individuals as a result of their failure to achieve success, honor, friendship.

The Negro has been the victim of this universal psychological response. But lately he has begun to benefit from the machine-made wealth and the natural democracy of the factory. The mass migration of Negroes to the North, during and after both world wars, (three million between 1910 and 1945) has made this possible. The continuing but long-delayed industrialization of the South is bound to have its effect too.

Already some Negroes outrank many whites in the South. One of the most important factors in race relations is the appearance of an upper-middle class Negro group—an educated, well-to-do people whose very presence will break down the old stereotype of the Negro as ignorant and unambitious, and who can give intelligent leadership to the continuing struggle for equal rights.

## The Good Community

There is little space left to speak of the place of government and law in the community. Perhaps enough has already been said to indicate the voluntary nature of much local government, undertaken as it is by amateurs serving for little or no pay. Instead of vesting authority in one man, decisions are often left to a board, or even to the whole community if it is in New England, to be voted by town meeting. There is reluctance to delegate power in such a way that one man might grow too powerful, or to make jobs too big for ordinary citizens to handle in their spare time. The mayor of a city as large as twenty-five thousand is usually a part-time officeholder. If you want to find him during working hours, you drop in at the drug store or the insurance office he operates.

With nearly 117,000 units of local government, well over half of them school districts, it is obvious that people put a very high value upon home-rule.

Many communities under five thousand have no local police at all; they do not need them. The prevention and punishment of crime become a more serious problem as the size of the community increases. The impersonal city lacks the social controls present in communities where everyone is known. Loneliness, lack of status and recognition encourage delinquency. Poor housing, ignorant parents, filth and disease are the crime breeders. Eliminating slums and raising living standards are regarded as the most effective approaches. Another is the use of social agencies to provide family counselling and to catch problems before the danger point is reached. Still another is the emergence of volunteer groups which seek by friendly means to deal with the underprivileged.

One of the most interesting of these is the Big Brother movement. Boys who get into trouble with the police are put in touch with a volunteer who undertakes to give them the love and understanding guidance they have lacked at home, and the absence of which has bent them towards crime. A man is chosen whose interests parallel those of the boy. He starts the youngster off in a positive direction, makes a pal of him, invites him home, takes him to games or on hikes, and may eventually lead him to a life career. In this way thousands of potential criminals have been turned into useful citizens—doctors, lawyers, craftsmen—men who in turn will raise good families and in their turn serve as Big Brothers. Nothing could be more typical of the American approach to a problem than this— with its voluntary action, its emphasis on human values, its Santa Claus aspect, its friendliness to the stranger and the underdog, its combination of the practical with the ideal, the sentimental with the hard-headed.

It is in the larger cities, where human contact and home-rule in the face-to-face group is lost, that problems of delinquency and crime become most acute and most difficult to deal with. But here, too, a way out has been demonstrated by such programs as that of Morningside Heights, Inc. in New York City.

Morningside Heights contains many of the finest American cultural institutions clustered around Columbia University—churches, hospitals, theological seminaries. It is a cosmopolitan area, with forty-eight countries represented in its population, many of the residents recent arrivals. But it was fast becoming a slum area, its residential property deteriorating, the schools overcrowded, church members and faculty members fleeing with their families to the suburbs, crime on the rise.

The fourteen leading cultural institutions formed a non-profit organization dedicated to making this run-down area one of the world's leading cultural centers. David Rockefeller, whose family had long been interested in the area, was elected president. With the Manhattanville Neighborhood Center as headquarters, they began to get people involved in the program. Merchants, professors, labor leaders and housewives began to survey the needs. A professional staff carried out expert planning. It recommended, as a start, a two-block slum-clearing new housing project. Six buildings costing $12,000,000 and accommodating about a thousand middle-income families were erected on a cooperative basis, each family owning its apartment. Two low-income housing projects were started by the city to accommodate another three thousand families. Thus forty acres of former slum have been turned into homes for 4,200 families.

But this is only a start. A non-profit corporation of property owners has been organized to rehabilitate the whole area.

Meanwhile steps have been taken to improve the critical school situation, to provide needed recreational areas, and to make use of other facilities which were not being used to capacity. For example, the Cathedral of Saint John the Divine offered the use of its choir school playing field to the boys of the neighborhood if supervision could be arranged. This the Y.M.C.A. supplied. The high crime rate has thus been tackled at its sources—poor living conditions, idle youth without facilities for play. Volunteers have come forward to help with counselling, athletic programs, dances.

The residents have learned that even in a large, impersonal city, community effort like that of the small town is possible. The people of Morningside Heights do not expect miracles. They know that progress comes slowly. But they have found a way to meet urban problems instead of being defeated by their size and complexity.

For many years Lewis Mumford has been writing about the necessity for rational planning based upon human needs, so that a new biological and social environment can replace the ugly prison of the modern city, its cultural advantages available only to the privileged, the basic decencies of life denied to many. He argues for a biotechnic civilization in which communities are framed to the human scale so that intelligent cooperation is possible. Each urban neighborhood should be a social nucleus, with school, library, and community center. It is characteristic of American thinking to re-gard the small, face-to-face community as the ideal.

Already in some places, as at Radburn, New Jersey or Green-belt, Maryland, the ideal has been achieved. Here urban populations have moved to garden communities where a continuous belt of park space separates domestic life from the noise and traffic of the street, and each area is planned in relation to its school and recreational facilities. Where such communities have been planned, with provision for group activity, a robust local political life, collective action and a sense of public responsibility have swiftly grown up.

The main stream of the American tradition has been intensely rural, the approach to city values negative. Provincialism, with its accent on the small community and on local self-government, has been a corollary of freedom in the American mind. When we try to cope with urban problems, we inevitably see the solution as a return to the small community with its reliance upon mutual aid and voluntary association. Urbanization may be confronting us with situations for which new solutions must be found. The loss of identity, the lack of meaningful contacts, goals and standards which afflict many people in our mobile, mechanized society present problems both grave and challenging. So far, however, the best success has come by breaking down big problems into smaller ones of manageable size. To work effectively for social ends, men must work in groups small enough to make the human contacts meaningful, as in the "home town."

The home town is an important symbol in American life. Often it is not the place where you live (especially if you live in a big city), but the place you came from. More than a dwelling place, it is a symbolic structure imitating that of the family, with its leaders representing fatherhood, brotherhood in the mutual relations of the intricate web of associations, and motherhood in the nurturing, protecting sense of togetherness, in "community spirit" and local pride.

The community is not an abstraction but a living thing. It harmonizes individual and social needs, enlarging the individual through his outreach in the groups he serves and joins. Says the anthropologist Ralph Linton: "Life as a member of a social unit large enough to offer variety in personal contacts yet small enough to permit the establishment of personal relations with the majority of its members seems to be the most satisfying life for the bulk of mankind." *

This is surely the case with the majority of Americans, who enjoy the feeling of being bound by strong ties of sentiment and obligation to their family, church, town, alumni group, neighborhood, profession or work group, social club, state, region and nation.

* *The Study of Man*, p. 218.

The harmony appropriate to a democratic society, they feel, comes from diversity rather than unity, from pluralism in associations, and from the division of power among many home-ruled units. Such a system is unavoidably full of tensions, strains, disagreements, conflicts. But it is dynamic. It is muscular from constant motion, sensitive to every pressure, alive to the need for change, self-regulating, and even—when the need for an organization has passed—blessedly self-liquidating.

It does not wait for government, but generates activity out of its own corporate body. Are slums menacing the American city? An organization known as ACTION springs into being—American Committee to Improve Our Neighborhoods. Is delinquency a rising problem? A community assembles its religious, social, recreational and educative resources, calls together representatives from its many organizations, and lays out a plan of action.

The sense of community, of belonging to a human group, is deep-driven in the American personality, its roots both psychic and historic. One cannot understand the United States until he has begun to grasp the import of that complex organism, the local community.

## CHAPTER EIGHT

# *Education*

Like so many of the attitudes and institutions in American life, the schools had a religious origin. Though Governor Berkeley could boast in the seventeenth century that Virginia had no public schools corrupting the youth with dangerous learning, New England had made them obligatory as early as 1647 as a means of outwitting the wiles of that old tempter Satan and raising up a learned ministry for the churches. When grants were made for the settlement of new towns, throughout New England and onward into the western country, portions of land were set aside for the support of the school. The early schools were often crude affairs, teaching only the fundamentals of language and arithmetic and keeping open only a few months in the year. But they laid down as a principle the right of all to be educated. And they led the way to the first system of universal public education in the world. (The United States also had the first public libraries, the first higher education for women.)

It was a hunger for the culture and learning denied them in cultured Europe that drove many immigrants to America, and their long impoverishment threw a burden upon American society and especially upon the educational system which accounts for some of the traits of our popular culture that more favored Europeans find fault with today.

Education in the United States is not a system at all. The Federal Government has no control over it. The strongest instrument of our democracy, it has no boss, no guiding council of educational leaders, no universal curriculum or method of certifying teachers, no common standard of achievement for graduates, no prescribed textbooks. Diversity is its most cherished value—the right of every local school district, every small college and big university to determine its own goals. Once again pluralism and local control provide the keys to understanding.

Belief in the importance and effectiveness of education is central to the American system. Today schooling begins at three or younger, and it extends with adult education to life's very end, with more and more programs for those in their last decades.

Do you want to learn how to write for money, to play the piano, to speak French? A correspondence course will teach you. Does the government need men capable of tracking down offenders against federal laws? It sets up a school. Does an industry need to acquaint its salesmen with new products? It hires an educational consultant and sets up a course, complete with the latest audio-visual aids. Newlyweds take courses in marriage and parenthood, youngsters are taxied off after school to dancing and music lessons, while even the dog gets into the act by attending obedience classes. Anyone can be taught anything; that is the American faith.

Along with this basic faith in education itself goes a conviction as to the job it is expected to do in a democracy. "The social role of education in a democratic society," asserted the President's Commission on Higher Education, "is at once to insure equal liberty and equal opportunity to differing individuals and groups, and to enable the citizens to understand, appraise, and redirect forces, men, and events as these tend to strengthen or to weaken their liberties.*

No wonder, since we expect so much, that we are always dissatisfied with our educational system. As the President's Commission points out, the recognition of the defects in democracy—"the extent of its unfinished business"—is essential to democracy itself. One function of the schools is to keep abreast of the changes by which democracy extends itself and constantly to revalue its own performance.

## School and Home

One of the healthiest symptoms of education today is the interest people are taking in the schools. This interest often takes the form

* *Higher Education for American Democracy*, p. 5.

of strong criticism and spirited controversy. The schools ought to teach our children how to live in a democracy, claims one faction.— Nonsense, that can't be taught. Give them the fundamentals—how to read and think, says another.

Parents think there must be something wrong with the schools, teachers are uneasily aware of the community's dissatisfaction, and as a result of constant experimenting—some of it wise, some pretty foolish—we keep building and rebuilding a school system which ever more nearly approaches but never fully meets the needs of a dynamic society.

Some of the conflicting views about education are merely technical, such as how reading can best be taught. Others arise out of basic cultural conflicts, as business, labor, the churches, women's clubs, veterans' organizations and civil liberties groups try to get their often conflicting views and beliefs into the school curriculum. This kind of pulling and hauling is an inevitable part of the democratic, pluralistic system. Since education is looked upon as the crucial instrument by which the minds of the young are prepared for their roles in society, inevitably every kind of opinion-molding force bears down on the schools. The august New York Stock Exchange was startled recently by loud but childish cheers from the balcony when the quotation for RCA appeared. The noise came from a school class of eleven-year olds who had studied the stock market in school, pooled their pennies, and put in an order for one share of RCA!

Since educators are, on the whole, likely to be more liberal than the social pressures surrounding them, an unrelenting tension between the school and the rest of society is inevitable. It is precisely because educators take their role so seriously, because they see the constantly widening horizon before them and feel the need to prepare the young for an age of increasing responsibility and leisure, that they come into conflict with the guardians of the status quo.

They have to cope with the fact that Americans have a deep and indeed almost unreasonable faith in the power of education, yet at the same time make fun of the intellectual life, the long-haired absent-minded professor. How are both respect and scorn possible? The respect arises out of our Puritan and immigrant traditions. The scorn comes from the self-reliant frontier where only the practical was valued.

Americans fight any signs of class superiority. Those who respect the learned man for his learning fear that he may create a hegemony, or that his learning will somehow endanger the hard-won status of the less-educated, or that his "crackpot" ideas will lead to higher taxes or other disasters. Parents resent the influence of the teacher because children cite her in combatting parental rules or in correcting their manners and grammar. At the very moment that the mother hands the child over to the teacher as to a surrogate parent, she both sighs with relief and begins to fear that the child will find the teacher better informed. Often a child does find in a teacher what he has failed to find at home, and so the fears are confirmed. Worse still, when he gets to college if not before, he stops going to church, begins to smoke and drink and stay out late —and all these signs of growing up are blamed on the teacher.

Parents commit their children to school to have them prepared for that future toward which American life is always oriented. It must educate for change. So the school comes to symbolize the divisive force between generations which as a matter of fact comes from the ideas of progress and mobility which are built into the culture. More is expected of the school than it can possibly perform, and as more of the family's functions are turned over to it (sex education, hygiene, etiquette, nursery training), parents feel guilty over surrendering their authority and guilty about the relief with which they have surrendered it. So they project this guilt on the teacher, and blame her.

They also take an ambivalent attitude toward her role in the community. She is held to a stricter private life than most parents hold themselves, yet she is not rewarded with a correspondingly high social rank. She is supposed to treat all pupils impartially, yet families of high rank expect (and often receive) special consideration for their children, while those of the underprivileged are, subtly or even unconsciously, made to feel unwanted. In defense of teachers, however, it should be said that many have taken special pains to prevent such discrimination, and are remembered all through life by those to whom they have given hope and inspiration.

The school, by bringing together children of all backgrounds and both sexes, is the greatest democratizing force in the society. They get accustomed to each other, sometimes forming deep friendships outside their socio-economic rank, and learn the habit of getting along with all which will form the basis of their adult lives. Sport and study are great equalizers, and the school gives the bright or the sturdy child a chance to go beyond those whose family rank is higher than his own. Especially in sports have the children of immigrants been able to quicken their climb up the ladder.

## Democracy and Education

From the moment when the tot in miniature blue-jeans or freshly pressed dress is taken to nursery school until the moment he looks down into the sea of faces from the platform where he has received his college diploma eighteen years later, school is the central fact in his life, in importance next to the family. The personality of his teachers is impressed so firmly upon him that years later he will find himself recalling their faces, their manners, their kindness or impatience.

Besides the subjects they are nominally sent to school for, children learn how to react to each other. The nursery school child learns that he cannot grab toys from others or go into temper tantrums without damaging himself. He learns things about the relations between the sexes: that girls are entitled to special consideration (though less than formerly) as more delicate and vulnerable, but still can often beat him in games as well as in classwork. For girls the lesson may be even harder, for they must learn not to push their successes too far for fear of outdistancing men and thus losing the chance to fulfill their biological function.

More and more the schools consciously teach the skills of group work and play, minimizing the competitive aspect which was once so prominent. The "project" has replaced the spelling bee. Pupils are encouraged to work together, say, on Africa. They will bring pictures, draw maps, play games, tell stories about their subject. The teacher, no longer an authoritarian, ruling with a birch rod, leads instead of driving. That is the literal meaning of education, anyhow—to draw out. She leads the children to plan with her, to discuss and to make group decisions as to what shall be studied, when and how.

The philosophical source of progressive education, as everyone knows by now, was Vermont-born John Dewey (1859–1952), who remembered the cooperative, communal, learning-by-doing nature of village life and applied it to education with an effectiveness which has influenced the world. Dewey saw the school not as a preparation for life but as a central part of life. The school reproduced society in miniature. Pupils should be encouraged to do more than recite. They should take an active part in the learning process itself. As a result they would be preparing themselves by experience for life; they would be learning by doing.

School was no longer confined to the classroom. Trips to the fire department or the post office, nature walks and excursions to experience the world in which they lived became a part of education. Above all, the child, rather than the subject, became the center of concern. To meet his needs and to fit him for his role in a democracy became the school's function, rather than to teach so many hours of reading, writing and arithmetic.

Inevitably this healthy emphasis on the child as a growing person rather than on the curriculum was distorted by educators of smaller stature and understanding than John Dewey's, and a good deal of nonsense came to be collected under the nominal head of progressive education. But when the excessive practices are separated from Dewey's theory, he remains one of the great liberating forces in the realization of an ever-progressing democracy.

It has been proved that the absence of genuinely democratic relationships with youth is closely related to crime, irresponsibility, egocentric boasting and unethical competition. The democratizing of the school, unless there are stronger opposing factors, should therefore lead to a healthier community life.

One of Dewey's important emphases was his view of the educative process as problem solving. An act of thought, as he had shown, was essentially the meeting and solving of a problem. So children should be encouraged to work out the answers to problems that were meaningful to them. If, for example, they raised the question of how water was supplied to their town, the progressive teacher instead of answering the question in a few words, would ask the class if it wanted to do a project on water supply. If they did, a project would be developed which might start with a trip to the town's reservoir and water works, and might go on to include experiments in humidity and condensation, the study of weather and how rain forms, arithmetical computations on the use and storage of water, the reading of poems about rain and rivers and lakes, the study of the world's principal river systems, and so on. Visual aids —movie films, picture books, slides and maps—would play a part.

Thus a child would learn how to tackle problems, how to ask the right questions and seek the answers for himself. The old method implied that there was a "correct" answer to every question the teacher asked. The new method took account of the fact that sometimes there are no correct answers—that we must learn to live with the problem, battling the waves and eddies without hope of conquering the tide. A sound education, surely, for our era!

The public school also attempts to:

encourage the child to develop recreational and creative interests;

permit him to progress at his own rate and in accord with his abilities;

look out for the child's health, call the parents' attention to any needs or deficiencies and find aid if the parent cannot afford necessary care;

develop the child's body through games, sports, exercises and the teaching of proper hygiene;

develop an understanding of the physical and social environment;

implant an understanding of and enthusiasm for democracy, and particularly the American form of democracy;

arouse a social consciousness which will carry over into adult life and lead to disinterested, positive attitudes and to voluntary work for the community;

provide the technical skills required by industry and agriculture;

give individual attention to each student and his needs;

make the school an integral part of the community and a focal point in the community's life;

help parents to understand the aims and ends of modern education.

Then there is the matter of teaching reading, writing, arithmetic, history, geography, science, arts, languages, and all the rest! No wonder if the school falls short of its goals.

## Who Runs the Schools?

No other society has devoted so much of its wealth and energy to education. One quarter of the population is directly engaged in the educational process. Over thirty-seven million students attend more than 165,000 schools taught by more than a million teachers, at an annual cost exceeding nine billion dollars. The number of students is rising not only with the rise in population, but because more and more students go on to high school, college, and graduate school. In the United States more than seventy-five per cent of the boys and girls between the ages of fourteen and seventeen are in high school—a record unmatched elsewhere. Forty per cent of the high school graduates go on to higher education. Education is compulsory, usually until the age of sixteen, and it is free.

About twelve per cent of elementary and secondary students go to private schools, many of which are church-operated. Still, American education through high school is massively and dominantly public. How is it controlled and managed?

Not by the federal government. There is no national ministry of education to coordinate this huge enterprise. The U.S. Office of Education is merely one part of the Department of Health, Education and Welfare, administering federal grants to the states and undertaking educational research programs. The federal government contributes less than four per cent of the funds spent on public education.

The United States has not one, but forty-eight separate school systems (or fifty-one if we count the District of Columbia, Hawaii and Alaska), for the Constitution left education to the states, "or to the people." It might be more correct to say that the United States has sixty thousand school systems—the approximate number of school districts. For though the states set up varying degrees of control, much power is left to the parents (and other voters) who

elect the school board. They also vote the taxes to support the
school. They run the Parent-Teacher Association which does much
to harmonize the conflicts between home and school and raises
funds to supply the extras for which careful taxpayers will not
vote. On average, about sixty per cent of the school's funds are
raised by local taxation, while forty per cent comes back from the
state which has raised the money by income, gasoline, liquor and
other taxes.

That forty per cent gives the state department of education a
halter by which to lead the local boards, yet most state systems are
highly decentralized, leaving each community to determine its own
needs. The local school boards are made up of representative members of the community. A rural area will naturally tend to elect
farmers, an urban area business and professional people, and more
recently labor representatives. Women are often elected. Reflecting
the views of the community, the board members may be timid
about raising taxes for improved facilities or asking for a bond
issue to build a new school. But because they are responsive to the
community, intelligent volunteer work can usually arouse sentiment for the new building or the rise in teacher salaries.

The state commissioner of education, instead of ordering the
board to do thus and so, must usually lead and coax. But in matters
of routine and in the professional aspects of teacher training and
guidance, the board is usually only too glad to let a state supervisor
do the work.

It may be argued that allowing the local board such power dis-
courages up-to-date education. But the tradition of the local school
goes back to a time before there was a nation, or even states, and
the right of the community to decide how its children shall be
taught is still cherished. What is the "right" system of education—
one devised in the teachers' college where the commissioner has
studied, or one which the community thinks suited to its needs and
the needs of its children?

Parents are nowadays encouraged to join committees which discuss curricula and other school problems, and to help in reaching
decisions. For each community the answer will be different. In
Scarsdale, New York, where most of the children go on to college,
the high school must emphasize a college preparatory program. In

rural areas where most of the boys will go back to farming, it is more important to give them the rudiments of scientific agriculture plus a knowledge of the world they live in, and the girls a knowledge of nutrition, child care and home-making.

## The School and the Individual

In elementary school all the children, boys and girls alike, study the same subjects even though in a progressive system they may select their own approaches. In high school * they share a common core—still struggling each year with the English language which they never seem to master, but with choices in social studies (history and government), sciences, mathematics, music and physical education, or occupational courses. Whatever the course, they will have at hand many facilities the primary school did not offer—radio and even television studios for voice work, a reference library, and more elaborate audio-visual aids.

If they go out for a school team, they will be supplied with uniforms and equipment. Or they may work on the school paper, take part in a play, or serve in the student government which takes charge of social and other extracurricular affairs. More and more the distinction between the curriculum and "outside" activities is breaking down, as students help plan the class work and as writing for the school paper becomes part of the class in journalism.

The classroom is becoming a laboratory where the students do their work by conference and by cooperation under skilled guidance—learning to work together, to assemble the facts, to reach common decisions.

The new method makes heavy demands on the teacher. To keep up with the latest methods, she attends many conferences during the school year, belongs to the National Education Association or to a group of teachers in her own subject (or to both), and often spends six or eight weeks of her vacation at summer school.

While the work of the classroom has come to emphasize the

* There are several ways of dividing the years. Most common is kindergarten beginning at age five, primary (or grammar, or grade) school in six grades beginning at age six, then three years of junior high followed by three years of senior high school, with graduation at eighteen. The junior high school has made it possible to start foreign languages and sciences in the seventh rather than the ninth grade.

skills of group cooperation, minimizing competition and individual differences, the schools have been developing a whole new department based on the recognition that each pupil is an individual. The guidance and personnel services, making use of psychological testing techniques and interviews, try to help the student with his personal and social problems, his physical and mental condition, his progress in school, his choice of a lifework and of the right college or trade school to fit him for it.

The fumbling, frustrated, angry parent is replaced by a psychologist whose tests disclose whether John is an introvert or extrovert, what Freudian symptoms are blocking his school work, whether he should go into engineering or the ministry, and hence whether he should continue to struggle with algebra or switch to Latin. It is all very reassuring—and a little frightening. Will it produce a generation of well-adjusted, confident, creative workers, or a race increasingly dependent on others to know what they want to do, what they should think, how they should feel, what their goals should be?

### Vocational Training

Dedicated to the practical, Americans have long placed emphasis on vocational training. The high schools, which once concentrated on preparing for college, now offer courses in many of the wood and metal working trades, in stenography and bookkeeping, in journalism and home economics and agriculture. Federal-supported vocational programs, operated through the high schools, are available to young men and women over fourteen who want to enter certain fields or have already begun work.

One boy who entered an agricultural course surveyed his home farm to determine its capabilities, then analyzed the market demand for crops he could raise, fixed upon hog raising, and each year for four years achieved the goal of a ton litter—a litter of pigs weighing two thousand pounds at the end of six months. Then he began to raise corn, following this with other activities which the farm and the market favored. Finally he bought land of his own and formed a partnership with his father.

Organized into a national body, the Future Farmers of America, such all-day vocational agriculture students also learn habits of thrift and public service which will fit them to be leaders in the rural communities.

Vocational training is a partial answer to the problem of the drop-out. Although the United States has the highest rate of high school attendance in the world, a quarter of its children—because of low mentality or relaxed attendance laws—do not get there. Many drop out because they are tired of studying, and because they like the idea of a weekly pay check with its lure of independence, new clothes, a car.

Among the efforts now being made to keep the success channels open are the guidance programs which encourage the gifted child of low economic status to stay in school, and the in-service training projects which help a worker to improve his skills. The very fact that a company has such a program convinces the worker that the economic system is friendly to his aspirations.

## Higher Education

The public schools, while they enjoy a good deal of home-rule, are forged into a system by the influence of state departments of education, teachers' colleges, and the endless conferences from the local level up to the national. But in higher education every great university and every country college invents its own recipe and dishes up its own repast. In their competition for the best students, they are always revising their programs and discovering some new principle of education, supplying some extra service or asserting some special distinction which will make them unique among their competitors. One college offers the study of a prescribed list of the classics as the infallible road to wisdom. Another alternates study with periods of employment. And there are institutions whose chief claim to fame seems to rest on their football teams.

There is no such thing as a typical American college or university. There are nearly two thousand institutions of higher education in the United States, and no two of them are alike. There are now about 3,000,000 students in these institutions. The President's Commission, which believes that about a third of the population has the mental capacity to complete a liberal or professional education, has set its sights on a goal of 4,600,000 students beyond the high school level in 1960. Yet already the United States has the world's highest percentage of college students—one out of every four high school graduates, as compared to one out of twenty in Europe.

Europeans often remark that American students seem less intellectual, and this of course is true. To get a fair picture, one would have to compare the top fifth of American students with all of those in European colleges, remembering, too, that the American college sophomore is about equivalent to a *lycée* graduate.

It is a mistake to think that, as so often abroad, two or three of the big universities offer a program superior to all others. Because of its size, its division into states and regions and its belief in diversity, the United States has many centers of learning. Often the best teaching will be found in a country college far removed from any city. Recent surveys have shown that of the fifty institutions most eminent in scientific training, thirty-nine are small colleges, and that of the eighty-eight per cent of top executives in the country who are college graduates, seventy-one per cent came from small colleges.

Many of the reformist schools are, as might be expected, private ones—Johns Hopkins which first introduced the European concept of graduate study, Swarthmore where the English honors system was developed in an American version, Antioch where classwork alternates with paid work, and Bennington and Sarah Lawrence where John Dewey's philosophy of education was first carried to the college level.

About two-thirds of the institutions are private, supported chiefly by gifts and endowments. The others are state or city institutions, supported mostly by taxation and therefore able to attract students by their low fees, while the private institutions, faced with rising costs, are constantly raising their prices. Some institutions, like Cornell or Syracuse, are part state and part private. While some are dedicated to one field only, the tendency is for each institution to offer all types of education. An American university sees nothing strange about including veterinary schools and nurses' training courses along with philosophy, law, medicine and the classics. By giving a common social environment to all professions, American institutions help to build the common social ladder which it is assumed all citizens have a right to climb.

Colleges and universities, like the institutions of any society, tend to be controlled by the dominant socio-economic group. Private colleges dependent upon gifts must choose boards which can make the gifts flow in. State institutions must deal with the politically powerful. Both depend upon the support of their alumni—a support which is nursed along by the emotional bond which football and other competitive events provide.

Here, amidst the martial strains of military bands, the ballet-like antics of girl cheer leaders and the throaty roar of the crowd, Americans achieve a number of emotional goals in one gala event. They get completely away from the job which is always driving them; they get out into the open air on a fine autumn afternoon; they recapture their past by meeting classmates and identifying themselves with the young heroes out on the field; they give free rein to their repressed aggressive instincts in a socially acceptable manner by cheering their team to fight on to victory; and they recapture the sense of belonging to something worthwhile—a great academic institution—by the exhilarating and unintellectual means of shouting and backslapping, rather than by painful effort.

What a bargain, all on a Saturday afternoon! And no wonder the grateful alumni support their college with gifts. If it wins games, that is. In the drama of success, one must always be on the winning side.

What does the young man or young woman learn in college?

To put it simply, he studies the three great divisions of learning in the modern world—science, social science and the humanities. All American institutions are agreed that an educated man needs to have a grasp on each of these three handles to experience, enjoyment and livelihood. But then each goes its own way in the teaching of them—in emphasis and order and method.

Every college uses the three basic devices of lecture, discussion and tutorial, though the larger the college (with some exceptions) the less it is likely to give individual guidance. For science the laboratory, for social sciences the interview and survey and statistics, for the humanities listening or seeing as well as performing are now taken for granted, and of course library and research work enter into all fields.

Beyond that, the variety is limitless. Progressive schools, such as

Sarah Lawrence and Bard, stress the importance of doing. If concentrating in music, the student should play and compose, not merely listen and read; if majoring in social sciences, he should ring doorbells and ask questions. Harvard and Yale have adapted the English plan of tutors and masters in order to bring a more individualized teaching to institutions that were otherwise growing too big for stimulating contacts between student and teacher. Area studies have drawn together the specialized knowledge of many disciplines, concentrating them upon one geographical region. John Erskine at Columbia revived an interest in the classics which led to the Columbia honors system and spread throughout the country in forms as various as those followed at St. John's College and Chicago, as well as in the formation of adult reading and discussion groups.

The salient qualities of the American undergraduate curriculum might be summarized as: emphasis upon individual instruction and group discussion rather than on lectures; a concern to fit students for adult life in a complicated world by sending them out well informed about the economy, the government, and the international world they live in; a rising accent on the arts and on their place in the well-balanced life; preparation for a job or for motherhood and child-rearing.

To pull together a system so various, an unknown genius devised the point credit system. For every hour per week of classwork, one point or credit per term. Five three-hour courses—fifteen credits per term, 120 points to graduate: how simple! Thus by a mathematical fiction it was assumed that a course in sociology at Harvard was equivalent to a course in wool-gathering at Podunk, and students could transfer back and forth as need or whim required.

Of course no one ever believed that such equality really existed, but academic bookwork has been greatly simplified and much face has been saved. And students may move from one institution to another even if the new one, to preserve its own pride, insists upon discounting the credits brought along, or depreciates as against its own currency the standard grades of A for excellent, B for good, C for fair, D for condition (requiring re-examination before credit will be given for the course) and E or F, failure. If a student gets too many conditions or failures, he may be allowed to attend summer school in order to keep up with his class. For him, and for teachers seeking to upgrade themselves or students trying to finish college in three years rather than four, summer schools thrive in most universities.

Thorstein Veblen, who took a sour view of the American university, claimed that the desire for pecuniary success led to a "practical" bias in the curriculum.

While Veblen's criticism is still valid in part, there has been a great change since his day, and a much higher valuation put upon the liberal arts, even by those whose major interest is "practical." Medical schools recognize the value of a rounded curriculum for their candidates. Industrial firms and engineering colleges are requiring that their students have some knowledge of the arts and of the social sciences which promote an understanding of the world they live in. The old elective system which allowed a student to pick and choose courses as he might buy an assortment of candies is dead. Certain basic courses in the three great disciplines are now required of all.

To make certain that each student follows a course of studies which makes sense for him, the adviser system has grown up, and in some colleges it is a close and continuous relationship requiring at least weekly conferences and sometimes involving tutorial work. American students soon learn that they may develop with their college instructors a relationship much closer than they enjoyed with high school teachers.

The aim of the skilled college teacher (or of any teacher) is not to impart knowledge by fíat or dispensation—though he sometimes uses the lecture as the quickest way of opening up a new world of ideas—but to make his students want to think for themselves, to infect them with the enthusiasm he feels for his subject.

"Wolfe is mad," jealous courtiers told King George. "Then I wish he would bite some of my generals," said the king, and sent him off to take Quebec.

It is a college instructor's business to bite his students—to hurt them a little with his criticism, to goad them, to inject into their blood-streams some of the rabid love of learning so that they will never be quite well of it.

In addition to his instructors who guide and goad him, the stu-

dent has a whole entourage of specialists looking out for his welfare. Surely no medieval prince ever had half the expert attendance
that is lavished upon the lowly undergraduate. First of all there is
the dean, who stands as a surrogate father to the whole college and
who tends to be idealized both for his strictness and his leniency.
When the boys play some prank which enrages the town (the
fight between town and gown is an indispensable part of small
college life), the dean administers the punishment. Yet after scaring
the wits out of the offenders, he somehow manages to make the
punishment not so severe after all, and even in the moment of delivering his stern reprimand, contrives to let them know that he
was once a boy too, that he is gown rather than town, and that in
after years this escapade will give them something to laugh over.
And the boys go away loving the dean, not knowing that they had
to misbehave in order to find through his handling of them the
ideal father they had been looking for, and against whom they had
to revolt in order to earn their manhood.

The dean's job is a tough one. In most small colleges, and in
many large ones, he undertakes to know every student by name.
Since he also has an academic field of his own and often teaches a
course or two, his duties sometimes conflct. A dean who was a
famous ichthyologist, when asked how he was getting along with
the new crop of students, complained: "Every time I learn a fresh-
man I forget a fish."

The dean must also meditate between his faculty and the administration. The faculty are usually fighting for higher academic
standards and sometimes they are fighting each other, but they will
always join and run with the pack when the horn blows for a
pursuit of the administration. In recent years the college budget
has been giving more and more to administration. Admissions, public relations, guidance, assistants to the dean, remedial reading, psy-
chiatrists, health service, residence hall directors, athletic directors,
libraries, employment bureau—all these persons and services in addition to those already established (bursar, secretary, registrar, buildings and grounds, alumni office) have grown up to serve student
needs in an increasingly complex world.

Administrative officers are concerned with keeping the alumni
happy by winning games and keeping "reds" and "pinks" off the

faculty, placating parents who think their children are being made
to work too hard or not hard enough, or are being taught "atheism"
or "pornography" if they read Lucretius or Rabelais, calming the
nerves of citizens who are roused in the night by the cries of
carousing students, attracting enough candidates so that the admissions office can boast of the high proportion of applicants it turns
away, and stroking the rich as ants stroke their "cows" for the
honey on which the life of the school depends.

The faculty complain that the quality of the students is always
getting worse; the admissions office shows them with charts and
graphs that it is always getting better. The faculty object that
they no longer have a real voice in determining policies, to which
the administration may retort: Do you want to give up any more of
your time to committee work? If the faculty are bold enough to
say what they really think—that academic salaries could be raised
by dumping out the whole lot of administrative sycophants who are
eating up the income, they will be answered that a college which
does not offer all these services would soon lose all its students to
one which does.

As the managers have taken over industry, so a managerial revolution has swept the universities. Between producer and consumer,
professor and student, are interposed a number of specialists offering services regarded as essential for the student's salvation, as perhaps they are, yet somehow compartmentalizing an experience that
once had been much more simple and direct though possibly not
nearly so efficient.

As in every department of American life, the trouble is that the
college has tried to do so much. Its ideals are sound; but it has to
do with refractory human material. For decades educators had repeated the classical ideal, *Mens sana in corpore sano*, to justify
athletic programs and competitive sports. But now a sound body
seemed to require many other props, including an expensive clinic
with doctors and nurses, and an infirmary for those enjoying the
childhood diseases which they had failed to get before coming to
college. Now mind and body could no longer be considered as
things apart like man and woman, night and day. So there had to
be a psychiatrist on hand. There had to be social activities, and
some solution to the explosive situation of having young males and

females together who were supposed to play around the fringes of sex without getting hurt. Here learning by doing could be a dangerous dictum!

The pretense that anyone can learn anything and that the properly balanced diet—whether it be food, work and play, individual and society, country and city, sex and religion, speed and relaxation, frivolity and seriousness, mind and body—will bring success and happiness is a durable folk belief. So the college diet calls for some study, some athletic activity, often some remunerative work, some conference with professors—if only to get practice in "contacting" people and perhaps raising one's grade a few points, some dating, some fraternizing with one's own sex and (if male) misbehaving enough to assert one's manhood, and a great deal of what is known as "student activity."

Student activities take the form of editing a newspaper (daily or weekly), getting out a school annual and a magazine, debating, going out for one of a dozen different sports in order to "make" the team, managing these teams, serving as class officers, planning dances and other social events, acting in plays or working backstage, singing in glee clubs and choruses, playing in bands, orchestras or chamber groups, taking part in literary, scientific or hobby clubs, joining the French or German or Spanish Club or House or Table, joining a fraternity and then serving as an officer or helping to fight the always losing (yet never lost) battle of keeping the house solvent and in passable repair.

All this activity—its variety and the drive with which it is carried on—amazes our visitors. Yet its logic is clear when it is compared with the life "outside." The student who tells a friend in another fraternity, "Get your house to support Lew Baker for student government chairman, and we'll back your man for football manager," is learning the give and take of business or political life.

Perhaps the most important skill of all is learning how to manage people—a gift highly regarded and highly rewarded. College students learn that the art combines business with relaxation—that you have to drink with the fellows, lie around on dormitory beds bulling with them, and meet them in the intimate body contact of sports, shrewdly assessing their strengths and weaknesses, and seem to give in when you know you have actually won a victory. If these are not arts highly valued academically, they are properly valued by society, and it is part of undergraduate wisdom to know this. Small wonder if American college students seem unintellectual to foreign observers. They have not come to college to become scholars, but to learn the magic formula, the balanced diet which will fit them for life.

## Women and Learning

A definite part of that life is women. Except in the east, most undergraduate colleges are coeducational. Boys and girls sit in the same classes, eat at the same tables, study the same texts, acquire the same enthusiasms, lie about on the green lawns discussing Life with a capital L, try each other out on dates. One of college's important functions, in a society which decrees exogamous marriage but gives the youngsters no help in achieving it, is to put them in touch with possible partners, and with members of their own age and sex with whom they can talk about their experiences and thus form their concept of the kind of girl (or boy) and marriage they want.

More often now students are marrying while they are still in college. Relieved of the tensions that otherwise upset them, they can live the kind of life for which they are biologically ready. The shift, initiated by the war which brought students to college four or five years older than the usual crop, has to some extent continued. Sixteen per cent of today's undergraduates are married. But some colleges and some parents still frown on the idea.

As for the college girl, her choice of studies is complicated by the fact that she will probably work a few years—many girls who marry at graduation support their husbands through law or medical school—then spend the rest of her life as a wife, mother and community servant. So she needs to study for two careers. Her professional education is her dowry and her insurance policy. If she marries, it will bring her a better husband. If she should by some tragedy fail to catch a husband, it insures her against want or dependence, and guarantees a better job.

So, having chosen a career, she will study for that. Often it will be teaching, since the great majority of public school teachers (three to one) are women. But it may be anything, for no channels are closed to women though they find it much harder to rise to the top, and are rarely paid equally with men. But as a potential mother the college girl will perhaps take more psychology, possibly a course in child training, and in some schools (though the more intellectual exclude them from the curriculum), courses in home economics. She will be as active as her boy friend in campus politics, for she, too, will later on be winning friends and influencing elections.

## Graduate Study

The jump from undergraduate college to one of the graduate schools of the university is in some ways as abrupt as that from high school to college. The 278,000 graduate students in the country are seriously preparing themselves to enter a highly competitive field of learning—law or medicine or philosophy or government. They have had to compete for a place in the graduate school and they know they will be dropped unless their performance is high.

There is no time now for campus politics, hobbies, athletics or night-long bull sessions. The graduate student shucks all this off as eagerly as he had embraced it a year before. Now he seeks a room by himself instead of one in a fraternity house or with a roommate. When he is not at lectures or seminars, he spends most of his time in the library or laboratory or poring over his own few and expensive text books late at night. Now and then he allows himself time off for a movie or a concert, a game of tennis or a date, but work is his staple.

Overseas visitors are impressed by the quantity of reading demanded by graduate school professors, by the required attendance at lectures, the tests and examinations, the demands for research papers of length and weight, the quality of the seminars at which these papers are discussed by professor and students.

One year of such concentrated activity (or sometimes two) will usually bring a master's degree. Three years are a minimum for a Ph.D., though most candidates take several more years to complete the dissertation which is one of the requirements. For medical doctors, several years of internship and residency follow the years of lecture and laboratory.

It would be interesting to know why American education is so arranged that there is an abrupt transition from high school to college, and then from college to graduate school. It is as if in each case the system, worried about having pampered the product too much and too long, tried to make amends by plunging off in the opposite direction—in the first case by a sudden sanction of social freedom including removal of family control, in the second a sudden gift of intellectual freedom combined with a sink-or-swim, survive or perish challenge, by Spencer out of Darwin.

Shortcomings of the graduate school include a premature and excessive specialization within a field, machine-made research, and unimaginative dissertations which display a good deal of mechanical activity, enormous bibliographies, and too little insight. The Ph.D. has become a required ticket of admission for the would-be college teacher, yet the Ph.D. discipline has little or nothing to do with the art of teaching, and it prepares a student not to want to teach, but to want to do more research. So teachers are produced in spite of the system, not because of it.

*Popular Education*

The President's Commission would like the universities to envision a still larger role—that of serving as the means by which the whole population is encouraged to carry education to the extent of its capacities.

Already the great state universities are approaching this goal, with their courses given by television, by mail, or by extension classes reaching out into various parts of the state, and by the encouragement given to forums, discussion and reading groups. About eight hundred thousand adults are enrolled in off-campus classes, while the number reached by correspondence and non-commercial television courses brings the total to thirty million.

Meanwhile the adult education movement has blossomed forth like a fruit tree all over the country. Ever since 1826 when Josiah Holbrook started the Lyceum movement in Massachusetts, the idea of education as a continuing process has been firmly rooted in the culture. In 1874 came the Chautauqua movement which by 1904 was sending its traveling companies throughout the country. Overnight a tent would go up in some vacant lot, and for a summer's week the favored town would be treated to lectures, music, "read-ings," and travelogs.

Nowadays adult education is centered locally in the public schools, whose facilities are opened at night to the general public. More than three million adults are enrolled in these evening courses, which teach everything from guitar-playing to mathematics, from metal-working to Spanish.

All kinds of organizations offer special programs—the Y.M.C.A's. and Y.W.C.A's., unions and farm groups, or associations established especially to offer a lecture series, a reading of great books, a dis-cussion of international affairs. Through the Extension Service of the Department of Agriculture about seven million rural people receive printed materials and demonstrations, attend meetings or join the 4H Clubs (Hand, Heart, Home, Health), which bring to rural children both recreation and projects related to better farm living. Into the country, too, go the bookmobiles—libraries on wheels which carry the latest reading, or the classics, to farm readers.

The public library (there are seven thousand of them) is an edu-cational institution in itself, for it not only lends books for home use and advises readers how to find what they are looking for, but offers book talks, story hours for children, discussion groups, rec-ord concerts and loans, film programs, reading lists, help to program chairmen of clubs, exhibitions, books in Braille for the blind, the use of meeting rooms for cultural purposes, and excellent reference collections for special interests such as local history, genealogy and fine arts.

A basic part of the adult education movement, ever since the great waves of immigration began, has been the Americanization program, by which new residents are prepared for the privilege of citizenship. In evening classes held at the public schools they study English, American history, geography and government. These classes are voluntary, of course, but they have brought to many their first taste of schooling, and so have made democracy seem synonymous with the right to know, as it should be.

The greatest failure in fully democratizing education in the United States has been the inequality of opportunity as between the various states, some having much better school systems than others, and particularly with regard to the schooling of Negroes in the

South. Until the Supreme Court decisions of 1954 and 1955 separate schools were operated in the southern states for Negroes and whites. This system no longer has the sanction of law, but a long and painful period of adjustment lies ahead before it can be brought to an end.

## Education and the Free World

One of the most exciting recent developments has been the up-surge in international education since the end of the Second World War. About thirty-five thousand overseas students and an additional fifteen thousand specialists are now studying in the United States, while about ten thousand Americans are studying abroad. The Fulbright Act, the Smith-Mundt Act, the Educational Exchange Act and many other laws have placed the resources of the federal government behind the largest international exchange program in the world's history. The Institute of International Education, a voluntary association, helps both American and overseas students with their plans. Often the college or university provides scholarships which cover the cost of tuition.

Not only college and university students and professors, but high school youngsters, labor, industrial and farm representatives and technical specialists are taking part in this cross-fertilization of cultures. The federal Office of Education administers a number of special programs for teachers, leaders and specialists which add up to about eight thousand people. Nearly three thousand are involved in a program which sends Americans to teach in the public schools of other lands, while teachers from overseas come to live and teach in American communities. The Office of Education also has a credit evaluation service to aid international exchange, and supplies valuable information on educational tendencies abroad.

Wherever a college or university has overseas students—and nowadays most do—the surrounding community is taking advantage of their presence to learn more about the countries from which they come. Many a town deep in the heart of the continent has in this way reached out to make contact with foreign nations. Students from overseas have in this manner found a second home.

Special summer orientation courses are arranged for a small number of these students, affording an opportunity to brush up on language, hear lectures on American life, take part in discussion groups with American students, and enter into the life of the surrounding community.

In international affairs, as in its internal development, the United States has planted its faith in education—in man's desire to know and to practice what is good, and in the power of knowledge to define and to overcome the problems and the malpractices which keep him from being what he should be. The American school system with its experimentalism and its local control suggests that internationally, too, we may have cooperation without control, harmony through diversity. But to have both harmony and diversity there must be a continuing exchange of ideas. That is what the new internationalism in education will provide.

Despite all the contrary evidence, the United States today is in the midst of a cultural renaissance, one of the exciting moments of history. This time culture is not restricted to an elite, as in the past. This time it is being offered to all, with results that will be considered in a later chapter.

Americans have always been shy of the word "intellectual". It is a word Marx used in developing his truncated view of society as a battle of classes. And it suggests a class superiority the American idea will not admit. Yet today, more than ever before, there is respect for the man of ideas. In government, the idea men, the economists and statisticians and sociologists, have been building a science of politics to replace the by-guess-and-by-gosh method of an earlier day. Impressed by results, the great middle class which includes most Americans has come to respect learning and scientific method as essential to the good life. Knowledge is power, and now that it has reached the ultimate power to destroy mankind, the need of the knowledge which will save it is a spur to still further learning.

Americans have always had the vision of a world with limitless horizons. Technology has now opened the door to this world. A little surprised to find that in their own generation the dream is capable of fulfillment, they are stepping cautiously up to the threshold. And they are turning for guidance to the educator, the scientist, the artist. The school system is facing a flood of students which threatens to shake it loose from its foundations. But in the process the whole society is going to have an educative experience from which it can never move back.

CHAPTER NINE

---

# The Political Animal

The American who takes any active part in politics finds himself mixed up in a maze of relationships. For politics is more than government, more than political parties. To some extent it is the switchboard where all the lines of human relationships are brought together. Political behavior is determined by family background, income, occupation, ethnic origin, education, religion, the place where you live, the clubs and organizations you belong to, and the people you talk to—especially around election time.

Once a voter has chosen his party, he is tied into another network of relationships, from the town or precinct up through the country and state organization to the national headquarters. Parties always need workers, especially during campaigns. Except in some cities where the "machine" tries to keep everyone but trusted henchmen out, the citizen who wants to become an active member is welcome. He can begin by attending caucuses or meetings of the party when they are announced, as they must be by law. Anyone who declares himself a party member is accepted without further formality. There are no dues, no conditions—except of course that you belong to only one party at a time. But you can switch parties as easily as you join them.

Since local meetings are often poorly attended, it may be easier to get elected to the town committee than to stay off it. The local committee is only the starting point. It must send members to the county committee and delegates to the state convention of the party, which will choose delegates for the national convention which nominates President and Vice President. An interested citizen willing to devote time to it can work his way up through all these levels. As he does so, he will find all along the way people he knows at other crossings of the social web—as members of the same service club, profession, hobby, religion. For all his other associations are set up with county, state and national organizations too. Unless he is a sleeper, he can hardly have avoided service on some of them at some of these levels. These relationships, in turn, will influence his decisions in the party, since he will naturally talk with the men he knows and be influenced by their opinions. As a party man, therefore, he redigests all his other relationships in making his decisions.

This web of relationships with its corresponding attitudes is the stuff of politics. Behind the judge, the legislator and the bureau chief, interests of all kinds are constantly clashing—economic, religious, ethnic; selfish and high-minded, corrupt and disinterested.

## The Political Consensus

American politics and parties are not based upon ideas but upon interests. It is misleading to attempt to classify the major political parties as liberal or conservative: they are both and neither. They are not parties in the classical sense at all, but coalitions of interests which are constantly breaking up and recombining. It is inaccurate to think of "industry" opposing "labor" because both industry and labor are made up of many groups. Some big business conflicts with some small business. Some business benefits from low tariffs, some from high. Business and labor agree in wanting a high level of employment and production, but disagree on labor legislation.

The result is a highly complicated organism with clash and conflict built into it. The constant sparring makes us tough and muscular—adept at shows of strength, quick footwork, a certain amount of bluff, and an ability to compromise, delay, make loud noises, and pretend to be making great sacrifices when our outrageous demands have been trimmed down to about what we wanted in the first place. The strength of democracy, as Samuel Lubell has remarked, lies in the way we have of battling ourselves into unity. Experience has shown that the system promotes an ever widening extension of benefits to an ever increasing number of people.

The task of the political leader is to judge all these conflicting claims and to forge a coalition which will satisfy all without giving undue privilege to any. The foreign observer finds a lack of ideas in our political life. This is because he is accustomed to ideological positions in politics—to closed systems which assume that problems can be met and dealt with on the basis of a preformed and therefore rigid scheme. The American idea is that each problem is unique and must be dealt with in its own terms, but that it also bears the seed of solution within it and if properly handled will crystallize a satisfactory result.

Yet behind the apparent lack of ideas in the American political method lie a number of basic propositions which everyone takes for granted:

1. The United States is a government of the people, by the people, for the people. Its authority comes from the people and remains with them, so that they may bestow it from time to time upon different leaders through elections, and change the rules through their power of amendment.

2. This authority does not derive from some unchangeable sacred lore, but from human reason, which is capable of adjusting to new circumstances without reliance upon any particular ideology or -ism. Although Americans complain about "creeping socialism," they adopt "socialistic" or "capitalistic" or "cooperative" or even authoritarian practices as the individual case seems to require.

3. The moral judgment of the masses is the most trustworthy guide to public affairs. This rather idealistic assumption has of late been supported by the results of public opinion polls, which have often shown the people well ahead of their representatives in Congress.

4. Government is a necessary evil. It is always trying to extend itself and must constantly be fought and controlled. The more things we can do for ourselves, voluntarily or at the local level, the less dangerously powerful will government become. With Tom Paine, we tend to believe that whereas society springs from men's virtues, government springs from their vices. To emphasize the voluntary and local, therefore, is to keep social what would otherwise become political.

5. Conformity comforts us, but we are always building a new conformity out of a late revolt. Almost every activity of government which we now take for granted was at one time or another

regarded as radical—child labor laws, the graduated income tax, anti-trust laws, unemployment insurance. President Theodore Roosevelt thought the twelve-hour working day for streetcar operators a proposal of radical socialism. Unhampered by any controlling political ideology, we assimilate any program which appears likely to meet a present need, whether it regulates industry, labor, farm income, hours and wages, inflation, or international alliances.

6. Being born equal, under the promise of the Declaration and the fulfillment of the Constitution, Americans have never had to fight a class war. Their philosophy denies the existence of rigid classes, and though they recognize privilege where it exists, they tend to see it as a challenge rather than a threat. Why tear down the mansions of the rich which someday they may themselves occupy? So reform takes the shape, not of depriving the mighty of their privileges, but of seizing those same privileges for all. In the place of social revolution we have put evolution—a luxury made possible by our human and natural resources and by some fortunate complex of temperament, voluntary association and energy out of which each advancing stage of social progress could be built on the former, instead of razing all and starting again from the ground.

So despite the battles and the tensions, a feeling of friendliness underlies our political life. The governor comes to town and makes a speech in which he says: "We want things to be right for the ordinary fellow like you and me." And he means it. Why not, when he was born abroad, brought to the country as the son of an immigrant, and has made his way up the economic ladder, then the political?

Even in our conflicts, the opposing sides are in essential agreement. It is agreed that we are all equal; the only question is *how* equal! It is perfectly clear to us that Marx's class conflict is a paranoid delusion. We cannot understand how reasonable men can entertain this nightmare as a valid description of the social order. And it is difficult for us to see why our own solution—agreement as to man's equality and constant struggle and realignment to bring it about—is not a perfectly sound system for others to follow.

7. Since authority is dangerous, it is best divided into many parts —among local, county, state and federal officers of government,

among voluntary associations, among the political parties. Wherever practical, the job should be a voluntary, non-paying one. Within the government, power is further divided by a system of checks and balances.

Perhaps the American attitude toward government was best summed up by Lincoln: "The legitimate object of government is to do for a community of people whatever they need to have done, but cannot do at all, or cannot so well do for themselves, in their separate and individual capacities."

## The Parties

Since the Constitution made no provision for political parties, they have had to develop their own rules, subject to whatever laws the states have established. (Federal laws regulating national elections also affect parties, though to a lesser extent.) The system that has developed is a loose one. Who, for instance, is a party member? Although seventy per cent of the voters are registered as party members, most of them take no further part than to vote in primaries and at elections, and perhaps to attend a caucus when candidates for local office are chosen, or to show up at a rally during the period of political fever known as a presidential campaign.

The parties, like the units of government, are organized from the bottom up rather than from the top down. Each local party unit organizes itself, decides how large its committee will be, chooses its candidates for local office and tries to get them elected.

At each level the party is free to run its affairs without direction from above. Each state party has its own rules and chooses its candidates for governor, for Congress and for other offices. The national committee has no disciplinary powers over the states. Nor can the President choose the candidates he would like to see in Congress, as Roosevelt's attempted purge in 1938 proved. Candidates opposed to the President's policies, though of his own party, can and do get elected.

There is no such thing as being expelled from a party. Not to expel but to accommodate is the characteristic motion of the American party. Each party is a coalition of widely divergent interests, joined together in order to win the election, and with the presidency as the grand prize. Each major party must appeal to some, at least,

of every type of voter—to labor and farmers, to Catholic and Protestant, to the Negro and other ethnic minorities, to North and
South, Midwest and Far West, to business men and professional
men, to rich and poor, liberal and conservative, international-
minded and national-minded.

Each party must promise to keep us out of war, yet be prepared
to win a war, to increase the benefits it confers upon the voter
while promising to lower the tax it takes from him, to keep the
economy booming, yet prevent inflation, to maintain farm income
without raising food prices, to squelch communism and subversion
at home while strengthening civil liberties, and to do all these things
better than the other party.

Then what *is* the difference between the parties?

De Tocqueville thought he saw the principle of division as between the haves and the have-nots, one party trying to limit, while
the other wanted to extend the authority of the people. It is true
enough that in the early years of the republic both Jeffersonian
and Jacksonian democracy arose out of an up-country equalitarian-
ism as opposed to town and seaboard commercialism and wealth.

The two-party alignments are historically rooted in this sort of
social conflict. With the development of industry, the conflict put
on other clothes, but its essence was the same. The Republican
rather than the Democratic Party became the first champion of free
labor and pioneered labor legislation, drawing its chief support from
Eastern labor and Western farmers. But then it let itself be led
into an anti-labor position, becoming the spokesman for big business. When the booming twenties ended in depression and the people voted in the Democrats to bail them out, it was the equalitarian
party of Jefferson they were looking to.

To say that either party is now the champion of the worker
would be a mistake, though low income voters incline toward the
Democratic Party. When organized labor has tried to make its
members support one party, however, the results have shown that
labor is no more addicted to bloc-voting than any other economic
group. So labor has learned the better strategy of letting both parties
bid for its vote.

Voters feel that the Democrats are for more government control
and spending, the Republicans for less control and more economy,

though recent budgets disprove even this handy distinction. Fear of depression therefore favors the Democrats while good times favor the Republicans, regardless of whether the voter is a worker or a business man, farmer or professional. Republicans have tended to emphasize the production of wealth, Democrats its distribution. Yet each must capture the majority of the middle and lower income groups in order to win a national election. So they differ more in detail than in principle. Both advocate the New Deal type of legislation; in each the liberal wing now dominates.

It is the lack of ideology which makes American parties stable, and which makes it possible for conservative Southern Democrats to stay in the same party with Northern liberals yet to vote in Congress with conservative Republicans on some issues rather than with the rest of their own party. Again, the American method is to harmonize its diversities. Ideologies are like medieval castles or the Maginot line. They fight a battle of position. The American party system is fluid, ever-changing, responsive to changes in the surrounding society—a mirror of the people's desires rather than a philosopher's dream of what the world should be.

Why is there no radical left or right in American politics? Simply because there are no votes (or few) at either extreme; because socially America has tried to wipe out or to ignore class differences; because the economy keeps spreading its benefits to more and more people.

As Samuel Lubell * has noted, the conflict among clashing elements of the party in power, rather than the conflict between parties, is the index to what is currently significant in the political scene. Not only is each party a coalition of varied and even opposing interests, but the President must attract support from both parties for a given measure, and each measure may require a somewhat different coalition depending upon the local interests involved. For example, the President can count on Congressman X to vote a foreign aid program, because this will stimulate industry. But the Congressman will vote against a bill which, by lowering tariffs, would permit the foreign country to get the dollar exchange to pay some of its debt, because his district manufactures shoes, and if the

* *The Future of American Politics*, p. 217.

tariff on shoes is lowered and some of his constituents are thrown out of work, he may not be re-elected.

American politicians are not concerned with ideologies; their concern is with people who have votes. The big city machines, powerful enough to act without much regard for the national party, got their power by catering to the vote of the poor—usually ethnic minorities of immigrant stock—for whom they did favors. Perhaps they prevented social disintegration. Along with this useful service, however, went an alliance with the underworld which was not so pretty. Shady characters who operated vice rackets and paid the police to leave them alone, who sold "protection" to small business men whose shops were smashed if they resisted, who "got something" on political leaders and threatened to make it public—such parasites too often fed on the political body of the big city. The national party could do nothing about such messes, for the local party was in no way dependent upon it—except perhaps for some federal appointments which a congressman might have to "deliver" anyway as the price of the machine's support.

Is this pattern changing? There are signs that it is. Social security administered impartially and almost universally, is a far bigger benefit than the boss's occasional handouts, and it is a thing he cannot control. The rise in education and living standards and the move to the suburbs have further undermined the machine.

Amateur groups are challenging the old pros. People are going into politics for the fun of it, enjoying the meetings and conventions and enthusiastically campaigning for a leader they believe in. The choice of a political candidate, particularly for President, has come to depend more and more upon popular feeling. David Reisman notes that politics has become more and more a matter of consumption preferences. The candidate must have "appeal"—he must smile pleasantly, exude confidence and geniality, seem like one of the boys and yet like a leader.

## The Presidential Convention

The national convention, once distant and mysterious, has now entered every home via television, with effects both on the people and the convention itself. When politics enters the parlor, when every voter is in effect present at the choosing of a candidate, pub-

lic preference is bound to affect political expediency, while knowledge of the political process should produce better informed voting.

The circus we call a convention is a strange phenomenon. It
combines modern machinery with a primitive tribal war dance,
frolicsome camaraderie with bitter hatchet-work, pompous speech-
making with astute maneuvering, deserts of boredom with oases of
high excitement. Is there any excuse for the hullabaloo of the convention floor?

The last Republican convention seated 1,323 delegates, the Democratic, 2,744 (allowing for half votes). There is also a large body
of alternates. These people are mostly strangers to each other; they
feel that they have to get acquainted. So they do silly things, like
strange children feeling each other out by showing off. They wear
odd hats or big badges. They make strange noises with peculiar
instruments. They bear huge banners showing the name or face of
their candidate. They parade and shout, hoping to arouse an instinct
of unity which will draw some of these other strange children to
them. For it is the lack of unity, and the need for it, which makes
them resort to the most basic appeal—that of the emotions.

Americans, inhabiting a vast land which has been settled by many
strangers and which still has great empty spaces in it, feel impelled
to make neighbors of these strangers. They do it at conventions of
Elks, Rotarians, Shriners, Garden Clubs, Boy Scouts. In the unceas-
ing urge to unify, the national convention with its simple emotional-
ism is a characteristic social feature.

A large emigrant party assembling at the Missouri River in the
1840's to cross the plains selected their leader in an interesting manner. Each candidate walked out onto the plains with his supporters
clinging in a line to his coattails. Others ran and hitched on until
all the emigrants were in one of the weaving lines. Then the man
with the longest tail of followers was declared the winner.

In some such fashion the presidential candidate is chosen. If the
system lacks dignity, it does generate enthusiasm; it provides an
emotional tone to unify men who cannot possibly agree on any
other level—whose only cohesiveness must come from a constant
tension, as the particles of the atom are bound together.

And the method does accomplish its object—to furnish a drama
of popular support for a candidate who must keep the party united

and win the election. Despite the smoke-filled rooms where political trading is done, the convention cannot frustrate the will of the people. It must choose a man people want or it will lose the election. Usually the candidate is from one of the heavily populated states since this gives him a head start on votes. Often he has been the governor of such a state, where he has had to meet in miniature many of the same problems the national government must deal with. Every successful candidate thus far has been a Protestant male of northern European stock. But men of Catholic and eastern or southern European stock have begun to climb into governorships and will eventually reach the White House.

As the Presidency is the great prize, so the glamor and gabble of the convention go mostly toward choosing the party's candidate. His running mate, the Vice President, is usually chosen in a great hurry when everyone is tired and ready to go home, though with an eye to unifying the party. If the President is a liberal, the Vice President may be a conservative, or favored by that group. The strange result is not only to unify the party but to give the losing faction a sporting chance to take control if the President obligingly dies in office.

The convention also adopts a platform drawn up by its resolutions committee. Here again the various factions within the party have been in dubious battle, with the result that the platform is usually so innocuous as to offend no one.

The presidential candidate nowadays must be more than a proven statesman, astute politician and unifier of his party. He must appear confident yet humble, genial yet dignified, sincere yet capable of shrewdness, well-informed but not too intellectual, sympathetic yet not soft, at ease both in the world's highest office and with the country's plain citizens.

## Campaigns and Elections

Local offices are voted for every year, congressmen and usually state offices every other year. But the big event is the one coinciding with leap year, with its extra day for a sport Americans take in much the same spirit that they take baseball or a prize fight. They demand that their candidate fight hard—the presidential campaign is a ruthless, gruelling experience whose nearest analogue is the contests of the gladiators in the Coliseum—on the apparent theory that only a Titan deserves to lead them. They expect him to win or lose graciously.

The presidential election is the one political choice which all Americans share. It brings national issues to the fore and forges a new coalition, a new consensus guaranteed to hold the country together through another four years of constant sparring and readjustment. The electoral system, which gives all the electoral votes of a state to the candidate who gets a majority of the popular vote, makes the big states the chief arenas in the contest. So the candidate must appeal to the big cities in order to get a majority of the 531 electoral votes (one for each senator and representative in Congress —which gives New York 45, Nevada 3).

In a presidential year many other candidates may be campaigning for office at the same time. So the parties will be active on all levels, and the candidates themselves will be scouring the countryside for votes—ringing doorbells, kissing babies, speaking at school commencements, clubs, meetings and rallies.

People like to see the candidates they are expected to vote for. If they are on the fence, they may vote for the candidate whose hand they shook. The things people say to each other also have a strong effect. But even more important are the voter's social and economic backgrounds.

In the North (as contrasted with the South) Protestants of old European stock are likely to vote Republican, while Catholics and those of recent immigrant background vote Democratic. Negroes, traditionally Republican, then swinging Democratic as a result of the Roosevelt program, have returned to the Republican Party to some extent as a result of their gain in civil rights under Eisenhower. Since the parties are now so equally divided and since the independent or shifting vote is so large, the Negro vote may determine the outcome of an election.

As the children of immigrants gradually climb the ladder, they move out of the city slums into the suburbs, become business men and professional workers, and enter the middle class. Ignoring the Marxian rule that they should grow more and more impoverished, they move into better homes, bigger incomes, more education for their children. More and more they control first eastern city politics, then state politics. Under Roosevelt they began to appear in important federal posts.

In the traditionally Democratic South a Republican vote is beginning to develop which may in time make the South politically similar to the rest of the country. The farm vote (West and North), having shifted from its traditional Republicanism during the New Deal, is now divided and uncertain, though trying to balance one party against the other.

Workers, still grateful to the Democrats, are doing so well that they, too, are taking a middle-class, middle-of-the-road attitude, and many of them vote Republican even when their leaders try to drive them the other way. Their prosperity makes them politically cautious, and even among their own ranks there is a fear of letting the unions grow too powerful in politics.

Everywhere the evidence is clear that rising wages have narrowed the cleavage between workers and employers. Prosperity and the middle-class spread claim an ever widening majority of the people. Like the modern highway, the whole road is now of the same good quality as the middle and there are almost no gutters any more—only occasionally soft shoulders to be avoided.

How then does a man decide his vote?

By tradition, partly—by what his father had done before him, by his sense of belonging to a social or ethnic group. By what his friends and neighbors say, and sometimes by what the candidates say or do themselves. By his income, and whether the candidate's program appears likely to endanger or enhance it. By the place he lives in, whether town or country, slum or suburb. By the appeal the candidate makes to his inner image of a leader—either as a destroyer of privilege or as a preserver of the status quo, as an idealized father or as the image of a hated boss. By his enthusiasm for some particular program the candidate is committed to: conservation of forest resources, civil rights, opposition to communism. By a determination to make his vote a protest—against big business, big labor, high taxes, mismanagement or ineptitude in office.

And in the end, perhaps, by sheer exhaustion when after having watched all the candidates on television and read their speeches in newspaper and news magazine, he walks into the voting booth still pondering and ends by voting Republican—or Democratic—as he always has, but with the feeling that after all this is where he belongs.

The two political parties, products of our history, our ethnic origins, our religious faiths, our occupations and our geography, are also the standard-bearers of a deeply held value system whose main items of faith hardly need be repeated here. Perhaps the greatest value of the strenuous contest every four years is its reminder that in spite of all the sectional, occupational and ethnic differences which divide us, we are deeply united on fundamentals. The magnitude of the contest tells us that we are free to argue and disagree. The sweep of it reassures us of our greatness and variety. The hotness of it asserts our strength in combat and our ability to challenge and defeat alien ideas. Each party fights the other as if it were an enemy threatening the very foundations of the republic, and thus we are assured that if ever the need arose we could fight a challenge to our chosen way of life.

But when the campaign is over and enough votes have been counted to designate the victor, the loser appears before the nation to promise his support to the winner, who has now ceased to be the hostile invader and has suddenly become the defender of the faith, like a medieval dragon changed by the kiss of the fair princess (the majority) into a shining knight.

"What unites us is deeper than what divides us," said Adlai Stevenson in 1956. "Tonight we are not Republicans and Democrats, but Americans." Thus we close our ranks, the battle over, patch up our wounds, clean up the debris, and get back to business.

## Local Government

We have already glanced at local government, and there is no space to describe its many varieties here. One rule of thumb can be followed, however. In New England the town or city is the characteristic unit, first developed at a time when there were no states and it was a virtually autonomous little commonwealth. In the South large estates took the place of towns, life was rural, and the county developed as the unit. In the middle and western states the county was generally the original unit, but as towns developed they became vigorous organisms, often influenced by New England ideas and settlers. So in these states the system combines the other two. New England counties remain unimportant except for their courts.

Large city governments, often centers of corruption in the past, have improved in recent years—partly because the rising standard of living has deprived the machines of dependent voters, partly because of the continuing light of publicity thrown upon them, and partly because of more efficient methods. Three forms of municipal government are in use—the mayor and council, the commission, and the council-manager plan which combines a group of elected councilmen to set policy with a professionally trained manager to carry out their decisions. To encourage good municipal government, research organizations like The Public Administration Service make studies and recommendations to cities requesting the service.

## The States and the Constitution

Fourteen of the states (Vermont and the thirteen original members of the federation) existed before there was a federal government. Vermont and Texas and California operated as independent republics before joining the union. The original thirteen had histories running back as much as 180 years before the signing of the Constitution, during which they had managed their own affairs in provincial assemblies, sometimes in bitter conflict with a royal governor, sometimes with little interference from Britain. Here they had learned the arts of government and learned them well, if we judge by such men as Jefferson, Patrick Henry, John Adams and Madison.

The states created the federal government; it was their child. Like parents who watch a growing son strike out on his own without knowing how to use his strength, the states have remained fearful and somewhat resentful of their child. Bigger and stronger than they are, he does not seem to have the proper respect for them. Though he showers them with gifts, he expects them to do as he says.

Its importance chipped away by a powerful federal government on one side and by growing cities on the other, the state is no longer as important as once it was. Yet it does retain all the powers which were not given to the federal government and specified in the Constitution. It, rather than the nation, confers upon its citizens the right to vote. It is the source from which governmental power, as set forth in its constitution, flows.

Loyalty to the state is one of the many loyalties a citizen is expected to feel. The feeling is likely to be strong and genuine—the result of birth and family tradition, or of adoption and preference, or of involvement in its affairs.

Though many states embrace strong contrasts—rural upstate New York as against New York City, Washington and Oregon split down the middle by mountains which have the effect of making the western half industrial, the eastern agricultural—yet each is held together by an emotional culture which plays its unifying ground bass against the varied ethnic, geographic or occupational tunes. What is said about the forty-eight states is also generally true about the two territories, Hawaii and Alaska, which most Americans believe should have been made states long since. (Also under the American flag are the Pacific islands of Guam, American Samoa, Wake and Midway and The Virgin Islands. Puerto Rico has the status of a free commonwealth.)

State legislatures generally meet every two years for a few months and are therefore manned by representatives who work at something else the rest of the time and who are paid only enough to cover their expenses. The system encourages corruption. A legislator merely by preparing a bill which would be costly to a given industry may be able to get a bribe for withdrawing it. But news coverage of state capitals and the necessity of reporting all income to the Director of Internal Revenue or facing prosecution have been spurs, if not to virtue at least to circumspection.

State government is important in establishing standards for the schools, in building roads, maintaining a system of courts, prisons, reformatories and institutions for the blind, the mentally sick and others unable to care for themselves, in administering unemployment and old age assistance, operating employment offices, state police and highway patrols, state parks, universities, and library service, in attracting tourists and new industries into the state, controlling rates and operation of public services such as electric power, and in a great many other functions. A great state like New York has a larger budget and in everything but the conduct of foreign

affairs provides more services for its citizens than many an independent nation.

The Council of State Governments, a joint governmental agency
of all the states, works to replace competition and chaos with cooperation and good order. It studies school systems, mental institutions, highway safety and governmental reorganization. It promotes interstate agreements in river control, conservation, mutual
use of facilities for the handicapped, crime control, road building.
It coordinates joint programs with the federal government, and has
helped develop a nation-wide civil defense program. It works with
the Governor's Conference and other associations of state officers.

The greater power of the federal government to tax has led to
many programs which are federally financed but turned over to
the states for administration. This practice also has the effect of
equalizing state services by using tax money from the richer states
to aid the poorer—an important balance wheel in the economy.
Federal funds support state programs of unemployment payment,
road building, occupational training, school construction and many
other services.

By specifying the powers of the federal government and leaving
all remaining power to the states or to the people, the Constitution
created a formula no one seriously desires to change. For while the
Constitution is rigid, it can be flexibly interpreted. Its creators had
no idea how many services the federal government would come to
perform, yet all of these services, from regulation of the railroads
to a practically universal pension plan have managed to huddle
under its broad umbrella.

It is an American belief that the founding fathers provided for
all future emergencies and that the Constitution, properly—which
means flexibly—interpreted and on rare occasions amended, will always meet our needs. To propose scrapping it for another would
be regarded as madness or heresy. We regard it as the last word
in political wisdom.

Why do we venerate the Constitution?

It is specific—a written document anyone can read. It is elastic—
with enough stretch in it to fit new situations. It works, as 170 years
of trial have shown. It has almost magic power to give unity to a
diverse people. The Tory defender of special privilege appeals to it;

the communist on trial for subversion wraps himself in it as in a coat of mail; the schoolboy knows it as the source of his freedom; the immigrant looks to it as the charter which will admit him to the privileges of citizenship. In a world full of tensions and upsets it has stood firm under our feet. It incorporates those inalienable rights which the modern world has none the less kept alienating, whether through fascism or communism, and it guarantees that so long as it stands we shall not suffer that alienation. Its system of checks and balances among the three arms of government helps to solve the old problem of reconciling freedom with order. So does the power of judicial review, which allows the judges to base their opinions upon the Constitution rather than upon the laws.

The special merit of the Constitution as a political instrument is that it gives the federal government direct authority over all citizens, parallel with but independent of that of the states. Then through the Supreme Court it establishes a living voice to arbitrate and decide all differences.

# CHAPTER TEN

---

# *The Drama of Politics*

In the great drama of national politics, Congress, the President, and a bewildering variety of interest groups play leading roles.

## Congress

No part of the governmental process comes in for so much criticism from all sources as the Congress. If it promptly passes measures requested by the President, it is "a rubber stamp." If it delays, it is "do nothing."

No one seems to be responsible for what Congress does. The President cannot control it, for even if his party has a majority in both houses, that majority itself is made up of many minorities, some of which are bound to be opposed to the President's program. The political leaders in Congress can rightly claim that they have little control over individual members. The members can say that they must vote as their constituents wish or else face defeat. The constituents, moreover, exert multiple and often contrary pressures so that a congressman, like a rat in a maze which is constantly being altered, must compete in a game where the rules are always being changed. Congressmen can, and do, help to bring about wise national legislation by explaining the issues at home. But self-interest too often blinds the individual voter to his larger interests—to the need for overseas aid or stronger civil rights laws. Congress mirrors the people it serves, demonstrating the old proposition that a people deserves the government it gets.

Yet Congress is a somewhat distorted mirror. Nevada, with a population of 160,000, has two senators as does New York with 14,800,000. This, of course, carries out the principle of state sovereignty and equality. But in the House of Representatives too there is inequality. Since state legislatures determine congressional districts, and since they usually favor the rural areas, city districts may have more voters than country ones.

Friction is built into the political system—friction between the branches of government, between parties, between factions in each party, between Congress and the President, Congress and the administrative departments, between the various congressional committees. Congressmen are harried by pressure groups, visiting constituents to whom they must be hospitable, committee meetings, reporters, mountains of documents.

Many congressmen are lawyers, and thus tend to take a legalistic rather than a social view of legislation. Yet the social viewpoint in the law has grown in recent times and is now beginning to affect law school graduates.

As a result of all these factors, it is difficult to pass important legislation of national interest, such as aid to education, civil rights laws or an immigration bill consistent with our world position. Bills favorable to local interests, thanks to the technique known as logrolling, slide through more easily. Ten thousand bills go into the hopper each year, many of them introduced without much hope of passage but in response to local demands.

Slow, clumsy, and local-minded, the system does have advantages. No one group can control it, and it is responsive to public opinion.

The effective political leadership of the House is with the Speaker and the majority leader, and they have more power than their opposite numbers in the Senate. But the Committee on Rules pretty much decides what legislation the House shall consider. Beyond this, it is hard to say how power is distributed, since it arises partly out of the committee system, partly out of the political parties. What is said on the floor of Congress is almost the least important of congressional activities. Since it has little effect on voting, it is oratory rather than debate, intended often for the ears of groups back home, which will hear of it by way of reprints from the *Congressional Record*.

"Congress is so strange," said a puzzled Russian visitor. "A man gets up to speak and says nothing. Nobody listens—and then everybody disagrees."

In the Senate, however, where persuasion counts, the debate is often interesting, and with a special flavor of its own deriving from the tradition of senatorial courtesy—which may extend all the way from hearty affection to the politest kind of genial insult and cordial invective. Harold Laski, incidentally, considered the Senate the most successful second chamber in the world.

The real work of Congress is done in committees. Every bill is referred to its appropriate committee, where a good deal of hard work is done on it, often with the help of experts in the field. As a rule, no important changes are made after it comes to the floor of the House, though the Senate often makes such changes. Each committee is so powerful in its own field that it is like a little legislature. It can kill a bill it does not like, while its chairman alone can block action for months or even years.

Since the chairmanships go to those with seniority, it is the men from settled and often conservative areas who hold the most important jobs. Members with the most seniority also get onto the most important committees and often have more work than they can do adequately.

In addition to executive sessions, the committees hold hearings at which government agencies sponsoring a bill are heard, and interested parties are invited to give evidence. Here again the chairman by his attitude can do a good deal to influence the outcome. The hearing is more useful as a propaganda weapon than as a source of information, for it is news; it gets into the papers, and those who testify have a chance to spread their point of view. The hearing also serves as a means of bringing out opposed views and developing a compromise.

Before a bill can become law, it must not only be reported out to the floor, but the two houses must reconcile their differences as to the kind of bill they are willing to pass. If there are wide differences, as in matters pertaining to appropriations, the compromise may be hard to reach.

## The Power of Public Opinion and Special Interest

At every stage of the legislative process, public opinion is essential in producing a decision. To mobilize this opinion and make it effective there exists a bewildering number and variety of pressure groups, associations or lobbies—the choice of word depending upon whether you approve their position. As Madison pointed out long ago, any civilization complicated enough to merit the name will develop groups whose interests are opposed. The activity of such groups, as David Truman has demonstrated in his able and thorough analysis of them in *The Governmental Process,* is an essential part of politics.

The activity of one group in suing for governmental favor inevitably gives rise to rival groups. Labor, industry, agriculture, professions, trades, veterans, ethnic minorities, religions, civil rights, international trade and friendship—all have their associations and their lobbies. Some are purely and commercially self-centered. Others are concerned about ethical issues. Each of these groups has a membership which it influences and whose desires in turn determine the kind of pressure the association exerts.

The Izaak Walton League, for example, favors conservation of natural resources. Its members are fishermen who fight stream pollution, overgrazing, and other sins against nature which some industries are guilty of. Since its members alone are insufficiently powerful, it will attempt to combine with other pressure groups and arouse public opinion outside its own membership to the support of its aims. A citizen may belong to a number of associations, and may even be supporting groups which take opposite sides on some issues. But such overlapping may actually help to stabilize a society made up of such groups.

Through his associations, the citizen exerts a continuing influence upon government and legislation. This may be one reason (though scarcely an excuse) for the disgracefully low vote cast in many elections—seventy-seven per cent of the registered voters, or sixty per cent of those of voting age in the last presidential election. Despite the danger that an elite group at the top may try to impose its views on the membership, many associations operate democratically, soliciting the views of members and passing them upward as a basis for policy forming. A certain bias, however, often results from the fact that it is the well-to-do who can afford to attend national committee meetings and thus tend to move into positions of power.

Often these associations, especially if they are nationally organized, contain within themselves a number of conflicting interests and thus are self-regulating. There are, for example, 2,300 chambers of commerce, with interests varying from North to South, large city to small town, and even within each local group the interests of manufacturers may clash with those of merchants, requiring local adjustment.

Often the group comes up against so many other influences that it can do little more than to stop legislation considered damaging to its members. So the lobbies police each other and no one gets an undue advantage. Political power has become atomized—scattered amongst a vast number of power-wielding groups which the legislature must attempt to placate and amongst whom it must mediate. Since interest groups also tend to be coalitions of varied interests, the effect of such groups as the American Legion upon voting is much less than they claim. For again, the Legion member may also belong to a union, a Rod and Gun Club, a civil rights group. He has to mediate even within himself! This mediating process—within groups, parties, regions, individuals—is one of the most significant processes in American politics.

In addition to capturing attention through the mass media, pressure groups attempt to convey the impression that their position is the "right" one, the reasonable one, and also the one to which most people consent and which is therefore bound to win. Slogans, word of mouth campaigns, petitions, letter and telegram assaults on members of Congress, even rumors may be resorted to.

Equally important is the group's access to Congress, the President, the state legislature. National associations work hard to gain the friendly interest of the chairman and members of the committee dealing with the legislation they are interested in—sometimes by means of "contacts," or by entertainment, by giving legal business to the firm a legislator is associated with (and of which he can legally remain a member during his term of office), or sometimes by less legal methods if they think they can get away with it.

Perhaps most commonly it is a natural sharing of interests which admits a group into the good graces of the legislator, whose business and regional interests, social status, friendship group and general outlook dispose him in its favor.

Pressure groups are often attacked as if they were an evil. Yet any candid analysis will show that this intricate network of associations, sensitive to the thousand divergent interests of the people, gives to legislators a set of readings as useful as those of the barometer and the anemometer to the weather man. As the political and the economic become ever more interfused as a result of government spending, industrial specialization, and the decision that it is government's responsibility to maintain prosperity, these constant pressures from all sides help to keep the car on the road.

Since Roosevelt equalized agriculture with industry, labor with capital, and consumption with production, the three big forces in the economy (labor, industry, agriculture) have exerted more or less equal pressure. Without doubt there are segments of the population who are not adequately represented by a pressure group—the white collar worker, the migratory worker, the subsistence farmer—and without resources or leadership to build an organization. But the road is there, and past experience suggests that when sufficiently aroused, they, too, will organize.

Government itself has encouraged the formation of voluntary associations to improve its contacts with economic groups. Outstanding is the example of the Farm Bureau, organized with the encouragement of the Department of Agriculture and now so intimately related to the agricultural extension program that it is hard to know where one stops and the other begins. The inter-relations of the Veterans Administration and the American Legion are like a tangled skein, while every other interest group tries to develop a similarly close working relationship with the appropriate department of government.

Another instrument for testing the public will is the opinion poll, now so well developed that it can give a reasonably accurate reading of what the public thinks about any given issue—even to the percentage of those who don't think at all! This fascinating device, while it often confirms the good judgment of the public, raises new problems, especially during a campaign. Given the large number of independent voters and the well-known human desire to be on the winning side, will the published poll results have the effect of swinging votes? And how far should a congressman follow public opinion as indicated in the polls? How can he tell whether opinion will have shifted again by the time the results are announced?

The most dramatic device Congress uses—ostensibly as a means of getting facts but often as a way of drawing public attention to a danger, a crisis situation, or even the personality of the committee chairman—is the investigation. Some of these, like the Truman investigation of government expenditures, have been paragons of what an investigation should be. Others have been disgraceful episodes of exhibitionism—vulgar and unfair in method and upsetting both the Congress and the country for weeks at a time. But on balance the work they do is useful and in the public interest.

We are always asking the impossible of Congress—as we ask the impossible of our economy, our educational system, our society. It is not surprising if we are disappointed; rather the surprise is that we so often get what we want. We expect our congressman to busy himself on our behalf, answering our letters, attending to our little requests, and yet we expect him to be present on the floor, attend committee meetings, keep in touch with the press and the communities at home, come back to make a speech whenever we want him, study the piles of legislation, the testimony at hearings and all the other materials that flood in upon him, and still have time for deliberate lawmaking.

When we criticize Congress—an indoor sport without an equal— we jump on the bad boy for disobeying his father. Yet it is for us he is disobeying; he *is* us. He is what we have made him. When we criticize, we are projecting our own guilt and attacking that. This is why we feel so personal an involvement in the behavior of Congress: it gathers up and battles out all the contradictions and disagreements of a diverse people. It enacts a play of sin and redemption of which we are a part, and each session is an act in the historic drama of the American people. From opening curtain to climax and dénouement, we can hardly wait to see how it will come out.

## The Presidency

That the American presidency is the world's most powerful office is a truism often repeated. It seems at first something of a paradox that a nation which cherishes home rule should have entrusted so many powers to its leader. Yet the powers are a function of the nation's strength rather than an abandonment of responsibility. There are sufficient checks to satisfy the most suspicious defender of liberty and irk even the most compliant president.

This mortal man is first of all a servant of the people, elected by them all. He is the chief of state, the ceremonial head of government like king or president in a parliamentary system. As chief executive he runs the government. As chief diplomat he heads up foreign relations, though dependent upon Congress and especially on the Senate in formulating policy and negotiating treaties. He is commander-in-chief of the armed forces. He initiates and recommends legislation to Congress, and uses his power to push it through. He is the leader of his party, and must attempt both to reconcile its conflicting groups and to lead it in the direction he and the people who elected him want it to go. He is the voice of the people, for once he has won their confidence and support no other power can equal his. He alone speaks, not for some segment of the nation, but for all.

When internal danger threatens, from strike or riot or natural disaster, he is the protector of the peace. He is the defender of prosperity, endowed with powers designed to keep the economy healthy. And he is a leader of the free nations which are joined to defend themselves against such imperialistic aggression and brutal disregard for basic human rights as the world saw in Hungary in 1956.

His many functions include preparing the national budget and submitting it to Congress, intervening in labor disputes that threaten national emergency, and taking a positive stand in the continuing struggle for civil rights.

One result of all this concentrated power is to make the President one of the most newsworthy men on earth. He can use the great power of the mass media to consolidate his position and further his program. He can extend this newsworthiness to commissions of responsible citizens who will study and make reports on needed legislation. By skillful use of his power of appointment, he can further his legislative program and weld his party together.

It is the President's job to keep the major economic interests in balance, to perceive the nation's deep needs, whether for better schools or for the defense of civil liberties or national security, and to keep his program moving on a broad front like a snowplough clearing a whole road instead of a gang of shovelers tossing mere bits out of the way or into one another's eyes.

Many of his powers are persuasive rather than absolute, as becomes a democratic office. Even his veto can be overruled by a two-thirds vote of Congress, and many other limitations have been put upon his strength. The bureau heads, who were in their jobs before he came and will be there after he has gone, can through their contacts with Congress frustrate a President's will. He must take account of that complex of economic and civic organizations which is continuously at work in and around the government. He must consider the effect of his decisions upon our overseas allies. And though he can often arouse public opinion, he is in the end subject to its will.

The body that devotes impressive energy and professional skill to keeping him in check, however, is the Congress of which he is paradoxically the leader. The United States has the only important legislature in the world over which the executive has no ultimate power of persuasion or control. Nor for that matter can the Congress unseat the President, except for impeachable faults. No impeachment has ever succeeded, and only one has been tried.

President and Congress play their appropriate parts in the national drama which involves us all. The President is our father-leader who knows what is best for us and whom we tend to revere and follow or hate and flout. Congress is the subconscious expressing itself—the hatred of father, of order and responsibility and authority. It is the child who asserts himself by demonstrating his lack of responsibility, thus punishing the parent whose authority he both rejects and desires. If this sounds too Freudian, one need merely read the papers when Congress is in session, or listen to popular political talk, to recognize some truth in the exaggeration.

Each of our Presidents has helped to fill out our conception of what the office is and should be—Washington with his dignity and sense of precedent-setting; Jefferson with his faith in a democracy based on the independent farmer and artisan; Jackson bringing the fresh raw wind of the West to the White House, and Teddy Roosevelt a verve and boisterousness which exhilarated the nation. Then in Harry Truman we saw, as our myth had asserted all along, that an ordinary man could with humility and hard work rise to the demands of the office and do big things in a big way.

But most of all in Lincoln have we found the man who embodies the meaning of our democracy. Poor and humble, largely self-taught, he rose by his own effort to his high office, and at a time when the union itself was breaking apart. To restore the union and at the same time to emancipate the slaves was his destiny, "with malice toward none, with charity for all," though for his devotion he was martyred, a sacrifice in the blood feud between brothers North and South, and an expiation of their guilt.

The shadow of Lincoln still broods over us, sorrowing for what still separates, hopeful of what brings us slowly together in that brotherhood for which he gave the last full measure of devotion. Rarely have a people been so blessed with a folk hero whose life dramatizes their conflicts, their strivings, their hope of a clear and final victory.

## The Administrative Network

The presidential office has changed somewhat since the days when Jefferson wrote out his letters longhand and then made copies by a process he had invented. Now the President has a dozen assistants, each specializing in one aspect of his many responsibilities, and an office force of more than three hundred. He has a number of advisory committees—the National Security Council, the Council of Economic Advisers, the Office of Defense Mobilization and the Bureau of the Budget whose functions are indicated by their names. He has his cabinet, made up of the men whom he has appointed to run the ten executive departments—State, Treasury, Post Office, and the rest. These men are not members of the legislature as in a parliamentary system, but are chosen in part so as to represent areas, religions and economic interests of political importance.

The Cabinet is not provided for by the Constitution, has no collective responsibility, and usually consists of men who have not had much political experience, though they may be specialists in their fields of agriculture, labor or commerce. Politically, a Cabinet post usually leads nowhere—which may be a good thing, since it leaves a man free to do his job without cocking an eye at some higher seat in government.

When Lincoln one day proposed an idea to his Cabinet which was voted down by all, he remarked: "Seven no's and one aye—the ayes have it." This just about describes the power of the Cabinet as a group. But as manager of his own department, each secretary has great responsibility.

In addition to all these offices, there are the independent agencies, such as the Civil Service Commission and a group of commissions empowered to regulate trade, interstate commerce, communications and securities. There is the Federal Reserve Board whose activities have much to do with keeping the economy in balance. And there are the services united in 1953 into the newest executive department, that of Health, Education and Welfare. There is the Government Printing Office which not only publishes official documents and reports, but a vast number of valuable and modestly priced pamphlets of information for the plain citizen, on everything from infant care to beekeeping.

Then there is the Tennessee Valley Authority, which is neither wholly government nor wholly business, but which is regarded throughout the world (except here at home where it still arouses arguments) as one of the great achievements of enlightened democracy, combining a critically needed program of conservation of land and forest, soil and stream, with production of power, navigation, and recreational resources. Still more important, it introduced a new concept in regional development, helped a rundown area to find itself, allied science with politics, and yet managed to work democratically by cooperating with the people involved instead of handing down orders.

It is a deeply grooved habit of Americans to groan about the inefficiency of their government, and no doubt any enterprise so large must have inefficient people in it. Yet the fact is that, especially since World War II, many federal bureaus are operated in accordance with the best modern business practices, and their methods have actually been adopted by business. Each department or agency also develops its own contacts throughout the sprawling governmental body, in Congress, with organized interest groups and even with individuals at the grass roots.

There remains the office of the Vice President, which Woodrow Wilson described in this manner: "The chief embarrassment in discussing his office is, that in explaining how little there is to be said about it one has evidently said all there is to say." Recent Presidents have made valiant efforts to make something of the office, and Mr.

Nixon has taken many chores off the presidential shoulders, serving as ambassador of goodwill, greeter, and member or chairman of several important committees.

## The Courts and Civil Liberties

The special genius of the American system is that it set up federal courts independent of the state courts, to try cases arising out of the Constitution and federal law. Every citizen is subject to the authority of both systems and may have recourse to them.

The federal system consists of the Supreme Court (a Chief Justice and eight Associate Justices sitting in Washington), ten Circuit Courts of Appeals and about a hundred District Courts. If the states have disputes with each other, or in some cases if a citizen of one state wishes to bring suit against someone in another state, the federal courts may be used. The courts serve an important function in interpreting and applying federal law and in deciding whether the legislative or executive branch has exceeded its constitutional authority.

Perhaps the most important function of the Supreme Court is to interpret the Constitution flexibly enough to keep pace with the changing times. By this device we can continue to revere the document on which our remarkably stable government is based, and at the same time let it swing with the tide while remaining at anchor. The trend of decision in the present century has been toward an ever broader concept of government's social responsibility and the rights of man.

Best of all is this seen in the recent decisions which put an end to segregation of Negroes and whites in the schools and in public vehicles.

"In the field of public education," the Supreme Court decided in 1954, "the doctrine of 'Separate but Equal' has no place. Separate educational facilities are inherently unequal." Despite the publicity given to areas of conflict, hundreds of schools have been integrated without incident. Despite the legal tactics adopted by some states to avoid integration, the trend is forward.

A recent two-year survey shows more than a thousand instances of racial barriers dropped in all walks of life. The Southerner who made the study concludes: "There is no longer a solid South of segregation. . . . The common notion that desegregation just can't work is plainly contradicted by the findings."

Instances of desegregation included housing, public health, private enterprise, public transportation and accommodations. They included the 164 colleges and universities which had opened their doors to Negroes, and the many Negroes elected or appointed to public office.

Jim Crow—an invention of the early twentieth century, and not, as many people suppose, an old institution—is on its way out. Open-minded Southerners know that a community cannot maintain such a system without damaging everyone.

In Louisiana alone the Negro vote rose from a mere 1,672 in 1948 to 108,724 in 1952, with similar gains elsewhere.

Perhaps the strangest sign of the times is that the Grand Dragon of the Florida Ku Klux Klan declared Negroes eligible for membership!

At last an attack is being made on the vicious circle of poverty, ignorance, disease and lack of opportunity which had held the Negro down. Many whites naively believed that the backwardness of the Negro was biological rather than a result of his lack of opportunities and his often wretched living conditions, leading to illness and crime. Many poor whites needed the Negro as a scapegoat, as a consolation for their own low status, and politicians were still willing to play upon this feeling to get votes. Too often the police and the courts intimidated the Negro, the merchant took advantage of him, and the press failed to publicize the miserable conditions in which he lived or the injustice he received.

Yet the press had become outspoken against lynching—a barbarous custom arising out of frontier conditions and often applied to whites as well as Negroes—which since 1951 seems to have disappeared from the scene, though other forms of intimidation or cruelty are still practiced.

Another aspect of civil liberties, provoked by the world-wide threat of imperialistic, totalitarian communism, was the so-called loyalty program. Enormous powers were vested in a Subversive Activities Control Board which, if its powers were misused, could rob government workers of their jobs and spoil their chances of reemployment elsewhere. The law also poses a threat to voluntary association, since it tends to make people shy of joining an organization which may later be investigated. The workings of this system after five years had produced over forty thousand pages of testimony about subversive organizations, but no *final* actions. If there is a real threat to our security, this system has failed to find it, but not for want of trying.

The domestic Red scare has now died down, as it has become apparent to most citizens that we are a united people, that the number of dangerous communists is small indeed, and that while we need to be vigilant, it is equally important to preserve our civil rights as the basis of our strength and moral leadership in the world, and in our fight against totalitarianism abroad. To protect these rights Americans again turn to voluntary association. The Civil Liberties Union is only the best known of many organizations fighting a continuous battle against those who would deny freedom of speech to those they disagree with, deny jobs or votes to minorities, or try to prevent workers from organizing. Legal Aid societies throughout the country offer free counsel to those who cannot afford to pay for it, thus assuring that no one shall lose a case for want of professional advice.

## Profile of American Democracy

What then are the characteristics of Democratic government in the United States?

First, its accent on home rule and local participation—a virtue so far as keeping government in the hands of the people is concerned, but a hazard in times of international crisis when local issues may befog international necessity.

Second, the importance of voluntary associations, acting as goads and guides in the governmental process—influencing legislation and legislators, interacting with government departments, performing many of the functions which in other nations would be undertaken by government. In an era where many political decisions are beyond the scope of the average man, and where many decisions have been transferred from the political arena to administration, this voluntary activity serves as a balance wheel against the weight of bureaucracy and the danger of a government separated from the people by its complexity and vastness.

Third, a continuous and even raucous criticism and analysis of government and its functions—by the press, by prominent individuals, by street corner critics, by Congressmen, by voluntary associations, and of course by visitors from across the seas.

The United States was first to adopt universal manhood suffrage (excluding slaves), first to achieve freedom of the press, first to separate church from state, first to abolish cruel punishments, first in free public education, prison reform, free libraries.

Fourth, it is preeminently a government for the people rather than for a privileged class. This, as de Tocqueville noted, makes for a society which is less elevated but more just.

Fifth, it is a government which rests upon its ability to translate the aspirations of its citizens into action. Though often slow and cumbrous in its motions, because the public will is a mixture of many separate and conflicting wills, it does in the end achieve this. Not by grandiose overall plans, of which Americans are highly suspicious because they seem always to be connected with rigid or totalitarian systems, but bit by bit, pragmatically, as the needs arise.

And sixth, it is a government based upon business and commerce. This is often mentioned as if it were somehow a unique disability. But every civilization worth the name has been built upon a solid economic base, for what other way (except pillage) is there to build one? Totalitarian systems are based upon one form of pillage or another. They use slave labor, dismantle whole industries in conquered countries and take them home, or expropriate the property of whatever class or group they have decided to make a scapegoat. The democratic system looks at property as a right to be defended, and while it may levy heavy taxes against high income or profits, it will not destroy the capital base out of which profit is built. For it sees wealth not as an evil, but as the source of its strength, from which all other benefits flow. Only a rich and productive country can give to its citizens all the benefits to which the democratic creed says they are entitled.

So in the United States economy and politics are interwoven. Each of the major economic groups cries bloody murder when government regulates or taxes it, yet each is constantly seeking government services and protection.

How then does this economy operate?

CHAPTER ELEVEN

---

# Life More Abundant

We live in revolutionary times. When our age can be seen in perspective, it may appear as the time when production and consumption entered a new stage, and the principles of economic democracy became as firmly established as political democracy had been assured (though not fully realized) by our first Revolution.

With only seven per cent of the world's population, the United States produces about forty per cent of the world's goods and services. Its national product when divided by the population is twice that of the most productive European countries, ten times that of Indonesia. Real Gross National Product was five times as great in the 1940's as in the 1890's, and this rate is continuing, so that an increasing amount of goods and services is available, as well as the higher income to purchase them. The output per unit of labor has increased by about two per cent each year for the past eighty years.

Between 1820 and 1930 the country increased the per capita supply of energy fortyfold. In 1910 laborers were twenty-one per cent of the total labor force. By 1940 they were only eleven per cent. More and more goods, produced by less and less expenditure of human toil.

Even since the end of the war the country has doubled its manufacturing capacity, with a capital outlay of $233 billion. Steelmakers and electric power producers kept expanding to meet the new demands. In agriculture, too, the rise in productivity has been miraculous. In 1820 it took seventy-two per cent of our working population to feed the country. By 1950 only eleven per cent were doing the farming, feeding themselves and the rest of the country.

The technological revolution has reversed the dour predictions of Malthus by enhancing the productivity of land, labor and capital, and by developing simple and effective methods of birth control. For the first time in history the means of overcoming starvation and disease are within man's grasp.

Any economy depends upon three basic things—natural resources, labor and capital. It has often been assumed that prosperity in the United States is a simple result of lush resources. Yet our resources are no greater in proportion to population than those of the U.S.S.R. or western Europe with its dependencies. They are no greater than they were in the thirties when we ourselves suffered a devastating period of underproduction and actual want.

The present standard of production is therefore not merely a matter of having the resources. New England, the poorest of our areas in resources, became the richest part of the nation during the nineteenth century by developing its industry, while the South though richly endowed went poor producing raw materials with slave labor. The Spaniards had the run of the whole hemisphere but failed to develop a lively, productive economy. Human enterprise, quite as much as rich resources, was the energizing force. The use of low-grade ores such as taconite shows how resources can be "created" by human ingenuity.

Although immigration supplied the need for manpower, labor was relatively scarce. So was capital. It too had to be imported. Scarce labor and high wages provided an incentive for high capitalization and mechanization. Profits were plowed back into more productive machinery, inventiveness produced more and more efficient machines. Now our increase in capital just about balances our continual lowering of man hours.

Growth is the distinguishing feature of the system—growth in gross output, in the number and variety of products, in methods of manufacturing, in output per worker, and in the purchasing power of those who produce.

## An Economy of Abundance

The United States had been able to start gradually, as had Europe, but it had outpaced the rest of the world partly because it was politically oriented toward producing abundance instead of maintaining scarcity. Its citizens had energetically, even ruthlessly, exploited its resources—not for a privileged class (though there was plenty of inequality and privilege in the era of the industrial tycoons), but for the use of all.

Its continuing output rested on several other assumptions: that while production was best left in the hands of the thousands of separate business enterprises and the shifting demands of the market, government had a responsibility to watch over the economy and to apply the brake or the goad as needed; that though government had the right to tax, it had no right to expropriate private property; that individuals and corporations should be free to contract for goods and services; that an acrobatic balance must be maintained among the main elements of the economy (labor, agriculture, corporations) in order to keep it healthy.

Perhaps most important of all, Americans have always assumed that wealth is dynamic—a thing to be used in the production of more wealth rather than hoarded. Experience has taught them that capital and labor can take more wealth out of the environment if they work together than by fighting each other. We pass laws to discourage monopoly (the Sherman Act) or to prevent disastrous price declines (Commodity Credit Corporation), to encourage labor to organize (the Wagner Act) or to curb its powers (Taft-Hartley), depending upon the situation. We built the TVA and let the government run the post offices, but turned over millions of acres to private industries to build the western railroads. Opposed to monopolies, we have let telephone and telegraph services develop as private corporations, but regulate them in the public interest. Similarly regulated are the railroads and airlines.

It is fashionable to regard the American economy as somehow old-hat, a survival from Adam Smith and Ricardo. But Frederick Lewis Allen argues that it has actually gone beyond socialism to a system which, by combining government control with private initiative, serves us better than either could do alone. We have socialized distribution rather than capital, by raising wages and heavily taxing big incomes. Our form of socialism is not to kill and eat the goose, but to get her to lay more and more golden eggs.

The American system of doing business has discovered a new principle—that of competitive cooperation. Manufacturers in the same field exchange valuable ideas, trade secrets, inventions. Then they go out and compete for customers. The system has, however, driven out many small independent producers.

We tend to take for granted certain advantages without which the economy could not function so efficiently: the existence of a lawful citizenry and a law-enforcing government, for example, which guarantee that contracts can be carried out; or the soundly established monetary system, and a banking system which makes the transfer or borrowing of funds a simple matter; workers who can be depended on to appear every morning and stay until the whistle blows at night. These are not things that can be taken for granted in all parts of the world.

Although the benefits of mass production were understood at least as long ago as Eli Whitney's development of interchangeable parts, it is Henry Ford who generally gets the credit for putting into effect the full cycle of mass production: a low-priced product which millions would want to buy, built by men whose relatively high wages were both a result of mass production and a source for mass buying. Low prices, increased production and higher wages producing greater profits and expanding markets—this is the cycle of abundance.

Inevitably such a program led to giant corporations. It led to a competition of products rather than prices. There is a negligible difference in the prices of Ford, Chevrolet and Plymouth. The customer makes his choice according to his preference for the car's mechanical qualities—or his wife's preference for its lines and color. The giants compete among themselves—aluminum against stainless steel, General Motors threatening to go into steel production unless prices are kept down, the big chain store threatening to manufacture its own cold cereals.

Will it end in monopoly?

History says no. The idea of monopoly is morally repugnant in the United States. The threat once posed by U.S. Steel and Standard Oil has long since passed and no one, not even the big corporations, would welcome monopoly today even if they could have it. For competition is their carrot; it keeps them moving forward. Monopoly would inevitably be government-controlled, and they know that a regimented economy could not possibly compete with one having 9,800,000 centers of initiative.

While the leading industries—automobiles, steel, oil—are each dominated by four to eight large corporations, there is still room for many smaller firms to prosper within the same industry. The four biggest steel companies leave about a third of the business to eighty smaller competitors. The top five in petroleum did three-fifths of the business, but five hundred others shared the remainder.

What John Kenneth Galbraith calls countervailing power operates to keep the giants from gobbling up the market. Big distributors like the chain stores are a countervailing power to keep producers' prices down. Big industries are balanced by big unions powerful enough to bargain for workers who would otherwise be at the mercy of the employer.

No one doubts that the big corporations are a basic institution in American life, even though many critics do not care for them. Yet they have proven their superior ability to supply goods in quantity and variety at relatively low prices. They are best equipped to carry on continuous research for better products and higher productivity. For the most part they rather than smaller firms pioneer increased benefits and better relations with their workers.

The American economic system, like so much of our society, defies simple description because it is plural, experimental, pragmatic. Although we shout private enterprise, everyone wants controls of one sort or another—on credit, on monopoly, on industry-wide unions, on crop prices. Among all the conflicting interests and demands, government must mediate—taking one tack in this situation, another in that. The goal is an economy favorable to all, one power balancing another, but all devoted to the ideal of maximum efficiency in production so that there will be more to consume.

*Productivity*

The United States benefits from a large, free internal market protected by tariffs and, to some extent, by the cost of transportation from other manufacturing areas. The lack of any customs barriers between the states and the rapidly developed transportation network has made it possible for manufacturers to produce in large volume for a national market, and thus to specialize each job for efficiency and cut prices to the point where the masses can afford to buy.

While Americans have always declared, with more sentiment than fact, for a free market, they have also insisted on restricting it so as to balance the demands of various groups in the community. Tariffs to protect industries that might otherwise succumb to foreign competition, social insurance and minimum wage laws to protect workers, subsidies to farmers, pure food and drug acts to protect consumers, credit controls to prevent inflation, the progressive income tax to pay for the vast federal program which protects or benefits all, collective bargaining to protect the union worker, regulation of utility and railroad rates, control of the airwaves and of airlines, regulation of securities to protect the investor—these are a few of the things public opinion has either insisted or consented that government should do in order to regulate industry and the market. In various ways these restrictions have strengthened the economy. Yet the question remains why the American system has resulted in such great productivity.

The Protestant ethic, as Tawney and others have shown, prodded men to work hard and to value productivity as a divine blessing. Equality of conditions and the lack of a class system, as de Tocqueville notes, encouraged men to get into commerce and industry. Independence from Great Britain gave a mighty push to home manufactures. Expansion westward and a rising population provided an accelerating demand for goods.

Efficiency became a fetish. Experts swarmed through the plants with stopwatches in their hands, changing the location of workers, introducing moving belts, reducing each man's work to a few simple motions. They went too far, and now the swing is back the other way, towards letting a man do enough to a product so that he can feel he has accomplished something. But they did prove that much effort had been unnecessarily wasted by poor arrangement of work space, flow of work, or work methods.

Standardizing the size and shape of products saved untold billions. More than forty types of hospital bed became one or two. Car manufacturers learned to make a few basic body types, frames and engines which could be used throughout a whole line of automobiles with minor variations.

Cost accounting, statistical research, job analysis, scientific research, business forecasting, inventory control, improved ware-
housing methods and quicker transportation of products—each
became a specialty further contributing to more efficient production.

American manufacturers learned how to join low production costs
with high wages—sure sign of efficiency. Another test: while the
Soviet needs one desk worker for every four at the bench, the
United States uses only one to seven.

While the old-style efficiency had prodded the worker to work
faster, the new type sought to improve his output by making him
feel more comfortable and satisfied. Music was piped in to offices
and factories all over the country by a specialized service which
even synchronized its choice of music with the known psychological
peaks and valleys of the working day. The result: less tension and
boredom for the worker, less breakage and fewer accidents. Employers could see the results in their balance sheets. Fifty million
workers listened to one musical service alone.

Similar results were also being claimed for color properly applied to walls and machines. Sometimes workers were asked to vote
on the colors they preferred. A large refinery selected red, buff
and orange for its machines, red and blue for the towers, baby blue
for loading racks.

Proper lighting, air conditioning and noise suppression have also
shown spectacular results. Comfortable, well designed chairs are
said to raise productivity ten per cent. Smart looking offices with
all these improvements and with modern furniture, machines, and
an arrangement designed for proper work flow can cut down the
time for processing an order from two days to two hours.

Said one happy employer: "My people not only work better.
They also dress better, speak better, and even walk more erect."
Even at less pay, girls prefer to work in such offices.

Meanwhile industrial research—2.6 billion dollars yearly of it—
is constantly bringing new marvels of production to birth. General
Motors has an automatic production line which makes two thousand automobile pistons each hour. Fourteen giant glass blowing
machines of one company produce ninety per cent of the country's
light bulbs as well as all the glass for electronic tubes. Despite the

fact that each of these machines requires but one operator, the glass industry uses half again as many workers as it did forty years ago.

Research is developing hundreds of materials—fabrics, detergents, medicines—that are revolutionizing man's former dependence upon the "natural" products of field and forest. Now huge continuous-flow chemical plants, looking like the science fiction dreams of an earlier day, spill out an endless stream of products—fertilizers, synthetic rubber, printer's ink, and the raw material for the plastics industry which has spawned a vast array of new things.

While chemists and physicists have already produced marvels, it appears likely that the joint efforts of chemists and physicists with biologists may introduce a whole new order of products and industries, perhaps even to producing food from light, air and water as nature itself does.

Invention is revolutionizing office work. One public service company with nearly two million customers has installed an electronic computing system, manned by 270 people, which can do in two days what formerly occupied five hundred clerks for a full week. Another machine, when stimulated by punched cards, sends out standard replies to every possible sort of complaint or inquiry.

Factory machines now in use can take in the raw material, watch for mistakes while the product is running through a complicated milling operation, correct any errors, stop and start, inspect the finished item, discard faulty units, count the number produced, and "remember" whatever aspect of the process is fed to its electronic brain.

Automation—continuous automatic production—has already transformed or greatly altered many industries, yet the age of automation is just beginning. Already it has kept the cost of electricity at about its 1939 rate while the cost of living otherwise has risen ninety-three per cent.

Some observers, looking only at the displacement of stenographers by dictating machines and typing pools, the displacement of book-keepers by calculating machines, the displacement of craftsmen like glass blowers and cabinet makers, see only evil in the result. Others stress the increased demand for engineers and technicians, the end of back-breaking labor and disease-breeding occupations, the shortening of hours, and the rising level of culture that more leisure will permit.

## The Corporation

The responsible center of this lively economy is the corporation. The word still has, even in American ears, a somewhat ominous ring, for we remember the days when uncontrolled and greedy corporations bred monopoly, great wealth and great poverty, shady financial dealings and political corruption.

How the times have changed! Nowadays the corporation shows an almost nervous concern for its reputation, hires public relations men to present it favorably to the public, welcomes visitors to its plants, courteously answers inquiries from stockholders and school-children alike, and encourages its people to be usefully active in civic affairs.

The great majority of employers, including corporations, are still relatively small. Ninety per cent of all employers hire fewer than thirty-one workers. But the top five per cent employ seventy per cent of all workers. There are about two million individuals and partners in business and only about half a million corporations. Yet of these corporations, about two hundred hold half of all business assets. It appears that by mergers and interlocking directorates or interlocking stockholdings these giants are growing bigger.

Such organizations are, like schools and churches, social institutions. Their impact upon attitudes and patterns of living is fully as strong. In fact, they influence in many ways what is taught in school and even what is preached in church, for the mind-set of business, especially that of the large corporation, permeates the society.

Who controls these giants, who owns them, and who benefits from them?

In most cases the ownership is very widely spread, and it is quite common for a firm to have more stockholders than employees. DuPont has 166,000 stockholders to 89,000 employees; General Motors 656,000 to 514,000 (and 88,000 more abroad); General Electric 296,000 to 210,000. Between eight and nine million Americans own shares of stock, and most of these people are little fellows rather than "capitalists" in the old-fashioned image.

The owners of a large corporation are therefore scattered throughout the country and have no effective control over the company. Control remains with top management and the board of directors. Yet the fact that stockholders can and do make trouble at annual meetings keeps the officers sensitive to the shareholders' interest. In an era of ever-widening economic democracy, the managers know that they must take a responsible attitude towards the social order or be restrained by government. So they accept a five-fold responsibility. Stockholders are entitled to a fair dividend, workers to wages which reflect their increasing productivity, the public to better goods or lower prices, or both, and the government to a share of the profits to be expended for the public benefit. The fifth share, which goes to replace or enlarge the productive plant, benefits all the other four by raising productivity.

It has come about, without anyone planning it that way, that the large firms have become political and social institutions almost as much as they are economic ones. The corporation thinks and acts more and more like government. In size, complexity, problems of coordination and impact of its decisions on the community, it has become a government in little, and not so little at that.

This bigness pleases some and alarms others. David Lilienthal, one of the country's distinguished public men, feels that it is a mistake to regard bigness as an evil, that the growth of corporations is inevitable because it raises productivity, providing the consumer with better and more varied products, and that these giants, competing against each other and curbed by big labor and big government, are sufficiently held in check. C. Wright Mills sees the corporations as dominating the society and imposing their will not by exploitation, but by leading us by advertising and suggestion to internalize what they would have us do, but he takes little account of countervailing forces such as unions, churches, and other groups.

While the pessimists rarely bother to compare big business today with its irresponsible and predatory forerunner of the late nineteenth century, they do assert that it is destroying small business, or unduly affecting it through the impact of its great economic power.

There still remains a large place in the economy for the millions of small businesses. The life of the small or medium-size town is still characterized by the activities of the professional men, merchants, service tradesmen and small manufacturers who with their wives give their time to the many voluntary activities on which the community's health and welfare rest. They provide a continuing leadership while the managers of the big business which has a branch in their town come and go. They may be affected by the prestige and consumption habits of the big business people, but these people in turn are dependent for social and community acceptance on the local elite. The forces are interacting.

"No business can prosper unless it serves the public interest in all of its many facets," says Crawford Greenwalt of duPont. "As a business develops and its policymaking decisions are delegated to an ever-increasing number of people, business conduct will in itself reflect the public interest as it may exist in a particular setting and at a particular time."

His firm, often subject to antitrust actions because of its huge grip on the chemical industry, has actually persuaded competitors to go into business. Then it builds the plant and supplies the necessary technical assistance to get the competitor started. This is a long step away from the monopoly mentality!

A more representative trend, however, has been for big corporations to acquire diversified production by adding new lines or merging smaller plants. General Electric, already in every imaginable electrical field, also manufactures jet engines and air conditioning equipment and has entered the field of atomic power. Secure continuity of operations rather than the drive for large short-run profits motivates today's corporation, which averages a return of less than four per cent.

Spurred by the federal tax on their profits, corporations have become more generous in giving some of their earnings for community welfare. Realizing that the future leaders of industry must come from colleges and universities, many of which have been hard hit by inflation, industries are also increasing their gifts to higher education.

If such giving is a product of enlightened self-interest, it also shows an increasing concern with the image the corporation etches on the public mind. The image they strive to present is that of a benevolent, public-minded institution, responsible for originating and increasing the flow of products and wages on which the nation's prosperity is based.

Perhaps the most instructive contrast is that offered by Henry Ford and his grandson Henry. The older Ford kept his vast industry within the family, announced high wages but by frequent demotions and firings kept employees from reaching the attractive maximums, was surrounded by bodyguards and attempted to hold his organization together by fostering intrigue and mutual jealousies. Henry II supplanted his grandfather's brutal handling of labor with a record of peaceful relations. He has combined business with public service as a delegate to the United Nations. With the money his grandfather left to the Ford Foundation he has encouraged broad programs of social research.

But Henry Ford II, as one born to great wealth and influence, is the exception rather than the rule. Studies of nine thousand industrial leaders have shown that a young man with nothing to offer but his ability has a better chance of ending in an executive post than his father or grandfather had. And his chances are best in big business. The proportion of laborers' sons in the management group has more than doubled in the past fifty years. But a college degree is still the best assurance of business success—better even than marrying the boss's daughter!

What makes a man successful in business? He is emotionally on his own. He has overcome dependence upon his parents. He fears failure and keeps working in order to avoid it. He identifies himself with his superiors. He is outgoing, enjoys working with people, likes the sense of being busy, knows how to make others feel good about working for him, and is able to channel his creative urges into service to the company, its products and policies. He is intelligent rather than intellectual.

Today's big business leaders have rarely run their own small businesses. They hold only minor amounts of stock in the company they manage. Seventy-two per cent of the top executive group are now in this category. A small number of these men are responsible for far-reaching decisions. At the top are men who move easily from industry into government, or from the armed services into industry, and whose decisions will affect the whole country. To regard them as freewheelers, however, is to ignore the importance of public opinion and many restraining pressures. Big business, in becoming big, has put itself in a position like that of government. It can lead only so far, push only so much. Public opinion is the final arbiter.

A more serious charge is that management people are losing their sense of individual values and becoming submerged in the group. The committee has replaced the leader, it is argued. Group decisions are killing individual initiative. But this criticism seems to ignore the fact that individual and group are complementary aspects of human personality. If the accent seems to some to be too strongly upon the group, this is doubtless a temporary emphasis which over-compensates for the once-praised rugged individualism, and will pass.

It is true, however, that staff work by experts in many fields has taken the place of decisions made off the cuff by the old style tycoon. With this change has come more stress on getting along with the group rather than getting ahead—or rather, one hopes to get ahead by getting along instead of by trampling on competitors.

Replacing the conspicuous consumption of Thorstein Veblen's day is the conspicuous production of a managerial group which wants its firm to look well in the public eye—to have attractive of-fices and shops, and products that are recognized from national advertising and respected by users. Management places high value on radio or television programs widely enjoyed by the public, good labor relations, leadership in the community, use of the latest ma-chines and methods, and a large body of satisfied stockholders who are kept happy by reasonable dividends and friendly letters and reports.

To get these results requires managers who are good at their jobs and who have been to professional schools of business administra-tion where such methods are taught. Companies compete for the graduates of these schools, and the modern ideal of the corporation which takes its social responsibilities seriously is thus more widely spread.

## CHAPTER TWELVE

---

# *Conspicuous Distribution*

Thorstein Veblen characterized our economy as one of conspicuous consumption. It might be argued that the age of
abundance has made distribution to an ever wider public the most
conspicuous factor.

Although there is plenty of room for improvement, workers get
a far bigger share than they have had in the past, and for fewer
hours of work.

This suggests a strange paradox. Will men, who now long for
more leisure and talk wistfully about what they would do with it,
soon be talking wistfully about the good old plant with its social
warmth, its tinted walls and machines, its perfect lighting, its coffee
breaks and air conditioning and comfortable posture chairs? Will
they tell their children about the good old days when they could
spend thirty or even forty hours of rhythmic activity at work instead of the parsimonious ten or twenty to which automation has
reduced them?

At present work provides many things besides income. Every
job carries its own ranking, and the job is thus a way of gaining
status. It makes human contacts which bring the pleasures—and
frustrations—of interaction. The work group often becomes an important source of satisfaction and of friendships. The job also af-
fords an opportunity for the use of skills which satisfy the owner
of them.

In this growing economy with its rising population, about half a
million people are added to the labor force every year. Manufactur-

ing employs only about a third of the non-farm workers. Another third are engaged in transporting and selling goods and in allied services such as finance and communications. Another third are in mining, forestry, fishing, construction, government and the professions. Production of goods is carried out by less than a quarter of the total labor force, and as machines make each worker more productive, this proportion gets smaller all the time. America's problem is no longer how to produce enough, but how to consume enough. This accent on consumption has had and is having an impact on the whole society.

Though fewer people are needed to produce, the number of women at work has been rising; in 1950 they made up thirty per cent of those in civilian jobs. Does this mean that as technology forces the number of working hours down, married women who work will expect their husbands to do an equal share of the housework? Or will these women tend to drop out of the labor market? In either case, automation will affect family life.

Although women fill many of the nation's jobs, they are often expected to take work that pays less. But they are steadily gaining more recognition. As automation makes physical labor less important, their role in industry is bound to grow more equal. They have already achieved status in many professions. Teaching, of course, is uniquely theirs, and so is that indispensable role of "office wife" or girl Friday to the busy executive who could not function without her.

World War II, which gave women the chance to show what they could do in industry, also brought benefits to Negroes. By the end of the war they held 9.7 per cent of the jobs covered by social security, and this was equivalent to their proportion of the total population. In five years their proportion of such jobs more than doubled in fifteen states outside the South, from which they had moved in response to better opportunities.

The whole working force is constantly being upgraded by replacing heavy labor with machines which require skilled or semi-skilled operators. European observers find this replacement of manual labor by trained people one of the three most significant aspects of American industry. The other two are, incidentally, the emergence of management as a social function and the disappear-

ance of the owner from management through diffused stockholdings.*

All Marx's dire predictions about capitalism have been reversed.
The level of living for workers has risen, their hours have been
shortened, and income has been more evenly distributed. Also, contrary to Marx's expectations, colonial empires are disintegrating or
being voluntarily relinquished, and agriculture is being subsidized
instead of exploited.

The loss in the number of hours worked is more than made up
by the increasing productivity of machines and by the fact that
men can work with more speed and precision during a short work-
day than a long one.

While hours have been going down, wages have been going up.
The average income of all those fully employed has now risen to
the surprising figure of $4,200 annually for men, $2,700 for women.
The percentage of the national income going to employees has
meanwhile shown a steady rise. Purchasing power per person has
risen at the same rate (2% a year) as output per man hour, and has
been ever more widely shared.

To help workers negotiate for a fair share of what they produce,
the government has enacted a number of laws—to permit collective
bargaining by unions on behalf of workers, to protect women and
children, to limit hours and establish a minimum wage, to provide
retired workers or their dependent survivors with a pension, to
care for the unemployed, to give vocational training, to enforce
safety measures and to assure compensation for injuries suffered
on the job.

Many of these advances, if not all, have been sparked by the
world's largest trade union movement. About eighteen million men
and women, one-third of the country's non-agricultural workers,
belong to unions. The bitter war employers once fought against
them has been replaced by negotiation between equals which is often
good-natured even when it is hard-boiled. Often these negotiations
are for a whole industry, though they may be on a local basis.

With the merger of the American Federation of Labor and the
Congress of Industrial Organizations in 1955, the great majority of

* The American Round Table: "An Examination of the American Economic
System." The Advertising Council, 1952. Statement by Peter Drucker.

union members became united under one set of leaders. As a rule, a worker belongs to the "local" of a national union for his particular trade—say the United Automobile Workers (an industrial union of many occupations) or the Lithographers (a union combining the several crafts involved in lithography). More than seventy thousand of these locals are scattered around the country. The locals of one trade or industry are united in a national union which is autonomous and self-governing just as the states of the federal union or the state political parties are autonomous. Federalism and the dislike of central control are not limited to the political sphere.

Collective bargaining is the union's most important function. Major items of negotiation are: 1) the nature of the agreement and its duration, provisions for renewal, and prevention of strikes and lockouts; 2) the rights of union and management, recognition of the union and its part in hiring; 3) compensation, including the wage schedule, setting of rates, increases, supplemeneary benefits such as pension and health funds and paid holidays; 4) tenure, hiring and promotion, layoff and reemployment; 5) working conditions, including sanitation, safety, speed of work and the length of the working day and week.

Public acceptance of unions is a thing of recent date, but has become a part of American life, even though employers may privately rail against them. There is, however, some feeling that labor in exercising its new-found power may press for benefits which will lead to dangerous inflation, while employers in accepting the power of the unions will merely pass along increased labor costs to the public.

Many unions have shown an intelligent awareness of the fact that the welfare of their members is bound up with that of the employer and the public. The Amalgamated Clothing Workers' Union, for example, helps employers organize the flow of work, establish production standards, introduce machines to take the place of hand work, transfer laid off employees to other jobs, and loan money for capital. The International Ladies' Garment Workers' Union has its own engineers who help employers to raise productivity. The most successful unions know that the only way to raise wages and other benefits is through raising productivity. Their concern is therefore to see that the employee gets his share of the increased output.

Leaders like Walter Reuther believe that labor should have access to company records in order to gauge its demands, and should lead the way in deriving social benefits for the workers from the expanding economy.

Labor has also decided that it is better off when it negotiates directly with the employer instead of working through government. In spite of its political action committees, its canvassing and its efforts to elect friendly congressmen, it is primarily business-oriented rather than politically minded.

This system has worked well for labor. In recent years labor has won acceptance of the union shop in big industry (1941), health and welfare plans (1946), pensions in addition to social security (1949), wage scales pegged to living costs (1950), and unemployment pay to supplement the federal plan (1955). It has achieved recognition of the idea that the welfare of labor is one of management's responsibilities.

The unions themselves have become capitalists, with huge funds safely invested in government bonds or other securities. The United Automobile Workers alone is worth about $40,000,000. Budget of the AFL-CIO headquarters is $8,000,000 a year. Unions pay their leaders well. George Meany, president of the AFL-CIO, gets $35,000. But the heads of some of the national unions get even more. David McDonald, president of the steelworkers, gets $40,000.

The union movement, backed at first by a friendly government and developed through the shrewd deployment of its own strength, exercises a countervailing power which has helped to spread the fruits of labor more widely, keeping the economy healthily vigorous.

If union and management fail to agree when renegotiating a contract, the Federal Mediation and Conciliation Service may be called to assist—but only if both parties desire it. Each year it settles thousands of cases which might otherwise end in strikes. The National Labor Relations Board may be called in to settle issues connected with the methods of collective bargaining, such as alleged unfair practices, or to supervise employee voting. Strikes have become relatively infrequent, and when they occur the atmosphere is vastly different from that of the bloody battles of the 1930's. During the steel strike of 1956 workers carefully banked the furnaces to prevent damage. A few amiable strikers leaned against company gates to check the maintenance men allowed to go inside, while others drew vacation pay from their employers and went off on a holiday with the family.

Just as professional managers have replaced the old-time owner-manager in industry, so professional labor leaders—including lawyers, economists, publicists and educators—have largely replaced the untrained, rabble-rousing union boss. The labor movement publishes six hundred newspapers and journals. In 1950 the International Ladies' Garment Workers' Union established a fulltime school for those who wanted to make union work their career. The University of Wisconsin runs a Summer School for Workers which provides a valuable campus experience. Labor unions like management have become active in community life, sitting on civic boards and helping with the inevitable fund-raising campaigns.

Labor's great power also poses new problems. Collective bargaining in the big industries is bound to have broad effects upon the economy—on prices, employment, and industry's decisions as to where to locate new plants. Too, the unions have the power to use strikes as a means of controlling the voting in jurisdictional disputes, to saddle their members with high fees, and to oust from their jobs men who resist the dictates of a clique in power.

In some unions the evil of bossism and the throttling of democratic procedure has become a national scandal, as in the Musicians' and the Teamsters' Unions, or the International Longshoremen's Association which the AFL-CIO expelled, having no power to discipline it, when it failed to get rid of its racketeers. In larger cities the building trades, supported by the contractors who hire them, have made a monopoly of the construction business, restricted union membership, enforced a slowdown, sponsored restrictive laws, prevented innovations in construction, held prices high and kept the building industry years behind the rest of the economy. Tie ups between labor and racketeers have been exposed.

Still the modern labor movement is clearly a response to the worker's need for security in a world where he is dependent upon the job for his livelihood, and where he has nothing else to fall back on. The unions have stepped forward as spokesmen and defenders of this dependent workman. Yet at present less than a third of the working force is organized. The South, the chemical industry and office workers are under-unionized, but the unions are preparing to tackle them.

One sign of labor's maturity as a social institution is the role it has played in encouraging union movements abroad after the Second World War. The AFL-CIO spends a quarter of a million dollars a year to maintain overseas contacts, gets out trade journals in foreign editions, supports a permanent bureau for Europe in Brussels, and gives its support to free unionism and better living standards for workers everywhere. Visiting labor leaders from overseas have also been the guests of American unions, and have seen for themselves how the American system works.

## What Do Workers Want?

When foremen in twenty-four plants were recently asked by the Labor Relations Institute (Newark, N.J.) to rate the things they thought the men under them wanted most from their jobs, they placed good wages first, then job security. But the men themselves had very different ideas:

|  | Rank as given by: | |
|---|---|---|
|  | workers | foremen |
| Full appreciation for work done | 1 | 8 |
| Filling in on company matters | 2 | 10 |
| Sympathetic help on personal problems | 3 | 9 |
| Job security | 4 | 2 |
| Good wages | 5 | 1 |
| Work that keeps you interested | 6 | 5 |
| Getting ahead | 7 | 3 |
| Personal loyalty to workers | 8 | 6 |
| Good working conditions | 9 | 4 |
| Tactful disciplining | 10 | 7 |

What the men wanted even more than wages and security was to be treated like people.

A Standard Oil affiliate was having trouble with chronic dissatisfaction among its workers until the president began to talk to the men about some of the company's problems. The response was immediate. The fact that the men had felt left out and unregarded was the principal source of their dissatisfaction.

Joseph Scanlon has stressed the importance of giving the worker a share in decisions affecting productivity and in the resulting profits. His plan has been adopted by a number of important manufacturers. For the individual who identifies himself with his job is motivated by inner impulses rather than by orders from outside. He works as a member of a team, rather than as a cog in a wheel.

A young Frenchwoman who recently visited seventeen American factories was struck by their cleanliness, their luxury, the synchronizing of men and machines which assembled a complete car in eighty-seven minutes, the ease with which the men did their jobs since everything was conveniently ready to hand. (They even had time to notice that an attractive visitor was passing by!) She also liked the piped-in music, the financial help given to workers who studied nights, the lack of class conflict, the workers and executives calling each other by first names, the democratic good relations in the plant.

And the suggestion boxes. Though our French visitor may not have known it, this pet of American industry has its own association—the National Association of Suggestion Systems, with eight hundred members reporting more than a million suggestions received in one year, more than a quarter million used, $7 million paid to employees for the ideas they offered, and many more millions saved. General Motors, for example, paid $3,230,000 for the 54,000 ideas it adopted.

The old gag of the boss opening the box to find there the suggestion "Drop dead" is no longer very funny. Not when a woman can earn $6,592 for discovering that if she puts fingernail polish around the edge of the belt on her polishing machine, it stops raveling!

While some manufacturers have found profit-sharing plans effective, others have placed the emphasis on giving meaning to the job the worker does—by helping him to see it in its place as part of a large, coordinated effort, by encouraging team work, by allowing workers to share in the governing of the plant community in matters of health, cleanliness, safety and relaxation. At General Motors, where the recreational program was entirely run by the workers, it was voted one of the chief sources of job satisfaction.

## White Collar People

Labor has the unions to look out for its interests, but who looks after the white collar worker?

Between 1870 and 1940 the office workers rose from twelve to forty per cent of the white collar group. Sales people and teachers are the other big groups. The income of labor has risen until many factory employees make more money than office people. White collar skills such as bookkeeping and stenography have been depreciated by accounting and dictating machines. Many professional workers, lawyers particularly, have become the servants of business.

As for the intellectual, C. Wright Mills remarks that unlike Europe the United States has not produced enough of them "who have been unemployed long enough or under such conditions as to cause frustration among them." * Sad case!

Mills sees the white collar class as the victims of industrialism, their prestige lowered, their jobs downgraded by the use of machinery, dependent upon the large corporation, robbed of initiative, anxious for the future. That the high school girls he pities for having to punch the keys of a machine would, in earlier decades, have been uneducated child laborers in a textile mill is not mentioned.

Instead of attacking the results of a mechanization which cannot be reversed, it seems more to the point to study how to channel increased productivity to the equal advantage of all—through education for all to the extent of their abilities, through the sensible use of increased leisure time, through unionizing of office workers.

The professional man in business for himself—lawyer, doctor, engineer, writer, architect—makes use of the apparatus business has developed: dictaphone, adding or calculating machine, filing system. He does this to a greater extent than his colleagues in other countries. He would also feel lost without the special tools of his trade, from slide-rule and microscope to the highly proficient technical services on which he draws. The independent professional is also a business man who must meet competition and make good use of his time and who therefore tends to have attitudes similar to those of the merchant or commercial man.

* *White Collar*, p. 156.

*The Stockholder*

Who owns the industries upon which the productive, expanding economy is based?

Communist propaganda evokes the old stereotype of the Wall Street capitalist with silk hat and cutaway coat, trampling the bodies of the poor. A State Department official who once had a couple of visiting Russians in tow, took them down Fifth Avenue in New York just as the churches were letting out one Easter Sunday. A few well-dressed churchgoers were walking down the avenue in silk hats and cutaways—probably for the one time in the year when they got into these largely outmoded costumes. The Russians nearly fell out of the taxi window.

"Look, capitalists!" they shouted.

They would not have recognized the typical capitalist if they had seen *her*. Of the 8,600,000 stockholders in the country, a little more than half are women. Thirty-four per cent of all investors are housewives. The mythical average investor is forty-eight years old, and lives in a small city of twenty-five thousand, on a family income of less than $7,500. A million of these investors earn less than $3,000 a year. One in every twelve adults now owns stock in a public corporation, another million and a half in privately held companies, and one hundred million are indirect owners through their holdings of life insurance or pension funds.

Investing has become so popular that brokers offer public lectures to help people understand the principles of sound stock purchasing. Investment clubs are springing up so that small buyers can pool their funds and buy regularly. Other schemes include the Monthly Investment Plan of the New York Stock Exchange, the mutual funds ($12 billions now invested) which permit the small investor to diversify, and the employee stock purchase plans which are turning workers into owners of the companies they work for. American Telephone and Telegraph has a quarter of a million worker-owners, while eighty-eight per cent of Socony Mobil's workers own stock.

"What would happen," Benjamin Fairless of U.S. Steel has speculated, "if our workers did own the company?" Pointing out that this could happen, he said, "There would be no walkouts to worry about because, after all, how can an owner go on strike?"

Although this is not likely to happen in a hurry, it is true that more and more little people are acquiring a small share of the producing machine even though the big stockholdings remain in a relatively small number of hands. Well-known, powerful companies are bidding for the small investor—by splitting their stock so as to make the price more attractive, by issuing annual reports in four colors, beautifully printed and so written as to make corporate problems clear to the average man, by holding annual meetings which are like huge picnics and where the $150,000-a-year president of the company listens patiently to a complaint from the floor —sometimes to an employee who as stockholder is talking back to the boss and demanding an explanation.

The rigid lines separating worker from stockowner, stockowner from consumer, are breaking down. Stockowners receive with their dividend checks descriptions of the products the firm turns out, and are urged to increase their own profits by using these products and recommending them to friends. What kind of economy is this, when ownership is so widely diffused? Instead of nationalizing industry, and thus merging political and economic power, the tendency of the American system is to spread out the ownership in so many individual hands that it becomes democratized.

In recent years the small investor has been encouraged by the soundness of the stock market, the regular profits and dividends, and perhaps most of all by the realization that while the purchasing power of money has (in twenty years) been cut in half, the value of common stocks has tripled in value. Investment thus becomes a hedge against inflation. The Park Avenue maid who saw her $4,000 invested during the early war years become a tidy $40,000 or the bootblack whose faith in one stock led to holdings worth $80,000 finds in stock ownership the gateway to sharing the great productivity of industry.

The dollars of these small investors have altered the face of Wall Street, and diminished its influence. The great industrial corporations now finance themselves instead of going to the financial houses of Wall Street, either by plowing back earnings (60% nowadays, twice as much as in the twenties), or by offering debentures to their stockholders. General Motors alone has working capital of $2,183,000,000 as compared with the $667,000,000 which the House of Morgan can command.

## Getting and Spending

All this investing, all this production comes to nothing unless the product is consumed. The paradox of so fertile an economy is that it no longer has to worry about producing; it has to make sure that the product is consumed as fast as it is turned out.

Since the economy has a great capacity to produce money and therefore credit, the volume of spending is to a considerable degree independent of the volume of income. The more money spent, the more money earned in this Looking Glass economy. For if spending is kept up, it generates employment.

So installment buying is encouraged, though if it appears to be getting out of hand the Federal Reserve Board can clamp down on credit. In spite of the spending spree, half the families in the country have no installment debt, and during 1956 consumers saved $20.5 *billion* dollars.

To encourage consumption, every possible device is used. New products are constantly being offered, and since customers are always eager to try new goods, they are offered more and more alternatives. Obsolescence occurs when some ingenious designer and manufacturer turns out a product which will persuade the consumer to throw out the old one. So a refrigerator in good working order may be discarded for one which comes in a pastel shade to match the new wallpaper, or which has shelves which revolve and a tap which supplies ice water.

Competition for the consumer dollar often leads to lowered prices as well as improved products. Electric refrigerators cost about $78 per cubic foot in 1922, as against $34 in 1955. The new refrigerator is also a much better product. Radio prices are low enough so that only three per cent of the homes in the country are without one.

The Consumers' Price Index supplied by the Bureau of Labor Statistics to show changes in the cost of living for moderate income families has had to add several new products to a list which already included radios, electric sewing machines and other automatic household devices. Frozen foods, electric toasters and television sets have also joined the list.

Through mail order houses and supermarkets with their lowered prices, through goods produced at lower cost through mechanization and automation, the American economy has spread its goods wide. Through market and consumer research it has tried to find out what people want, and has then produced it.

The widening market has broken down class distinctions. Nearly everyone wears ready-made clothes. The plumber or steelworker is very likely to dress as well as the doctor or even the millionaire. Rich and poor smoke the same brands of cigarette, buy the same packaged foods, read the same magazines, go to the same movies, ride in the same cars of a train, buy the same electrical appliances.

Income too has been levelling out, as in any mature private enterprise economy. Between 1935 and 1950, the lowest fifth of American families saw their real incomes after taxes increase forty-two per cent, while the top five per cent experienced a small loss. One out of every five families engaged in crafts receives more than $7,000 a year, only one in six of professional and technical groups. Thus class lines are growing blurred. The share of income going to property has declined while that to workers has increased. Special occupations of all kinds are increasing, while common labor is holding steady or declining.

Thirty-six million people have life insurance, thirty million have savings accounts, four million families live in their own homes. And several million baby sitters in 1956 earned about a billion dollars! This new specialty symbolizes many things—the need of the small family for outside help, the new function for the old and the teen-ager which this need supplies, the availability of money for such a purpose and for the recreational spending which the presence of a baby sitter implies, and the quick professionalizing of the service. In Hollywood the Baby Sitters Guild, with 4,800 registered sitters, screens its members with great care. In Detroit an elementary school gives fifth-graders a course in baby-sitting. No one has yet given the babies a course in how to be sat, but it will no doubt come.

Automatic washers, vacuum cleaners, frozen foods, mixers and all the rest have lightened the tasks not only for women who in earlier decades would have had servants, but for millions who would not.

Especially to the farm woman, who once had to carry or pump her water, wash and scrub and clean by hand, can her vegetables and meats instead of freezing them,* the mechanized house has brought release.

## The Hucksters

An economy which depends upon rapid consumption for its vitality cannot afford to sit and wait for customers. The raucous advertising which distresses so many of our visitors and many of us is an inevitable necessity if people are to be converted from a psychology of scarcity and saving to one of prosperity through spending. Advertising, aided by psychologists, and by polls and market surveys instills the desires, prods the timid or indifferent, and teaches people to be consumers.

One might argue that some of the money squandered on advertising and on the products it offers might better be spent to build needed schools, roads and hospitals. Aware of this criticism, the Advertising Council, a voluntary association, has organized to make the great power and reach of national advertising available for social ends. Its principle is to advise the nation of dangers—such as the shortage of schoolrooms and teachers—which voluntary groups can then tackle locally in the traditional American manner.

Another answer to the offensive blatancy of advertising is the institutional approach. Du Pont presents a series of radio and television dramas based on American history. It advertises no products, simply identifying the firm as a manufacturer of things for better living through chemistry. The Texas Company provides the nation with an afternoon of Metropolitan Opera every week throughout the season, without commercials.

Advertising has indeed become an institution of social significance, ranging all the way from the vulgar and offensive to the aesthetically aware and socially conscious. Its raucous crudity is a product of the forces that gave it birth—competition for the consumer's dollar, and the nervous need of an ever widening market to keep the giant productive mechanism operating.

This need also leads to the policy of consideration for the cus-

* Thus destroying that old joke: "We eat what we can, and what we can't, we can."

tomer which sometimes surprises visitors. Mail order houses and department stores accept returned merchandise with little or no question. Salesmen are given courses which stress friendliness, courtesy, and genuine interest in helping the customer. Standardization and brand naming produce goods the buyer can rely on. Installment buying, telephoned orders, door-to-door salesmen and delivery services make it easy for the customer to spend his money. Upon his willingness to spend, the economic health of the nation depends.

*Problems*

Even in the midst of this booming economy there are pockets of gloom, or at least of doubt. How can we maintain this healthy growth? What would happen if real disarmament made it possible for us to slice our fantastic military expenditure of over $40 billion a year? What can we do about the resources which are giving out as a result of our heavy use of them? Would we have the courage to use the monetary and fiscal stabilization tools now at hand to avert a really serious depression, or would we do too little, too late? Can we continue to broaden the fruits of our productivity so as to wipe out the frightful pockets of poverty which still exist? What can we do to meet the needs of farmers? Will the current inflationary trend reach the dangerous stage, and how can we control it?

These are a few of the problems the economy still faces.

The clear and present danger is inflation. When the demand for goods is strong, both industry and labor find it easy to pass rising costs along to the consumer. Government control of prices may be the only alternative to runaway inflation.

To keep the economy stable it is necessary to offer incentives to industry which will keep its spending on capital goods steady, and to limit the fluctuations of private bank credit so as to minimize their effect on the volume of consumer spending.*

Another problem area of the economy is housing. Too many Americans still live in slums, rural or urban. Slums are profitable to landlords, and the corrective measures required are so huge that they can only be undertaken by government, or through voluntary pooling of resources such as the Morningside Heights program.

* Sumner Slichter, *The American Economy*, p. 80.

The federal government, cooperating with cities, has launched slum-clearing housing programs in about 750 urban centers. Only families of limited income may move in. Rent is usually one-fifth of gross income. Rooms are assigned according to the size of the family, thus avoiding the crowding which makes slums. In Chicago four-fifths of the original tenants of the three oldest projects have moved to better private homes. Thus the housing project upgrades the family's living standards, leading the way to private ownership.

While the abundance produced by industry has brought prosperity to its workers, the abundance produced by agriculture has brought a relatively lowered income to farmers. We appear to be able to absorb the products of industry without limit. But we can eat only so much. Even improved eating habits with more protein and fresh foods and a rising population will not absorb what the farmer with his greater productivity based upon machinery and scientific farming can send to market.

Programs to supply food deficit areas abroad and to provide free or low-cost food to the poor, and to schools and institutions at home, cannot consume the surplus. Federal price support programs only aggravate the surplus problem. Rewarding the farmer for limiting his acreage only leads him to produce still more abundantly on the remaining acres.

From the wheat fields of the great northern plains to the central corn and hog country and south to cotton and tobacco, from the lush irrigated valleys of California to the rugged grassland country of Vermont and New Hampshire, from the 920,000-acre King Ranch in Texas to the share-cropper on a few eroded acres in Alabama, American agriculture embraces so many varieties that no single program could meet its needs.

Farmers have helped themselves through cooperatives which supply them with twelve per cent of their needs at wholesale prices and market their products to best advantage. The great voluntary associations such as the Grange and the Farm Bureau have brought other advantages, including social and educational activities at the local level and increased political power in state and national capitals. The many federal aids—soil conservation, rural electrification, crop insurance, irrigation projects, agricultural research, pamphlets, visits from agents of the extension service and credit services—make the farmer the best-served of all our citizens.

Still his income does not keep pace with that of the rest of the economy. Price support programs benefit most the large farmers or corporations controlling great acreage, and these are least in need of help. Untouched by them are the million and a half migratory workers who travel northward with the crops, do the backbreaking labor, and have to put up with poor housing, primitive sanitation and inadequate medical care. As transients they cannot establish a voting residence, enjoy the benefits of community life, or allow their children an uninterrupted education.

"The way to stop producing surpluses is to stop using price supports as a means of increasing farm incomes," according to Geoffrey Shepherd, Professor of Agricultural Economics at Iowa State College.* Shepherd believes that the annual surplus of half a million farmers resulting from a high farm birth rate is responsible for low farm income. Even the average wheat or dairy farmer with good land can count on only $2,000 or so of net income. The way to raise this is to reduce the farmers, not the acres, and then to improve per capita production. But this plain and logical answer is not likely to please those who prefer to increase farm votes instead of lowering them, or who believe that farming is a way of life which should be open to all who want it. The sentimental regard for rural life, as well as the belief in its superiority, are powerful factors.

*Foreign Trade*

The United States, producing forty per cent of the world's goods, has only about one-tenth of the world's trade. By tariff concessions, gifts and loans it has tried to do its share in restoring world production and trade. It has successfully encouraged regional economic organization abroad. It has negotiated many reciprocal trade agreements, and played a leading role in establishing the International Bank for Reconstruction and Development and the International Monetary Fund. The trade agreements program has reduced our tariffs from an average of fifty-three per cent in 1930–33 to less than 15 per cent by 1951. This, for a nation so long committed to high tariffs, is a good deal. Industries affected by foreign imports

* The American Assembly, *United States Agriculture*, p. 77.

are constantly using their influence to limit this program; congressmen, elected by men and women who may lose their jobs as a result of competing foreign products, are under heavy pressure to protect American industries.

The United States is rapidly using up its supplies of copper, zinc, lead, petroleum and other essential resources. It should buy half of them abroad. But again local interests intervene. What would become of the miners forced out of work? The communities dependent on their wages?

As long as American wages, productivity and living standards remain above the world average, we will continue to be embarrassed by our dealings with the rest of the world. Even the impulse to generosity seems to bother us. We are almost apologetic about it abroad, while at home we have to pretend that we are really too tough to give things away, except for some military advantage. Yet it is clear to us that we too will benefit from higher productivity throughout the world.

## Business and Government

The idea that government is responsible for regulating the economy so as to insure prosperity is relatively new in the United States. Government, because of its mediating role and its huge spendings, is the dominant factor in the economy. Thirty-eight per cent of the profits of corporations (except small ones) go to government. Then the stockholders pay another tax on the portion of the earnings they receive.

What we have seen in our lifetimes is a quiet revolution which has socialized capitalism, harnessing its immense productive power, its freedom of choice and experiment, and distributing it like electric current through a network of substations (the great economic groups—labor, industry, agriculture) and transformers (the voluntary associations) to the consumer. After a long period of open resistance and rearguard action, capitalism has virtually made its peace with government. It has accepted the idea that an economy must benefit all the citizens in order to benefit any. The wall between business and government, economics and politics has been pulled down, and they are now seen as aspects of a social order whose purpose is the welfare of the people. This socialized capitalism has broadened the benefits and narrowed the gulf between rich and poor more effectively than any socialist or communist state. Estate taxes have put an end to huge family fortunes.

Our system is far from perfect, but it is constantly moving—and in the right direction. Abundance and freedom: the two appear to be inseparable. In the United States they have been achieved by a social pattern which combines individualism with voluntarism and federalism in a constant tension of counterbalancing forces. This pattern has brought widespread ownership, diffusion of initiative and decision, and a continuously widening distribution of the abundance the system has produced.

With abundance assured, Americans are showing an increased preference for non-market values and for activities which are not related to piling up material goods. In addition to voluntary civic activity which has always been one of their strong points, they now value the things which renew and strengthen them as individuals and members of society.

Material values are likely to be most important to those who desperately lack the essential materials for an adequate life. There are many signs that the coming of abundance shifts the emphasis to other values. The profit motive has always been placed at the center of the economist's description of human behavior, but it is obvious that other motives are coming to have an increasing effect.

Material plenty is often confused with materialism. The marks of material abundance are plain in the United States; they often seem more important to visitors than they do to us. We like our shiny gadgets, sometimes with the innocent delight of a child, sometimes for the comfort they afford. But their long-range effect is to free us from materialism—to make time available for non-material things if we care to use it that way.

The United States is already wrestling with problems yet to be faced abroad. What happens to culture when class differences are virtually wiped out, when the majority have leisure and money to spend? What satisfactions and frustrations does the individual experience in a mechanized economy? How may the productive economy be employed for the attainment of goals that are not purely economic? What is its impact on taste, sensibility, style? How does it affect the arts, both fine and popular?

## CHAPTER THIRTEEN

# *The Arts*

Someone is always discovering that the arts are dead or dying in the United States. If not the theater, it is opera, or poetry, or painting. Our taste is atrocious, we are told. We are cultural barbarians. We lack the eye or the ear for what is refined and aesthetically reputable.

Like all generalizations, these accusations are partially true and patently false. The United States contains many publics, and they consume everything from the ugly chromos for sale in cheap furniture stores to a canvas by Matisse or Jackson Pollock. They devour badly written Westerns but also some of the finest criticism being written in the world today.

They attend more art shows, buy more books and toot on more musical instruments than ever before. Someone reads all the new books—more than 12,500 new *titles* a year. There are audiences to support more than two hundred symphony orchestras, and 2,100 cities provide regular classical concerts. If Broadway is caught in an economic straitjacket which makes possible the production of only the safest and most popular hits, community and off-Broadway theaters are flourishing, and here experimental work can be tried.

There are many soft spots in the cultural picture—the difficulty a serious painter has in making a living, the problem of survival for the accomplished young soloist, the low per capita expenditure for books despite the great upsurge in paperback production. Only seventeen per cent of the American people are reading books at any given time, compared with fifty-five per cent in England. Yet when a television program recently praised *The F.B.I. Story*, fifteen thousand orders poured in.

Meanwhile there has been a renaissance in the minor arts. Textile and pottery design have leaped ahead. Furniture has become simple and functional. More and more homes are tastefully built, decorated, furnished and lighted. Month after month the magazines specializing in better homes gush a ceaseless fountain of new ideas, many of them excellent. Packages, displays and shop windows are quickly influenced by trends in the higher arts and are frequently distinguished. Whatever one may think of automotive design, it is constantly on the prowl for new ideas. If only we could have a little less chrome and a little more headroom!

Museums and art centers sprout like spring dandelions. Many private collections, thanks to tax law and impulses to attain immortality, have become public. When a group of international students visited the Clark Museum in Williamstown, Massachusetts (population, 4,300), they looked at the walls full of French masterpieces and then turned to ask: "But these, of course, are copies?" It was hard for them to believe that a town they had never heard of could house such treasures.

Summer schools of the arts are now common throughout the country. From Breadloaf in Vermont to Aspen, Colorado, they bring practitioners in the arts together with young men and women who want to learn writing or painting, music or dance. And of course the arts now play an important part in college curricula. The word has got around that the most successful man in the professions is also at home in a museum or at a concert.

Louise Bogan sees in the burgeoning art centers, the regional romanticism and the feeling for folklore, an artistic vigor which will lead us away from mannerist art and literature to a natural renewal of romantic idealism.*

All these activities help to conserve the cultural pluralism which is the source of our artistic vigor at the very moment when the mass media threaten to wash over it. For in the arts as in other aspects of the national life, it is variety which makes for strength.

---

* For this and other suggestions in this section, I am indebted to the series of essays on "Our Country and Our Culture" published during 1952 in the *Partisan Review*.

"The American novel" or "the American style in painting" is non-existent.

## The Arts in a Classless Society

Is there then any kind of art particularly appropriate to a mobile and virtually classless society?

De Tocqueville thought there was. Its literature, he thought, must be easily obtained and quickly read. It must depict strong emotions. Its style will be vehement and loose, dealing with the unexpected and the new in order to astonish more than to please, to stir the passions rather than to charm the taste.

Although de Tocqueville's comment applies very aptly to the mass media, it fails to take account of the widely varied audiences made possible by education and abundance. Yet it points clearly enough to the dangers art is subject to in a commercial civilization.

De Tocqueville could not foresee that the time would come when man, freed from toil, would develop his tastes and even become an artist after hours if he chose to do so. He could not foresee the astonishing development of expertise among plain citizens, who now consume classical records at the rate of $100,000,000 worth a year, and not only know the music but critically compare one conductor's performance with another's.

While Americans have often been irritatingly boastful about their material accomplishments, they have generally been bashful about putting a cultural foot forward for fear the cut of the boot or the clod of earth clinging to it would appear inelegant to European eyes. We were willing to concede culture to Europe, while we claimed democracy, freedom, prosperity, comfort and mechanical ingenuity for our own. Europe became for us an image of what was old and effete, not modern and manly. So we left the cultivation of the arts to women. And art became more and more feminine in our eyes.

The picture is changing now, but the stigma still clings.

The fact is that our turning away from the past toward the future, a factor de Tocqueville astutely noticed, was in part a turning away from the symbolic forms which are the realm of art. For art, by its dealing in myth and symbol, manages to convey the tragic sense of life, manages to say something allusively true about man's condition and destiny. But America was the new land whose future did not admit tragedy. Its myth was one of hope.

To coin this promise one must do more than poetize. Offended by ugliness and poverty and degradation, Americans were determined to do something about them. We felt the need of grappling with them—not merely realizing them through art but correcting them. So we turned to social experiment and social science.

The same energies and motives that might have inspired artists have gone into the studies of man undertaken by sociologists and psychologists—the same patient desire to understand human purpose and motivation, the same effort to explain the meaning of human behavior. Only the end product is a textbook, a family welfare service or the emergence of psychiatry in medicine.

Driven by a thirst for knowledge—Americans make a fetish of "the fact," even the unassimilated, useless fact, as witness the TV quiz programs—we are suspicious of ideas. Ideas, that is, which imply strict adherence to an ideology regardless of the human results. We have seen what happens to men who follow that road in politics. We have earned the reputation of being unintellectual because our approach to problems is experimental and pluralistic, rather than abstract and monistic. The results keep assuring us that we are right in refusing to be snared by simplistic theories such as communism, fascism, Freudianism or any other ism pure and simple. The world and human nature are much too complicated and delicate to be manipulated by formula. We like the feel of the tiller in our hands, the reassurance of wind on the cheek.

So we have adopted the method of the artist—the immediate response to experience—as our way of steering. Driven by an immense curiosity, we have probed our world as a child explores a hole in the seabeach or a poet some mood or moment in nature. But where the end product of art is a work which clarifies existence, our end product has more often been a work which changes conditions.

When talents have been turned to the arts, the impelling force is still, often, a desire to change conditions, or at least to discover the special meaning of America, to see it more clearly both in its beauty and its squalor. So Grant Wood paints the flat prairies into the faces of his farm folk and Walt Whitman struggles to encompass the whole sprawling, throbbing, muscle-tensing nation.

Although we have had great poets, and will again, the natural direction for literature to take in such a culture is towards journalism. To a world which moves so fast, both in its public events and in the discoveries of science and their application to everyday life, journalism is indispensable. Now that the plain descriptions of science exceed the former fancies of poets, and the wonders of nature as Walt Disney can translate them to the screen surpass the marvelous wanderings of Odysseus, we need practical men to guide us through this maze of marvels—men who can say what is there so that we can understand.

Do you want to know what is going on in the world? There are the weekly news magazines, or John Gunther with his political guides to the continents. Psychology? The Overstreets with their shelf of sane and deceptively simple books. These experts know how to use the narrative skill of the novelist or dramatist. And since the materials they deal with are fascinating, they have to an extent replaced the novelist and dramatist.

Journalism has also spilled over into the novel and the play. As Upton Sinclair used the novel in muckraking days to expose the sins of meat packers and oil kings, present-day novelists are giving us the low-down on Hollywood, the advertising game, or life aboard a carrier. While news magazines are using the arts of fiction to make the events of the day palatable and memorable, fiction is using the arts of the journalist to give credibility to its portrayals of modern life. The movies, too, grow increasingly topical. Instead of stories which exemplify the basic human relationships we get relationships which exemplify problems—racial relations, alcoholism, delinquency.

The mechanized world which persuades us into journalism also supplies the machinery to disseminate what is written and painted and composed. "Materialism" is responsible for the outpouring of classical records, paper books, films, and beautiful color reproductions of paintings. *Life*, a popular magazine, prints the difficult verse of T. S. Eliot, Hemingway's *Old Man of the Sea*, splendid reproductions of the old masters, accounts of world religions. It also prints cheesecake and crime photographs. But the high culture seeps down to those who have never been exposed to it before. And who can tell what roots it will water, or what growth it will nourish?

Modern technology and artistic impulse have interpenetrated to produce the recording, the televised opera, the reproduced painting. The idea of reserving culture for an elite who can feel superior because of the exclusive patent they hold on it is advocated only by a minority. Truly great art, we feel, makes a universal appeal.

It is this popularizing of art which shocks some visitors from overseas, as if the spreading of it also profanes it.

## Literature

One might expect that our literature, following Whitman, would utter its barbaric yawp over the rooftops of the world; that it would reflect the pioneering crudity, the vital optimism, the healthy pragmatism of the surrounding culture.

Not at all. Said W. H. Auden: "Coming from Europe, my first, my strongest impression is that no body of literature, written at any time or in any place, is so uniformly depressing." * Why, he wondered, should a nation reputed to be the most optimistic and the freest on earth see itself "as a society of helpless victims, shady characters, and displaced persons," with heroes "whose sole moral virtue is a stoic endurance of pain and disaster."

One answer is that many American writers are at heart idealists who take seriously the promise of American life and who rebel against every defilement of the ideal. They are the obverse of the coin which is stamped on one side with the image of the booster. It became the writer's function to keep an eye on the slums. Perhaps the novelist, in that characteristic counterbalance of American life, is merely trying to compensate for the advertiser. Possibly, as D. W. Brogan asserts, the pessimism comes from the competitive strain of life as it is lived here.

Powerful novelists have thrived on this fare—from Garland, Dreiser and Norris through Sinclair Lewis and Upton Sinclair to Dos Passos, Hemingway, Faulkner and Steinbeck, and on to a younger postwar group. Between 1925 and 1940 the American novel was the most influential in the western world.

Hemingway's stripped, spare style and his determination to pre-

* Quoted by Frederick Lewis Allen, *The Big Change*, p. 271.

sent experience as it felt instead of describing how it appeared was most influential of all. Implicit in his work was the terror of modern man at losing control of his world. His people fear the loss of self-control, so they talk in a minor, muted key. His heroes are usually defeated physically, and whatever victory they have is a moral one, like that of the Old Man who won his battle with the fish and the sea but lost the prize. Destruction and death dominate these books and these people.

John Dos Passos, angered as many Americans had been before him by the passage from Jeffersonian agrarian democracy to a Hamiltonian economy dominated by big business, saw the little man of the thirties as homeless and deprived of his heritage in his own land. With new techniques of camera's eye and newsreel and biography he took up the cudgels for the unemployed, the underpaid. His heroes never have a chance to fight as Hemingway's do; they are already defeated—made helpless by the impersonal metropolis.

William Faulkner found violence, degradation and the abnormal in his study of Southern life. Here the past infected the present, pride mingled with shame, and rural slums cursed with the burden of racial intolerance were seen to be even more horrible than the nightmare evoked by industry. The stories had the quality of nightmare, even to the vague and undefined elements floating through the text. Yet Faulkner found tragedy in this mess, which was better than meaninglessness.

Other writers, and good ones by the score, took equally dim views of the American scene from one vantage point after another: Erskine Caldwell from Georgia, James Farrell and Meyer Levin from Chicago. John O'Hara has found life equally empty among the well-heeled, while Budd Schulberg found coarse self-seeking in Hollywood and corruption spawning in the fight ring, along the waterfront, or wherever power tempted men to ignore social norms.

Out of the regional diversity of the land has come a literature somewhat more heartening because it deals for the most part more realistically and less depressingly with life as it is lived. Dorothy Canfield Fisher has not only presented village life in Vermont but has shaped our understanding of Yankee culture. Walter D. Edmonds and Samuel Hopkins Adams have spoken for upstate New York, Martha Ostenso (and before her Willa Cather) for the lonely immigrant farmers of the northern plains, A. B. Guthrie for the mountain men of the far Northwest, Conrad Richter for the past as it was lived in Pennsylvania and the Southwest, Clyde Brion Davis for many places but chiefly for Missouri and Colorado, Marjorie Kinnan Rawlings for the people of the Florida back country. Ben Lucien Burman has made a special place for himself in evoking the riverboat culture.

When we come back to the South, violence and decay set in again, yet many of the most talented novelists are Southern, including Carson McCullers, Lillian Smith, Eudora Welty and several more to be mentioned in a moment.

Immigrants all, Americans had built a rich literature on the experiences of the "greenhorns," the new arrivals in the country, their past in Europe and other continents, their struggles and gradual acculturation here. Irving Fineman writes with sensitive perception of the old Jewish life, Herman Wouk with a sharper thrust at present patterns. Oliver La Farge in *Laughing Boy* and other works looks sympathetically at the Indian's struggle between two cultures. Richard Wright describes the effects of discrimination upon the Negro, as do many other Negro writers. A page could be given to the names of those who have filled out the picture of our complex ethnic portrait.

As Americans reached out from their own cross-cultured society to understand the international world they were getting more and more involved in, the novel again bridged the way. Pearl Buck wrote movingly of China, James Michener rediscovered Asian cultures. Americans had always written novels based in Europe. As interest shifted to Africa they eagerly read novels (though not always by Americans) in an effort to understand the tragic implications of that land and its problems.

If the view of the United States as seen through its novels is primarily a gloomy one, there are still some outstanding writers who take a more balanced view. John Steinbeck's reverence for life, his feeling that it is worth the struggle, balances his angry view of what the elements and social irresponsibility can do to men. J. P. Marquand, satirist and puritan, shows how human power may be wasted by those who live by the standards of a past generation or who are pressed into conformity by wealth. Yet his tone is warm and sympathizing, not irritated and hopeless.

Robert Penn Warren has been able to infuse a genuine sense of the tragic into his pictures of life—often Southern life—with its way of turning good intentions to evil results. He sees the irony that often makes good things spring up out of what is evil, as Willie Stark explains in *All the King's Men.* Hope lies in the fact that men still long for justice, even when they are robbed of it or when they pervert it themselves.

James Gould Cozzens has ranged over many themes, but always he sees man's struggle within a framework of spiritual values, his central problem the striving to know good from evil and how to choose that which is worth the choice. These are books that confront evil but are not overborne by it.

Edna Ferber, Gerald Warner Brace and Hamilton Basso are also among those who are not swept up by the wave of evil, and who are interested in recreating the common life and the interactions of individuals and the community.

From the list of many other promiseful writers it seems unfair to abstract a few names, yet Nelson Algren and Saul Bellow perhaps stand out for their interest in the ordinary or even subnormal man and their ability to recreate character through an approach to the reader which is personalized.

Historical fiction, in a land proud of its history and able to live with all its past because it is so recent, is always popular. Of the many skillful story tellers in this field Kenneth Roberts, Samuel Shellabarger, Thomas B. Costain, Bruce Lancaster, and Van Wyck Mason must serve as representative examples for a large tribe.

The novels which recreate World War II are mainly based on Dos Passos for their structure, since they need his techniques for handling collective heroes, on Scott Fitzgerald for mood, on Steinbeck for humor and Hemingway for action and dialogue.* Typically they pick a squad or platoon which brings many ethnic strains together. Prejudice flares up, but in crisis it is the man of despised race who turns out to be the hero. The intolerant are either killed or converted and the group in their ordeal of fire become blood

* This observation, along with several others on the new fiction, are to be found in Malcolm Cowley's *The Literary Situation.*

brothers. In addition to prejudice, hatred of officers and of women back home who prove unfaithful are recurrent themes. Though the men may resent discipline, they accept the war as inevitable and somehow assimilate it as a condition of their lives. But they fight without sense of mission, without idealism, hoping that the muck and the horror will at least entitle them to the breaks when they go home. Hopefully, the books are full of good men—plain men whose heroism in crisis takes the form of standing up for the oppressed.

No one has yet written the story of life as it is lived in a typical small city with its constellations of groups clustered about schools, churches, jobs, and clubs, its ball games and parades and square dances, its political battles and economic ups and downs, its broken homes and happy homes on both sides of the tracks, its streets glowing with colored lights at Christmas, its ridiculous pride and simple good-heartedness, its response to the danger of fire or flood, the heroism of the little and the degradation of the great, the feeling it has for itself and the security or the fear it communicates to the youngsters it nourishes.

Because of the melting pot, American writers cannot count on having readers attuned to slight shades of meaning. Rather (as Margaret Mead points out) they have to depend upon an invocation of objects which have overtones rather than on words carrying their own aura. This has perhaps led them to satire, caricature and portrayal of the abnormal where the signals are easily read.

This is one reason why poetry has given up the attempt to communicate to a wide public, becoming an exercise for intellectuals, and not many of them. Of the great generation which brought about a rebirth of poetry forty years ago, only Robert Frost continues to speak in an idiom so universal, so blended of earth, that it is widely loved and understood. Yet many fine poets, young and not so young, still speak to those who have ears to hear.

Readers are turning more and more to non-fiction in their efforts to understand a world which somehow grows more complicated even as more tools of learning are developed to explain it. They devour the many fine books dealing with the nation's most traumatic experience, the Civil War. Biographies, popularized but none the less distinguished, accounts of everything from the Dead Sea

scrolls to the prospects of travel in outer space, memoirs of states-
men and generals, treatises on diplomacy, and calls to the spiritual
life continue to be popular. The international tone of the output is
one of its distinguishing features, as Americans try to explore their
way in a world which is inevitably their concern.

The reading of books has soared upward with the sudden emergence of paperbacks costing from a quarter to a little more than a
dollar. At last it seems as if technology has found an answer to the
high cost of books. For while the price of new titles has been rising
along with everything else, the sale of reprints (and some originals,
chiefly in the popular fiction field) at the price of a magazine has
let out a flood of books over the land. In place of a mere five hundred bookstores there are now over fifty thousand outlets, with
every stationer and druggist displaying racks full of books. A housewife can even pick up a few as she shops for groceries. More than
300,000,000 paperbacks were sold in 1956. Now that the book can
be thrown away like the magazine, now that it has been geared to
the overall economy of low cost and quick obsolescence, it has
caught on with millions.

Some of the titles are trash, as their lurid covers indicate. But a
surprising number are classics, ancient and modern, or serious treat-
ments of abstruse subjects. Never before have such riches of the
intellect been so accessible.

In addition to paperbacks, 115,000,000 hard-cover books and 95,-
000,000 books in the booming juvenile field were sold, and on top
of these a great number of Bibles, encyclopedias, text and technical
books, for an estimated total of 800,000,000 a year.

Book clubs with several million members further stimulated sales.

Writing for the theater, always a dubious gamble, is inhibited by
the economics of Broadway production, but Tennessee Williams
and Arthur Miller can be counted on for interesting and often distinguished writing. Meanwhile the little theaters throughout the
country, including university theaters, perform plays both old and
new. Their experiments in acting style, staging and writing are
often exciting. The summer theater has become a special institution. In barns, town halls and specially built theaters wherever there
are enough vacationers to make an audience, Broadway talent com-

bines with young hopefuls to act everything from Shakespeare to the latest farce.

## Jazz

When the King of Thailand joins Benny Goodman in a jam session and ends by presenting him with a royal decoration, when Louis (Satchmo) Armstrong plays his hot trumpet with the Royal Philharmonic Orchestra in London's Royal Festival Hall, when audiences in the Middle East which have never heard jazz before go wild with enthusiasm at the concerts of Dizzie Gillespie—then it is clear that the world regards jazz as a new and exciting contribution to culture. Said Louis Armstrong of an audience he played to in Germany: "They got tired of applaudin' with their hands and started applaudin' with the chairs." The police ended by turning on the fire hoses.

Gillespie and his band reached Athens at a time of anti-American feeling. But the same students who had thrown rocks at the American Embassy came to hear and stayed to dance in the aisles with the police who had been stationed there to preserve order. They carried Gillespie home on their shoulders.

Jazz was born and raised in the United States. Its folk roots developed by the greatest technical virtuosity, it spans the whole cycle of art. It blends two great musical traditions, the European with its mastery of harmony and counterpoint, and the West African with its mastery of intricate rhythms. It is, of course, preeminently a Negro contribution, developed out of the field holler and work song and spiritual, polished and packaged by whites. Or more accurately, it is a product of assimilation. Significantly it developed in New Orleans where Creoles of color (with French and Spanish blood in their veins) blended the two cultural streams.

If the Negro had been thoroughly assimilated from the beginning, or if he had been thoroughly segregated, jazz would never have developed. It is a product of his equivocal position in a society which admires his best qualities but is still not sufficiently advanced in the faith of the Christian and democratic principles it professes to afford him full status. Yet like the timid rabbit in his own fables, the Negro has subtly triumphed over his stronger brethren, for his music is regarded almost everywhere abroad as the most significant art to arise in the United States.

Ragtime, Dixieland, blues, swing or bop, jazz has gone through a continuous evolution. Like the society of which it is a part, it is always changing, always renewing itself through the discovery of new rhythms, orchestral combinations, or melodies surging up from a people who still create work songs and spirituals. It readily absorbs new approaches to tonality, counterpoint or harmony.

Why does jazz make such an impact, even on audiences who have never heard it before? Because, says the president of Hamburg's Hot Club, "A jam session is a miniature democracy. Every instrument is on its own and equal. The binding element is toleration and consideration for the other players." * Even the novice can catch at once the spontaneity and craftsmanship, the individual creativeness and the inspired teamwork required of an art performed at its best without written notes, dependent upon sheer skill and faith and mutual understanding.

That scientific spoilsport, the psychiatrist, has another explanation. He says that jazz is a form of protest against authority and that the reason it appeals most to adolescents, intellectuals and Negroes is that they all feel a need to compensate for the manner in which they are discounted by society.

Sensitiveness to one art easily carries over to another. Jazz, once the despised music of the brothel, may be the channel by which the great public will refine its responses to the arts!

But what *is* jazz? Marshall Stearns defines it as "a semi-improvisational American music distinguished by an immediacy of communication, an expressiveness characteristic of the free use of the human voice, and a complex flowing rhythm; it is the result of a three-hundred-years' blending in the United States of the European and West African musical traditions; and its predominant components are European harmony, Euro-African melody, and African rhythm."

It should not be confused with the popular songs, a few of them catchy and memorable, most of them standardized and uninspired, which appear in a constant stream.

* Quoted, p. 296, in Marshall Stearns' readable and authentic *The Story of Jazz*, to which I am indebted for this brief résumé.

## Other Music

Negro spirituals, important source of jazz, are still being created today. In their simple sincerity, their direct expression of great joy and deep sorrow, they stand near the top of musical expression in America. Other folk music still lives in our midst. Leadbelly's work songs, the modern ballads of Woody Guthrie and Cisco Houston, the preservation of old English ballads by singers like John Jacob Niles, the cowboy and lumberjack and railroad songs—these remind us that the country echoes with many strains of music brought here from all parts of the earth and shaped to new conditions.

American composers have mined this folk art in their search for themes on which to build an American concert music. The out-pouring has been so rich and copious that its significance can only be suggested.

Though neglected and unknown throughout much of his life, Charles Ives (1874–1954) has gradually come to be recognized as an important composer, having anticipated some of the innovations of Schoenberg and Stravinsky. The American idiom is built into such works of his as the second piano sonata, *Concord, Massachusetts, 1840–1860*, the suite titled *Three Places in New England*, and his many songs (about 150) and pieces of chamber music. Folk themes provide the core for much of his writing, and he enjoys evoking the mood of a revival meeting, a Negro gathering or a New England town. Despite this popular material, Ives developed a style far in advance of his time, involving polyharmony, polyrhythm and dissonance.

By drawing upon the jazz idiom, Aaron Copland brought a fresh vitality into concert music. His *Lincoln Portrait* and the ballet, *Appalachian Spring*, are recognizably American, the latter including a theme from a popular hymn. In his composing for radio and the movies his ability to combine folk themes and folk feeling with the modern concert idiom has given him access to a wide public.

Roy Harris like many other composers found inspiration in the poems of Walt Whitman, on which he based his Symphony for Voices, while folk music formed the basis of his Folksong Symphony.

So much good music has been written on American themes and

from an American background that even the specialist can hardly know it all. Arthur Farwell searched Negro, cowboy and Indian sources for themes. Douglas Moore has written charming operettas based on folk tales. In country fiddles and brass bands, in dance halls and circuses he found many of the suggestions for his lively rhythms, his sparkle and humor, and his evocation of scene. John Alden Carpenter, influenced by jazz, put folk humor and the sounds of the streets—hand organs, dogs barking, riveting—into his scores. Mary Howe wrote a stirring chain gang song for orchestra and chorus as well as instrumental music which combines modern and traditional techniques in a rich, evocative texture. Virgil Thomson's scores for such moving pictures as *The River* and *The Plough That Broke the Plains* gave his music a wide public. He frequently uses folk themes.

William Grant Still, one of the foremost Negro composers, exploited the rhythms of jazz and wrote a cantata about lynching and an Afro-American Symphony. Randall Thompson's Second Symphony, to name but one of his works, in its syncopation and folk feeling, its lively rhythmic sense, provides a concert music which is both recognizably American and acceptable to the modern ear.

Best known of all American composers is George Gershwin, who succeeded in merging the jazz tradition with that of the concert hall, and whose *Porgy and Bess*, combining tunefulness with reality, pointed the way to the popular opera or musical drama which is the best known of all American music. The whole world knows and loves the songs from *Show Boat* (Jerome Kern), *Oklahoma!* and *South Pacific* (Richard Rodgers) and *Kiss Me, Kate* (Cole Porter). In such productions, with their sparkle and verve, their musical evocation of universal moods, their easily remembered and even haunting folk-like tunes, an idiom suited to the American scene has found full development.

In addition to all this outpouring of music which is clearly American, many of these composers and others too have been writing music in styles which the influences of Stravinsky, Schoenberg and Hindemith have made universal. On this ground too American composers can risk comparison with the rest of the world. All the experiments with tonality, with rhythm and polyphony which characterize modern music are in full swing here. Henry Dixon Cowell introduced the idea of tone clusters played by the whole forearm on the piano. Samuel Barber used an electrical instrument to imitate a radio signal beam in his Second Symphony. Otto Luening mixes tape recorded sounds with instrumental music. Carl Ruggles, strong and intense, seeks to burst out of the limitations imposed by the usual orchestra and the range of its instruments. Most audacious of all the experimentalists is Edgar Varese, French born, but settled in the United States since 1915. Varese believes that music grows only by constant experiment, that the great composers have always been experimenters, and that music to be free must constantly fight academic restraint. The physical impact of such a work as *Deserts* with its recorded sounds booming out of loudspeakers in addition to the din of the orchestra is usually described as "overwhelming."

The United States has benefitted from the naturalization or long-term residence of such musical masters as Stravinsky, Hindemith, Schoenberg, Bartok and Milhaud, and their influence is as apparent in American as in European music.

Among the hundreds of capable composers writing in the modern idiom there is space to mention only a few: Roger Sessions, Walter Piston, Louis Gruenberg, Vladimir Dukelsky, Lukas Foss, John Vincent (who tends towards modal music), Leonard Bernstein, Paul Creston (Bach-like, but with the "sourness" of modern tonality), Leo Sowerby, William Schuman whose bold originality is often expressed through polytonal writing, Colin McPhee whose *Tabu Tabuhan* is a stunning evocation of Balinese rhythms and tonal patterns, and John Cage who likes to use a modified piano that may call for a celluloid Santa Claus to be placed between the strings! Gian-Carlo Menotti's charming operatic style carries a lyric expressiveness and rich chromatic color which has become known to millions through television performances of *Amahl and the Night Visitors*. Composers like Howard Hanson and Deems Taylor have retained a romantic coloring in their operas and symphonic works.

With all this activity, American music can no longer be thought of as provincial or derivative. It is a respectable and respected voice in the polyphony of international music, both influenced and influencing.

## A Culture Set to Music

In 1955 more than thirty-five million people paid to hear serious concerts, while there were only fifteen million paid admissions to major league baseball games. Americans spend more on music than does the rest of the world combined.

Public libraries have opened listening booths for those who want to hear music in the library, and also charge out records, like books, to those who want to take them home. Many radio stations specialize in music, and all day long play classics, light classics, modern and popular pieces. Record clubs, since the advent of long-playing records, are becoming as popular as book clubs. Millions of music lovers who never had a chance at a musical education are learning to love the works of Vivaldi, Bach, Mozart or Brahms in towns far from symphony orchestras. The Metropolitan Opera's Saturday broadcasts have become a national institution, listened to by about twenty million people.

Music is not only being listened to; it is being performed, by more people than ever before. More than a million Americans now play the accordion, and an equally impressive number the guitar. The church has been the traditional focus of musical life in the small town, and music is now integrated into the school program. From the rhythm groups in kindergarten to the sometimes surprisingly well trained choral and symphonic groups in the high school, music has become in the United States what Plato wanted it to be in his ideal republic, a means of cultivating the youth.

As with everything else, voluntary association rather than government direction has marked out the course for music. Thousands of groups throughout the country have been organized to sing or play. Among the more famous are the Bach Festival at Bethlehem, Pennsylvania, and the group which performs the Messiah annually at Lindsborg, Kansas—amateurs under expert direction giving performances of professional quality.

Colleges and universities have become musical centers, often requiring of their students some knowledge of music as part of a liberal education, presenting concerts of distinguished, and often otherwise little heard, music both ancient and modern, and serving as purveyors, often at no charge, to the surrounding countryside. They combine studies *about* music with composing and performing.

With summer comes a whole galaxy of camps, conferences and schools devoted to music. Here a group of amateur performers assemble to play new works for and with their composers. There a summer camp is organized around music as the core, and teen-agers put on amazing performances of great music, choral and instrumental. Great orchestras like the Boston Symphony perform regularly under the stars in rural locations, with thousands of listeners spilling out beyond the huge open shed to the spacious lawns beyond.

If you are a solitary musician who plays, say, the oboe or the violin, you can buy from Music Unlimited recordings which leave out the part you play. Thus you become the soloist with a professional symphony!

No longer dependent on Europe, the United States now trains its own musicians. Three out of four professional performers are now American, and everyone agrees that musicianship is extremely high, technical proficiency here, as in Europe, at a level the world has never known before. Many of these excellent performers, however, thanks to a star system dominated by a few managers, have little opportunity to share their talents with the public. The American Federation of Musicians has imposed restrictions on the playing of music which hamper its natural growth.

The increase in musical consumption has tended to commercialize music, for if the audiences are huge, one must consider their tastes, and the larger the public (at this stage of our cultural development anyhow), the less one can experiment. The very need of appealing to so large an audience may inhibit the composer and prevent him from an untrammeled expression of what is in him. At the same time he becomes secondary to the performer, the packager (radio station or movie studio), the advertiser. On the other hand, the standard repertoire comes quickly familiar through reproduction and demand grows for novelty.

Yet here, too, counterbalance is at work, for the university, free of commercial considerations and government interference, can provide a permissive environment for the composer and a receptive audience.

Finally and briefly we may ask, why has music become a passion-
ate avocation with Americans?

The answer is to be found partly in the availability of leisure
time, partly in a surfeit with words which pour upon us from every
side. Music is our escape from materialism, from the production
line and the marketplace. It is symbolic, yet untranslatable. It speaks
and speaks deeply, but in a wordless language, in a significance that
is more deeply rooted than the verbal. It releases us from the burden of conscious thought while its effects enter literally into the
heart to raise its tempo and into the blood to hasten its coursing.
Its symbols embrace ambivalence, and thus the complication of life
itself. They do not argue or preach; they do not even represent
emotion. They *are* emotion in the sense that they recreate the
onrushing, illogical, richly textured and often confusing life of the
feelings in which we are all constantly immersed and on whose
varying currents we are borne.

"Music is our myth of the inner life," says Susanne Langer in an
admirably suggestive phrase.* Perhaps this myth is particularly attractive to Americans because the surge and sweep of music is symbolic of their own society, begun on so small a note and grown to
so sizable a symphony. The very pluralism of musical form with its
promise of unity has its analogue in American social development.

But these are speculations. The fact remains: Americans bathe in
an ocean of sound. It surrounds them at work, at play, even in
sleep. A popular radio model shuts off the music after one has gone
to bed and, as Montaigne prescribed, comes on to wake the drowser
to the new day. Whatever meaning America has must necessarily
be set to music.

## The Dance

In their exploration of the arts, Americans have suddenly discovered the dance again—it was always a part of their lives in the old
days when reels and square dances lent gayety to the country life—
and have adapted it to new needs and media. Building on the work
of pioneering Isadora Duncan, Ruth St. Denis and Ted Shawn with
their troupe brought free dance forms and ethnic dances to many
American audiences. Much of their work had spiritual meaning and

* See her treatment of musical symbolism in *Philosophy in a New Key.*

was even danced in churches; many of their themes came out of the American heritage.

Other great dancers—Martha Graham, Doris Humphrey, Charles Weidman, José Limon, to mention only a few of the masters—evolved an art which by combining movement and gesture with music could express not only human moods but social injustice, personal tragedy or triumph, and aspects of nature.

Meanwhile the ballet, once regarded as a vested interest of Europe, acclimatized itself with the formation of several outstanding American companies. Agnes de Mille led the way in adapting distinguished dancing to the needs of the musical comedy, and when she used ballet as well as modern dance and folk dance in *Oklahoma!*, this art was finally at home in the United States. Dancing was now not merely an adornment, but an indispensable part of the whole dramatic ensemble. Into the movies too, already enriched by the skillful dancing of Fred Astaire and Gene Kelly, dance went as a functioning partner. In *Seven Brides for Seven Brothers* it was so much a part of the plot and the development of character that moviegoers hardly recognized it as dance—which was the best compliment they could have paid it.

Choreography has become even more important in television, where many of the best young dancers are now appearing. Here, as in the work of the mimic Iva Kitchell who pokes fun at the dance itself while getting enmeshed in her veils and robes, the tone may be comic as well as serious.

To Martha Hill and Margaret H'Doubler goes much of the credit for pioneering the dance education which produced both the dancers and the audiences, and the academic support which made it respectable.

*Painting and Sculpture*

Any impartial view of American painting will conclude that over the years it has compared favorably with that of any country except France, which has led the world. Realism has been its dominant mood—a realism however which has often glowed with a romantic aura. Great landscapists like George Inness and Thomas Eakins, Winslow Homer with his chronicles of the sea and those who follow it, James A. McNeill Whistler and Albert Ryder with their individualistic styles full of lyric and mystical overtones, John Singer Sargent with his aristocratic portraits, and a whole group of painters (including Childe Hassam and Mary Cassatt) who at the end of the nineteenth century had adopted French impressionist principles—these made a solid foundation for the painting of the present century.

Spearheaded by Robert Henri, John Sloan and George Bellows, who with others formed the famous group known as "The Eight," there followed a vigorous movement away from academic painting and European domination and toward full freedom in the choice of subject and technique, with emphasis on the American scene treated realistically. This was the source of the "Ash Can School," whose members were not afraid to paint what they saw.

The critical date in modern painting is 1913, when the Armory Show in New York brought to the United States for the first time a full awareness of what the masters of painting were doing in France. From then on, modernist movements flourished among us— Fauvism, cubism, expressionism, Dada, surrealism and many more. Most important, the artist adopted the modernist attitude (which was really an ancient one) of looking at the world as if it were something new, and painting from an inner motivation freed of traditional restraints. The Armory Show caused a revolution in industrial design, clothing, interior decoration—even plumbing and hardware. Private collectors began to buy the "new art," much of which later went to museums not then in existence.

Early disciples of abstraction included Max Weber, Charles Demuth, John Marin, Stuart Davis and Arshile Gorky. Ultimately from the work of these artists developed the American school of abstract impressionism, the leaders of which by the forties were Jackson Pollock, Robert Motherwell, William Baziotes and Mark Rothko. Their paintings were not about things, but about the act of creation itself. When Jackson Pollock in 1948 laid a huge canvas on the floor and began throwing and dribbling paint on it, he had achieved what appeared to be the ultimate in the effort to transfer the "explosive motion of creation" to canvas.

From among the many fine abstractionists working today one can mention but a few—Willem de Kooning whose huge canvases delight in mockery, Mark Tobey whose calligraphic painting is influenced by the Orient, Clyfford Still's map-like splashes of color, Franz Kline's black and white paintings which have been hailed in Japan. Emphasis on color, and on free-gesture brush work, are the clearest marks of this group as a whole.

Concurrently with modernism runs the older tradition of realism based on American themes. Charles E. Burchfield in Ohio, Thomas Hart Benton in Missouri, John Steuart Curry in Kansas and Grant Wood in Iowa were leading exponents. Edward Hopper, with a deep regard for the common scene before him, managed to make his concern for what he painted show through, catching in the passing scene the aspect of eternity. Though he had little use for abstraction, his own paintings by their suppression of unimportant detail and their concern for broad planes and areas of color offered a hopeful bridge between abstraction and representation.

Others who combined selective realism with formal design include Georgia O'Keefe, Charles Sheeler, Peter Blume and John Atherton.

It is likely, however, that the average American asked to name the painter whose works he likes best would hail Norman Rockwell, whose name rarely gets into the art books but whose technical virtuosity and photographic style, tinged with warm humor and even with slapstick, and whose love of emotionally weighted domestic drama have endeared him to those who want their art to tell a story.

A tremendous surge of interest in art on all levels has been evident during the past twenty years. The depression made art respectable by recognizing that unemployed artists had as valid a claim on government as unemployed truck drivers. The murals they painted awakened popular interest in art, while the beautiful drawings of folk arts in the *Index of American Design* were part of an interest in the past which led to such restorations of our cultural heritage as the rebuilding of colonial Williamsburg, Virginia. Through the W. P. A. and the Painting and Sculpture Section in the Treasury Department (dealing with art in and for federal buildings) the U. S. Government found itself one of the world's leading patrons of the arts.

Museums, most notably the Museum of Modern Art in New York, also sprang up to preserve and encourage contemporary

painting. Even small, poor communities raised money to bring exhibitions of controversial art to their people. The Virginia Museum
of Fine Arts established the first state-wide visual arts system, with
a traveling artmobile to take exhibitions into the remotest areas.
In museums large and small throughout the country art came to
life as children were encouraged to come and fingerpaint or put
on their own plays, while adults could make pottery, weave, or attend life classes. Half a million people now paint in oil.

Sculpture, too, departed radically from its former anatomical
realism. Jacob Epstein, though American-born, went to England
where, as Rudi Blesh remarks, he has been "frightening the English
with his sculptures until at last they have knighted him." * Paul
Manship, popular and decorative, has done many monumental
works. The portraits of Jo Davidson, the laborers of Mahonri
Young, and the work of Gertrude Vanderbilt Whitney, Gutzon
Borglum and Malvina Hoffman are worth noting. Boldness in the
rejection of academic formulas, working directly in the wood and
stone, and the adoption of surrealist ideas have characterized the
work of a whole group of outstanding sculptors—William Zorach,
Isamu Noguchi, Chaim Gross, Robert Laurent, and others of equal
note. So great has been the distinguished output of artists in the
past twenty years that it is dangerous to name a few when justice
demands the naming of hundreds.

Alexander Calder with his mobiles, and a group of men working
with various materials to create constructions which emphasize
open spaces as part of the work, represent the latest development.
Millions of Americans have become familiar with this form of art
through the construction made by James Ernst for the television
show, "Producer's Showcase."

*Architecture*

The roots of functionalism strike deep in the United States. The
simple home-made tools, furniture and household goods of the early
settler often resulted in designs so beautiful that museums now preserve the hayrakes, wooden mixing bowls and pewterware of earlier
generations. The plain saltbox house of New England or the log

* *Modern Art USA*, p. 25.

cabin introduced by the Swedes into Delaware combined simplicity with practicality and the best use of available materials.

As early as 1840 Horatio Greenough, standing on the threshold of the industrial age, defined the functionalism appropriate to it. "By beauty I mean the promise of function," he wrote. In clipper ships and bridges and machinery rather than in art with a capital A he found his principle realized. Structure, he argued, should be based on a scientific arrangement of spaces and forms adapted to function and location. Democracy, science and industry in his view formed the basis for aesthetic standards.

Greenough's principles were realized in John Roebling's design and construction of the Brooklyn Bridge, begun in 1869, which established criteria still in use.

But in spite of this clean functional beginning, the United States like Europe fell into a phase of showy ornamentation. Unfortunately this period coincided with the time when most of the country was being built, and as a result we have more than our share of monstrosities to live with.

But with the work of the "Chicago School" of architects, led by Henry Hobson Richardson (1838–1886) and Louis Sullivan (1856–1924), American building returned to its earlier functionalism. It was no accident that in Chicago with its agrarian Populism, rather than in finance-minded New York, a functionalism based on democratic needs came to flower. Richardson designed façades which expressed the internal organization of the building instead of confusing them with irrelevant decoration. Sullivan, though he did not invent the steel frame or the tall building, produced structures (such as the Wainwright Building in St. Louis and the Schlesinger department store) which became models for half a century. As early as the 1880s Sullivan announced his famous dictum that form expresses function and function determines form. Socially conscious, he called for an architecture which would satisfy the needs of the community and which would be a tool of progress.

Frank Lloyd Wright (1869–    ), Sullivan's pupil, carried the master's ideals into the homes he built, fitting the house to its natural setting, using parallel planes to make it grip the earth, and treating the interior as enclosed space rather than as a collection of rigid boxes. Instead of starting with a conception of how the house should look from outside, Wright designed it to fit the needs of the dwellers within. Furnishings and furniture were so far as possible incorporated into the organic design, with simplicity and repose as logical results of building organically conceived.

Wright, a master of plan, structure and mechanics, was always devising striking new forms like that for the Guggenheim Museum, or originating new techniques of building.

The earlier tradition of simplicity and efficiency which characterized handicraft production has finally established itself as the one most appropriate to an industrial age. Structures like Wright's laboratory for the Johnson Wax Company, the General Motors Industrial Research Center or the factories of Albert Kahn are triumphs of the functional viewpoint, beautiful in their simplicity and their appropriateness.

The battle for functionalism was won first in industrial buildings —in skyscrapers and factory structures where simple and efficient design resulted in better output. Then it moved to home construction and schools, and finally to churches and libraries, where tradition is likely to dictate the repetition of old forms. In homes, the multiple use of a given space is now taken for granted. Three boxy rooms—parlor, living room and dining room—have been merged into one large area. Even the kitchen, now that the housewife customarily does all her own work, is often built with only a counter dividing it from the living space.

As Wright had his influence in Europe, so a number of European architects have enriched the American output. Coming to the United States, Richard Neutra, Antonin Raymond, Marcel Breuer, Walter Gropius and Mies van der Rohe have established the international school here. Though spending only short periods in the United States, Le Corbusier has also had a strong influence here as throughout the world. Through Frank Lloyd Wright (who designed the Imperial Hotel in Tokyo) and others, many elements of Japanese architecture have influenced American design.

These influences, combined with the technical advances which brought new and cheaper materials, have changed the face of the land and are still changing it. Skyscrapers carry the chaste and severe lines of the functional to scales of grandeur. Mass housing developments (many of which are still poorly designed), recreation areas and shopping centers surrounded by acres of parking space announce the new day. More and more the trend is to design homes and communities for relaxed living—for intimate family life, for the use of increased leisure time, for a merging of outdoor with indoor space, for group play. An architectural renaissance seems to be under way.

## CHAPTER FOURTEEN

---

# *The Mass Media*

As we step from the communication of art to the art of communication, we are aware of certain uneasy connections between them. The mass media use the talents of every art, and sometimes the product deserves the name of art. But the mass media also include activities that are not artistic, and their motivation is profit rather than creativity.

Advertisers spent about ten billion dollars in 1956, most of it in the mass media—television, radio, newspapers and magazines. Advertising keeps these outlets alive—the 626 magazines of general circulation, the 1,700 daily newspapers and 9,000 weeklies, the 2,947 radio stations and 465 television stations. Inevitably the advertiser's point of view seeps out of the advertisement and the announcement to affect the content of the article, editorial, or teleplay. Advertisers seek customers by supplying them with entertainment, and since every cigarette and soap manufacturer is out to get more business, he wants to sponsor the most popular radio or television program, or advertise in the magazine of greatest circulation. Networks and magazines are also competing with each other; *they* want to attract the largest audiences.

*Television*

But what attracts the largest audiences?

Thirteen million people tuned in to the television production of *Fledermaus*, about fifteen million to *La Bohème*. When the National Broadcasting Company put on Laurence Olivier's *Richard III* at a cost of $500,000, it drew the largest daytime audience in history—fifty million people. Despite the recurrent talk about twelve-year-old mentalities, it seems that the public will go for a good thing when it gets a chance.

No one needs to look at television very long to discover that it is not all *Fledermaus* and *Richard*. But what is it?

Several things grow clear from watching television continuously for a few days. One is the tremendous potential it has—for pure, relaxing entertainment, for intimate immediacy and directness of appeal, for the human touch, for raising the cultural level of a whole people. It hops from United Nations headquarters in New York to sunken ships in the Suez canal, to a fire in California, and we go with it all the way. It brings distinguished ballet to homes that never before knew the meaning of the word. It rocks us with laughter, grips us with fear, involves us with the people who come before its cameras, binds us together with a new knowledge of our world, the look and feel of it, and shows us in a hundred ways that we are truly one people, both here and abroad.

Another thing that grows clear is that television can run the whole gamut from superior to plain lousy, and often does not seem to know the difference. Obviously, with networks and local stations grinding out programs eighteen hours a day month after month, much of the product must be mediocre. The trouble is that in its major efforts it has not yet learned any rule of thumb by which to tell the distinguished from the pathetic. But neither has the theater in its several thousand years of operation—except by trying the show on an audience.

Another surprise television provides is the continuous interest in family life. The domestic stress crops up everywhere—in the way contestants are always queried about their families, in the frequency with which children are brought before the camera to be adored, and in the light comedies of home life with their muted but repeated lesson that humor and consideration conquer all difficulties. Television with its intimate focus on the uninhibited expressions of the young reminds us over and again how cute and wonderful the little devils are, and how symbolic of our young, growing, irrational, sticky, frightened, outgoing, boastful, generous, impulsive culture. Our love of children may be narcissistic, but we find it purifying. Television has discovered our weakness and capitalized on it.

On a lower level, the soap dramas play upon the fear of poor or unhappy women by presenting them with a fantasy of the lost or unfaithful husband, at the same time allowing them to vent their aggressions upon the bad woman, while identifying with the wronged wife or noble big sister who sets things right. In one of these daily droolings the characters keep saying, "It's an awful mess," which is quite true, though they are referring to the situation rather than the show. Yet these plays do serve a purpose, helping young women to adjust to their role at home, confirming the importance of a woman's place as moral arbiter and guide.

In a society which has no made marriages and where boy and girl must somehow find each other, the mystery of mating is necessarily stressed. Meeting a stranger is always a crisis, for who knows but what he might be "the one and only"? The zest of these meetings, so important in real life, carries over to television, along with the attitude that "a man chases a girl until she catches him." Many a teleplay is essentially that. Behind the humorous treatment of the attractive, but scheming and assertive, woman there lurks perhaps a fear that she may displace the male from his dominant role.

In the quiz shows which shower their gold upon the lucky winner —perhaps identifying gold as the symbol of sexual fertility and confusing love with material success—the American myth appears in all its crudeness, optimism and good will. In "Queen for a Day," for example, several tired, worn-looking women—and one pretty young one to hold whatever males may be watching—compete for the shower of gold. A cheerful, slightly overbearing master of ceremonies barges into their lives, gets them to expose their most personal troubles and hopes to millions of viewers, then lets the audience by its applause choose the one on whom the shower will fall. Thus the democratic myth is shaped: everyone, no matter how poor, and the neediest most of all, may find riches. The common folk themselves are the makers of queens and fortunes, are judge and jury.

Other programs combine easy riches with a minimum of competition. Their crazy optimism only exaggerates a hopefulness which is unmistakably American. Allied to it is the idea of humor as a way of life. Most popular of all teleshows are those of the comedians—Benny, Silvers, Caesar, Marx, Allen. But in almost every other show as well, humor as a mental tone, as an indicator of good breeding and good health, as a breaker-down of barriers and builder of intimate human contact between performer and viewer, is cultivated. In every drama of the sexes the point is made—and most popularly in "I Love Lucy"—that good humor can overcome all difficulties, all the differences ethnic and religious and regional and occupational that make for tension in American life. Humor, in fact, becomes the only solvent which can blend us all together.

In this spirit, advertising makes fun of itself in the very process of pushing a product. Hiram Holliday ridicules the adventure drama by the ease with which he overcomes the insuperable. He satisfies our need for adventure, and with his humor makes it both ridiculous and at the same time acceptable—letting us have the cake of adventure while we eat the satire of it, thus both being involved in and superior to it at the same time.

Humor provides a symbol system far more intricate than we generally realize, through which tensions we are too frightened to look at directly can be brought into the open and resolved. Have you quarreled with your wife? Are you ashamed of the flash of hatred you have felt for her? "I Love Lucy" transforms your wife into her younger, charming real self, makes fun of her feminine quirks and her interfering ways, assures you that married people do quarrel but that love underlies all conflict.

Jack Benny displays your own suppressed tendencies towards parsimonious and gauche behavior. You are not laughing at him but at personal shortcomings you cannot admit to yourself, except as humor symbolizes them. The intimacy of television, entering the living room with its colloquial tone and familiar faces, is ideal for humor.

Whatever Americans will laugh at, they will sooner or later accept, as they once hooted at Duchamp's "Nude Descending a Staircase" and went on to build up the world's finest collection of modern art. The laughter that rises so readily in this fortunate country is not childlike. Sometimes it rides close to tragedy, as express trains pass on neighboring tracks. It indicates a deeply held belief that conflicts can be resolved by good will, that the essence of a thing is what is funny about it, that to laugh is to conquer.

Visitors complain that we lack the tragic view of life, and this is true. But is there a merit in the tragic higher than in the comic? To cultures built upon slavery, special privilege, brutality, exploitation, and mass starvation the tragic is appropriate. But America, for all its faults, is not that kind of culture. It asserts the positive. It believes that universal education, material and cultural well-being for all are within reach. Naturally, then, its genius is comic, and humor is its chosen way of looking at life.

Another thing television does well is to combine drama with documentary. The *Andrea Doria* sinking is reconstructed from actual film interspersed with re-enacted scenes. A teleplay about a prison operated on the honor system distinguishes itself with a natural style of acting and a simple message: trust the rootless and give them roots if you would overcome crime. A play about a doctor who finds a new life in serving a simple Caribbean community, unobtrusively gets its point across: every culture has its own way of life and its own goals, and all are worthy of respect.

Not only the twenty-six educational stations, but many commercial ones are putting on distinguished programs in every conceivable field of learning. Anyone who stuck with one of these programs day by day, and took notes on what he heard, could get a liberal education in his own living room. The use of television for educational purposes has scarcely begun. The National Citizens' Committee for Educational Television—a voluntary association, naturally—is working to raise TV standards generally. But already fifty million people are within reach of educational TV.

Whatever may be television's shortcomings, it has at its best achieved a high level of acting, directing, pacing, staging and inventiveness. And it is a fertile, lively medium of communication. It has also become the meeting ground of all the mass media. It uses the news and photo services of the press associations, magazine and book sources for plots, directors and actors borrowed from radio, and whole shows produced on film by Hollywood.

From the viewer's vantage point, television's most irksome trait is its insufferably long, repetitive, and sometimes insulting commercials. Most irritating is the pre-emption of the hallowed symbols of youth, beauty, happiness, domestic bliss and Christian morality in order to sell a pack of cigarettes or a new soap.

Why is it so often soap, one wonders? Only a nationally distributed product can afford to buy network time, of course. But is there not also a symbolic reason? The finer points of housekeeping and the social graces are learned with difficulty, but any woman can wash. Associate washing with the social graces and you not only catch a customer; you make her believe that she has elevated herself socially by using the product. If we are not a people scrubbed to sterile cleanliness, it is not the fault of the advertisers.

Both in the advertising and in the shows which fill in the time between commercials, the sponsors know what they are up to. They understand perfectly well that the unconscious mind of the viewer incorporates the material of the story as its own. Three basic obsessions—with what is socially tabu, with authority and omnipotence as symbolized in the father, with security—are put to work to involve the viewer in a story, softening him up for the commercial.

The television code of the National Association of Radio and Television Broadcasters pledges its members to supply the best in education and information as well as entertainment. Recognizing its duties as a public service, it runs many spot announcements and programs free of charge, urging viewers to go to church, to contribute to Community Chest, or explaining mental health and welfare programs. It makes time available to government, which more than in any other nation is dependent upon the commercial media since it has no networks of its own. (C.B.S., for example, spent a million dollars on a series about air power which it produced with Air Force cooperation.) As a commercial enterprise which can stay in business only if it makes a profit, the television or radio network or station has to consider economics first. But is it necessary for every program to appeal to all? Even a "small" television audience consists of millions. Does not the station have a moral responsibility to meet the needs of the intellectually curious as well as the lethargic?

Against the main disadvantage of the mass media—their tendency to seek the lowest denominator—several counterbalancing influences can fairly be named. The very size of the audience, its inclusion of all varieties in taste and experience, leads to tolerance in the presentation. Such an audience also imposes a kind of coarse vigor which prevents effeteness. Its unexpected enthusiasms for the best in drama, ballet and music prove that its tastes are higher than the soothsayers had thought, and thus gives commercial incentive to the raising of standards.

## Radio

Since the advent of television, radio has taken a back seat. But it still reaches great masses of people, there are still times when it can be used while television cannot, and in competing with television it has rediscovered its own special strengths.

Soap operas continue to reach women who are too busy to sit down in front of a television set, or who prefer to stick with the old friends they have followed for years, or who like to project their own world of fantasy, and resent the embodiments of the television screen. Radio still presides in kitchen, bathroom, bedroom and car—wherever people are busy with hands and eyes but have an ear to spare. It is the welcome companion of a camping trip or a day on the beach. Built with transistors and batteries, it can be slipped into a pocket and carried anywhere. It has rediscovered its strengths: simplicity, informality, immediacy, brevity, narration.

People now turn to the radio for news, weather reports, or the very latest bulletin when crisis or disaster makes them avid for information. They turn to it for the continuous stream of music which comes from at least one station in every metropolitan area, and for the all-night shows when a disc jockey talks informally between records, becoming a companion to the lonely.

Radio now has to be programmed in short units for those who stay with it only while they shave, eat breakfast or drive to work. To hold those who might be listening longer, it has devised long programs broken into short units, each sufficient within itself though leading to another unit designed to retain the listener. Like a newspaper, it jumps from late news to an interview with a congressman, to an overseas report, to a new scientific discovery, to women's fashions.

Syndicated platters now bring top entertainers to local stations, while networks provide shows with station breaks into which local ads or announcements can be fitted. The advantages that only big money can buy have thus become available to small stations and local merchants.

*The Movies*

Television delivered a body blow to the movies. Weekly theater admissions dropped from ninety million to fifty million, then climbed back to fifty-five. Television was not the only reason, but it was important. The high cost of movies, especially to a family which either had to buy tickets for the children or pay a baby sitter to stay at home with them, was a factor. Drive-ins helped, for then the children, who went in free if they were small, could sleep in the back seat if they tired of the show.

After trying for a while to pretend that television did not exist, Hollywood decided to join what it could not fight, and began making teleplays, releasing old pictures for TV, and lending its stars, who usually got a plug for some new picture they were appearing in. It also began to make better pictures—which it always seemed to be able to do when driven by desperation from mediocrity to distinction. It drew on assets television would never have—size, spectacle, large casts, movement and epic sweep. At the decisive moment a number of technical improvements helped emphasize these qualities—the wide-angle lens, the wide screen, and even more beautiful color.

Hollywood, of course, had always been prolific of devices. Slow motion, underwater photography, ships sinking and trains colliding, whole cities burning, animated cartoons with their humor, charm, and brutal destructiveness sugar-coated with comic and immediate restoration—these had taught audiences all over the world to expect the marvelous from Hollywood. Two hundred and seventy-six major arts and crafts were needed to make a movie.

Something in the Hollywood magic spoke to all men everywhere, and Hollywood became the sex symbol, the dream symbol for the world. Even those who condemned the product continued to consume it. Thus they could enjoy the inner fantasies which Hollywood projected for them, and throw on Hollywood the blame for their own shortcomings.

One reason for Hollywood's international success was that it had learned from the very beginning, because of our large immigrant population, how to appeal universally with story patterns anchored in basic human needs and fears—tabus and fantasies of omnipotence or security. The cowboy film with its projection of inner tensions and its outlet for aggression, the gangster film with its chase in which the pursuers are man's guilty conscience and the screaming police sirens like Greek Eumenides, the amorous film which allows the viewer to possess in fantasy the body of the buxom heroine—these speak a universal language. South Seas natives, with their genius for going to the heart of the matter, divided all movies into two types—bang-bang and kiss-kiss. They liked both.

Unfortunately for America, the innocent viewers of these universal fantasies came to believe that all Americans were gangsters and cowboys and lovers, though they would never have made the mistake of thinking that all their own people were like the persons portrayed in their own movies or plays. The price of Hollywood's success was a false and depreciated image of the United States throughout the world, one which persisted in spite of every effort to tell the unvarnished truth about the country and its institutions, and one which communism gleefully exploited. Like Pagliacci, America seemed doomed to amuse the world and never to be seriously understood.

Since howls of protest arose every time the films presented a Mexican, an Arab, or any other recognizable ethnic type as the villain, Hollywood had long since determined to have no villains but Americans (or maybe communists of indeterminate origin). Thus we manfully and for a price shouldered the job of being the world's villain. Those who resented the inevitably growing power of the United States in world affairs found that we had made it easy for them to hate us, for had we not ourselves said that we were gangsters, saloon brawlers, rich idlers?

The stories often had a special twist that characterized them as American. The girl who appears bad but is really good is a special type in American films. Her badness—a projection perhaps of the male writer who likes to imagine a girl who will readily fall into his arms—helps to establish and carry on that chance acquaintance which is essential in a culture where the young must find their own mates. Her readiness helps the hero along, helps him to overcome a natural shyness derived from a maternally imposed morality. Then, when she has aroused his desire, a situation which appears

to compromise her turns out to be innocent. In the end they happily marry.

The special conditions of American family life determine some
themes. The hero often puts his parents behind him, insisting upon
his right to choose his own way of life. Emphasis is on the family
he makes rather than the one he comes from. Youth is exalted. The
father figure is often bald, ineffectual and ridiculous. In melodrama,
however, the father figure is bad and dangerous and tries to overcome the hero. In Freudian terms this may be a means of excusing
the son for outdistancing the father as he is expected to do. The
dangerous world he has to fight externalizes his own guilt in sur-
passing the father, while the suspicion in which the police hold him
projects his own self-accusation.

Thus a persecutory fantasy lies at the root of the crime film. It
is usually an independent investigator, not the police, who solves
the crime. He symbolizes the renegade son, who has to flout the
law (symbol of the father's authority) in order to secure justice.
Symbolically the American is the young man who has rejected the
fatherland for the new world, and who then turns away from his
father's house and occupation to find wealth and happiness in an
ever newer world to the west. There he must take the law in his
own hands; there he must set up a new household which again will
be forsaken by the next generation. Resistance to paternal authority
is the root of democracy with its fraternal equality, and is therefore a constant theme of our popular art as of our politics. Youth,
initiative (of women as well as men), striving and winning, having
a good time—these are stressed.

Those who damn the movies for their undoubted failure in
quality overlook the fact that they are not the closet drama of an
intellectual elite, but the folk drama of the world. As such they
will continue to be based upon the same fantasies, the same fears
and desires, which folktales have always exploited.

The movies would be better if they were less paralyzed by censorship. The industry, hoping to overcome the headaches of multiple censorship, set up its own Production Code under the Motion
Picture Producers and Distributors of America. No dog could sniff
at a post, no baby wet its pants under this sterile regimen. No toilet
could be shown in a bathroom, no legally married couple could be

shown in a double bed. Adult problems and passions, especially those relating to sexual relations, were banned. Catholic "Legions of Decency" and some Protestant Church groups kept constantly at work to prevent Hollywood from presenting adult themes.

Their concern was understandable. Movies are seen by children. Those around nine are especially susceptible to themes of physical danger, those around sixteen to sex. But the prohibitions laid down have stamped out the picture of wedded sex while flaunting the unwedded variety. They have permitted crime and violence, and created a false world of black and white. The censors have tried to change humanity by changing the films, and they have ignored the real causes of delinquency—slum areas, indifferent or hostile parents, lack of adequate recreation programs, and the provocation to crime provided by an acquisitive society which values wealth too highly— because it is easier to blame the movies than ourselves.

Recent Supreme Court decisions have tended to weaken censor- ship codes. Independent producers can now get films shown without the Code's seal of approval. Television, which operates without such a code, has broken through some of the Hollywood tabus.

But even if the censorship problem could be solved, a basic prob- lem would remain. Hollywood is an industry trying to produce an artistic product, and the two are in conflict. Experimenting, or any deviation from the supposedly proven formulas, is discouraged by the banks which supply the money. Yet artistic imagination and originality, as the box office has proven over and again, do pay off.

The successful films are being produced, with increasing fre- quency, by men who combine the work of writing, directing and producing. Combining the artistically creative functions and giving more power of decision to them are bound to make better use of the excellent talents that exist in Hollywood—often in a state of frustration—and to produce better films. But this will probably not put any quick end to the bitterness which exists between "front office" and directors, directors and producers, producers and actors, actors and agents.

As for the actors, those modern folk heroes who with their fickle and flagrant loves, their lavish living, their often putrescent pub- licity and their sudden dramatic appearances among us commoners, more nearly resemble the gods of Olympus than any other mortals have done, their lives are not as easeful as their admirers imagine. When they are making a picture, they must work long and hard, yet at the same time suffer long periods of waiting around and many irritating retakes of the same scene. Between pictures they are bored and frustrated, and their lives run to empty partying, sexual adventuring, and searches for amusement which turn out to be dead ends. They must live according to a style determined by their income, which in turn is determined by their box-office appeal. Though they earn more than anyone else in the country, they are bound by serf-like seven-year contracts. They are glamorized for the public but hated by those who do the job. But the public, confusing them with the characters they portray, idolizes them to the point of embarrassment.

The product they star in continues to capture a world audience. Why?

The Hollywood movie at its best is an expert evocation, through the absolute technical mastery of a difficult and complicated medium, of emotions which lie at the root of our being. It simplifies and orders experience, enlarges our world both in time and space, takes us through the horror of murder and brings us out safely, lets us release our aggressions and fears and hatreds, revel in borrowed luxury, be clever with the comic, brave with the hero, triumphant over the villain, and at last possess the lovely girl as our just reward. What a bargain, for only sixty cents!

*Newspapers*

American newspapers use up sixty per cent of the world's newsprint. In content they vary all the way from popular tabloids such as the *New York Daily News* (Sunday circulation, 3,694,851) to the *Christian Science Monitor*, the *Wall Street Journal*, and the *New York Times*, which can boast the fullest news coverage in the world and whose Sunday edition uses two hundred acres of forest. There are small local papers which emphasize personal paragraphs and community activities, and which play an important part in defining a community's spirit and upholding its morale. And there are papers like the *Cleveland Press* whose editor, Louis Seltzer, having risen from a childhood of extreme poverty, makes his paper a voice of conscience for the whole community, plugs the need for cleaning up Lake Erie or establishing a zoo, and has one employee who spends her full time promoting letter exchanges between American and foreign children.

It was America's immigrant population which determined the nature of the popular press. Joseph Pulitzer discovered first in a German language newspaper what immigrants of German stock liked, and his *New York World* rose to popularity through the support of second generation Germans. Similarly, Hearst developed his papers with Irish support. Both learned from the foreign language press the value of sensationalism, news of social and group activities, and advice to readers.

With advertising as the main source of revenue, sensationalism became the chief spur to circulation. With its sports page, society news, comic strips, news of books, arts, homemaking and how to do your own repairs, its syndicated columnists both humorous and serious, its medical and personality advice, the newspaper tried to appeal to everyone, young and old.

The great wire services—Associated Press, United Press, International News Service—not only send telegraphed news throughout the country, but now by telegraphic impulses punch a tape which can be fed directly to linotype machines for type setting. Syndicates —nearly two hundred of them—supply every sort of column and feature. Thus small papers, which otherwise would have been absorbed by chains, are able to bring world news and well-known features to their readers, even though at some sacrifice of originality. Newspapers in return supply the wire services with important local news for dissemination to other subscribers, so that a mutual service is in effect.

*Magazines*

Of the five hundred magazines of general circulation, fifty-four have sales ranging from 700,000 up to 11,000,000 copies. *The Reader's Digest* with its huge circulation not only in the United States but abroad, tops everything else and would merit special analysis if there were space for it. Its optimism combined with exposés of waste and fraud, its quick capsule articles, its easy story-like style and its skillful presentation of personalities, popular science, personal advice and humor both meet and illustrate American habits of mind.

Thousands of trade magazines, learned journals (many among the world's best), company publications, school papers and news bulletins of organizations add to the voracious consumption of paper.

Magazines vary from the lively but intellectual *American Scholar* to the lively but unintellectual comic book. In between are many varieties, including a whole rash of pulps purporting to reveal the dirty truth about famous people (usually movie stars), abortion rackets, and all the slime that can be scraped from the gutters of a society which bears its full burden of human greed and depravity.

Since mass audiences are needed to get advertising, there is a constant search for material that will pull them in, no matter how lurid or base it may be. Yet the encouraging fact is that magazines which offer the best writers and the best in photography and layout top the circulation lists, while the gutter scavengers fall below not only the news and picture magazines, but below many religious publications.

Some Americans favor censorship to wipe out the trash. But the country as a whole still feels that freedom of speech means nothing unless it means the right to publish all but the flagrantly pornographic. The way to fight trash is by education and the offer of something better, not by suppression.

## Criticism

If the mass media are capable of sinking to low levels, they have their critics to tell them so. Movies, radio and television, the press, and also music, dance, theater, recordings, literature—all are under a constant and on the whole healthy barrage. Never before has so large a corps been employed in the critical sifting of a culture.

The critics are, as a rule, severe. American novelists had strong and sometimes bitterly criticized the nation for its shortcomings. Now the critics are probing the novelists. Literary works are studied from every point of view—with relation to the writer's own development or his attitude towards society, with close attention to the text, or as symbolic action. John Crowe Ranson introduced a method which came to be known as the new criticism, its purpose to study the literary work as a separate entity with its own laws of being.

Literary quarterlies flourish. Men as distinguished as Edmund Wilson, Kenneth Burke, Lionel Trilling and Joseph Wood Krutch established their reputations primarily as critics, while poets or novelists like Mark Van Doren also wrote first-rate criticism.

The novelist's criticism of his country, and the critic's criticism of the novelist might give the impression to outsiders that the United States is in a bad way. The fact is that both novelists and critics hold to idealistic standards. This is the other side of that America which optimistically expects the best of everything.

The growth of critical awareness becomes apparent to anyone who listens to the knowledgeable talk of teen agers about jazz or internal combustion motors, who reads the excellent critics of the leading papers, or who notices that criticism, too, has received the sanction of syndication, along with comment on politics or sports.

American critics do not restrict themselves to American output. Some of the best criticism of English literature originates in the United States, while according to a French observer the most abundant and the most distinguished criticism of French art and literature outside of France itself is being written in the United States.

American criticism, fortified by the insights of psychology, sociology and anthropology as well as by the older disciplines of rhetoric, history and philosophy, is broadening its base and deepening its understanding. American critics, sure of themselves and of the methods they have developed, are doing their part to guarantee, as Delmore Schwartz put it, "the survival of that critical nonconformism without which the very term intellectual—and the reality of the intelligence—is meaningless." *

*Taste*

But has American taste improved any? Or is it on the skids?

One answer was provided when television began to show movies that were ten or fifteen years old. Films which at the time of their release had seemed adequate now appeared antiquated as to technique, awkward in dialogue, thin in content, naïve in conception.

* *Partisan Review*, XIX (1952), p. 596.

This contrast with contemporary television and movies demonstrated a rising standard.

The competition for a mass audience, and the resulting search for what appeals to the millions, often seems to keep standards lamentably low. But against all that is cheap and shoddy, a growing counterweight of good artistic output must be balanced. Europeans accustomed to finding a small artistic elite may recoil at the trash they see on the newsstands or on television. But Americans, keyed to change, look at tendencies instead of regarding the product of the moment as a fixed thing. So looking, they feel that they have succeeded in opening vast channels of communication to all, and that through these media they are gradually raising the standards of taste of a whole people in the greatest cultural advance ever known.

The real problem is where to find enough good material to fill the hungry maw of the mass media, and how to encourage advertisers to support the best. Perhaps the need will be supplied by creative talent which is now staying at home instead of going abroad. No longer is there some other cultural haven to which the creative artist can fly from American stupidity and vulgarity. As a result, noted Lionel Trilling, there is a marked cultural improvement. Wealth is now ready to submit itself to the rule of mind and imagination, justifying its existence by a show of taste and sensitivity. The members of a constantly expanding intellectual class stimulate artistic output, and thought is more generally received and valued than ever before.*

As Americans had raised their political sights from purely local issues to international affairs, so now as they stood on the threshhold of a rapid cultural expansion, one might hope that their artists would speak positively and boldly in an idiom the whole world could understand.

* *Partisan Review*, XIX (1952), pp. 319-21 and 434.

## CHAPTER FIFTEEN

---

# *Recreation*

American soldiers likely to be stranded in South Pacific jungles during the war were taught to have a piece of string in their pockets. On the approach of a suspicious or hostile native they were to take out the string and start playing cat's cradle. Often the native would join them in this universal game. The symbolism of play could be counted on to break down hostility and, where a common language was lacking, build a bridge of understanding.

From the games and festivals of antiquity to the modern Olympics, from ancient temple dance to modern square dance, men and women have sought forms of bodily action in which to express a whole complex of instincts and desires. Play form like art form tries to make order out of chaos, meaning out of confusion. The games a people devise illustrate their goals and their interpretation of life as clearly as their arts.

What can we learn from American games and use of leisure?

### Games and Sports

The square dance, though an offspring of European folk dance, is uniquely American in several respects. It is rural in tone as befits its country origins. In its pattern of four couples to a square it acknowledges the biological pair as the unit and stresses the skill of group cooperation. Thought and motion are fused in the quick and graceful figures of the dance, as the pioneer's quickness with musket or hatchet fused thought and action into one.

The square dance is a microcosm of man in society, each individual indispensable to the social order, the actions of all combining into a graceful whole. In fact, the square dance symbolically expresses the whole pattern of the society. Stress is placed on the individual (individualism) and his responsibility to the group which he voluntarily joins (voluntarism) for mutual benefit. The party is further composed of several squares, each working separately but harmoniously under one law (federalism). Counterbalance is found in the opposing motions of male and female, interpenetration in the intricate motions of the dance which mingle men and women, and fusion is the tendency, expressed in those figures where all eight members join hands in a circle.*

So, too, our major sports demonstrate the same pattern, with their accent on the individual performer within a *team* which competes with other teams in a *league*.

Baseball, a representative American game, depends on teamwork, but every individual has the chance to exert himself to the fullest. Accuracy and speed, a quick eye and a strong arm, are rewarded. The player must be able to make the most of unexpected opportunities, to know what is going on in many parts of the field at once and to calculate rapidly what action will do the most good. The team, moreover, works harmoniously together without orders. It depends on mutual understanding and mutual aid. (Is this one reason why, in wartime, American soldiers do their most courageous acts, not in killing the enemy but in saving other members of their outfit?)

Basketball, too (started at Springfield, Mass., sometime before 1893), depends on team work, quick thinking, fast response, opportunity quickly seized.

Football, the American form of which developed after 1867, has the teamwork and combination of quick headwork and legwork, the speed and the constant movement, but it emphasizes the more brutal impact of body against body. Its surrounding symbols also stress warfare—the military band, the fair maidens and elderly, one-time warriors upon the walls or bleachers beseeching their heroes to capture the field and save their honor for them, the tribal yells of encouragement, the totem animal (the lion for Columbia, the Princeton tiger) as a symbol of unity.

The spectators seem to benefit as much as the players. From our

* For an analysis of this sixfold social pattern, see Chapter 17.

earliest frontier days, when law either did not exist or was weak, we have felt greater safety in identity with the group than in reliance on abstract justice, and we carry this feeling into our sports. We project ourselves into the skillful team, feeling ourselves united to all the thousands of fans around us and thus to our society.

*Hobbies*

Hobbies, too numerous to list, take up the increasing leisure time. There is a marked return to the ancient handcrafts as men and women seek to recover that pride in work which their ancestors possessed. Garden clubs and flower shows flourish. Collections of everything from stamps to buttons, figurines to autographs, are burgeoning. Other hobbyists may breed chinchillas or Siamese cats. The do-it-yourself craze has opened alleys of achievement to many who had never worked with their hands before, creating a new $6,000,000,000 business in books, tools, materials. Hi fi—the building of fine phonographs—has become a cult, with high priests uttering magic formulas in many a magazine.

Every hobby has its club. People are discovering new friends through their hobbies. Bird watchers rise in the dark to meet at some rendezvous where they hope to add another species to their collection—not by shooting, but merely by observing it. A string of ancient cars rolls down the highway: it is a club of enthusiasts on an outing, perhaps dressed in the linen dusters of fifty years ago, the old cars restored to their pristine glory by the proud owners. Musical groups form to sing folk or classical music. Los Angeles has a symphony orchestra made up entirely of doctors.

Community theaters attract those with dramatic leanings. Those who can't act but love theater are put to work making scenery or costumes. Pageants like *The Lost Colony* which is performed each summer at Roanoke Island, N.C., the many western rodeos, the Albuquerque fiesta with its folk dancing and folk drama—all add to the richness of the cultural texture of a people who after working hard to build up the country are now taking time to enjoy it.

The use of the rural schoolhouse as a community center is an old custom. That ideal, revitalized by the depression, activates many public schools today. It is a rare night when the high school is not blazing with lights as men use its shops to learn how to make

furniture, parents its auditorium for a meeting of the P.T.A., teen-
agers its gymnasium for a record dance, and a Great Books group
its library for a discussion meeting. Some towns are big enough to
have a special recreation center for such events.

Playgrounds, begun late in the nineteenth century for city youngsters without recreational facilities, are now thought essential to
any alert community. Where the community feels unable to afford
one, volunteer groups have often pitched in to do the work. By
1956 over seventy-six thousand paid recreational workers, fulltime
and seasonal, directed such programs.

Parks are now designed for use rather than for the more formal
arrangements of an earlier day. Most noteworthy of all are the great
national parks which from Maine to the state of Washington preserve the natural heritage of the people while opening it to their
view with modern motor roads. Yellowstone, the first and largest,
covers an area of nearly 3,500 square miles, its geysers and hot
springs and bubbling pools of colored mud, its magnificent views
of lake, forest and mountain making it one of nature's great works.
Historical and battlefield parks, though smaller, preserve such
precious memorials of the past as the log cabin believed to be that
in which Lincoln was born, the Gettysburg battlefield, and the area
of first English settlement at Jamestown, Virginia.

Also open to the public are 150 national forests with their 4,400
camp and picnic areas, hunting and fishing, skiing, wilderness hiking
trails and water sports. For a small rental, land can be leased and a
private home built in one of these refreshing wildernesses. Nearly
every state also has its own historic shrines, and parks with camping facilities.

Americans on vacation pour into these places in such numbers
that some of the parks can hardly accommodate the traffic. Possessed of a great curiosity to see the sources of their history, they
herd the children ahead of them to see Plymouth Rock, the indoor
weathervane at Jefferson's Monticello, or the Alamo where Davy
Crockett fought and died. The better informed carry along one of
the excellent state guides which the depression and the Federal
Writer's Project produced. Never perhaps in history has there been
so wide an interest in the past, or so lavish an effort to preserve and
reconstruct it. Old Salem was rebuilt, then old Williamsburg, old

Sturbridge, and now old Plymouth. If the tendency continues, we may soon have more "ancient" buildings than Europe!

The summer vacation, now extended to thousands of workers who never had it before, sends families off in their cars to all parts of the land, extending their contacts with the nation and its people, its comforting sameness of gasoline and cigarette brands, its exciting variety of scenery and history. For the children of those who cannot afford a family vacation, there are fresh air camps and homes, the latter freely offered by small-town residents.

All this moving around seems to have aided the trend toward less formal clothing. Riding long distances in a car, camping, fishing up mountain streams, working in a cellar workshop persuade a man to roll up his sleeves and shift to a pair of blue jeans. Women also take to slacks or shorts, and even the best hotels hang out signs urging "Come as you are."

Informality is also the new style for friends who entertain one another. Without servants, hostesses plan meals that can be cooked in advance, brought hot to the dining room, served buffet style and then eaten on the lap or at bridge tables scattered around the living room. More informal and more popular still is the outdoor barbecue, where the host dons apron and possibly chef's cap, grilling a juicy steak over an open charcoal fire and serving his guests at tables on the lawn.

Families, with more leisure time to spend together, develop more resources within the home. The workroom or workshop is coming to be an essential part of the house. Toys which promote positive play patterns, approved by psychologists, are put before the little ones. As they grow up, they are sent off to take lessons in various forms of play which the school does not provide—dancing, piano, tennis, even horseback riding.

Another form of play has entered the home with the sanction of psychology. This is the love play between husband and wife. The old tabus and fears have given way to the recognition that sexual love is the basis of a sound family life, that the instincts for sex play are natural and fitting, and that many of the tensions of modern life are relaxed by uninhibited experiment and the indulgence of moods all the way from laughter to passion.

To meet the relatively new need of recreation for the retired, whole programs have sprung up to open new activities to them and bring them together with companions of their own age. Throughout the land groups calling themselves Senior Citizens or Golden Age have been organized. Members plan their own programs to fit all tastes, from discussion groups to dancing. Many retired executives find deep satisfaction, after a lifetime of competitive strife, in serving their communities without pay—as members of the school board or other civic groups. With retirement now often mandatory at sixty-five and the life span ever lengthening, the nation has a valuable resource in the available time of these citizens.

Not all recreation is as productive, unfortunately, as the programs we have glanced at so far. In Las Vegas, Nevada, gambling capital of the country, Americans (and some foreign visitors) gambled $60,320,000 in 1955, arriving at the rate of 3,861 a day in the scramble to throw their money away. The nation spent a fantastic $5.3 billion for tobacco in 1952, and twice as much for alcoholic beverages.

## Leisure for What?

The varied uses of leisure, the almost anxious concern Americans show over having a good time, evince a determination to enjoy the fruits of their labor, to get something immaterial out of the wealth they have worked so hard for. So, with their usual overcompensatory drive, they go at relaxing as if they were conquering another wilderness.

At the root of all recreation, as the word itself implies, is creativity. In the past, Americans have associated this spirit of creativity with their professions and their crafts. Work itself has been zestful, has been like food and drink to them. Out of the abundance their work has created has come the necessity to consume what has been produced, to spend less time making and more time using up. This fundamental change has brought about a change in attitude. Where once the American found morality in work, now he finds it in fun. And he is still a little too earnest about it. Leisure patterns, like anything else, must be learned.

Already Americans are recovering from the blow which industrialism dealt to craftsmanship and the arts. As technology provides the media by which the dramatic arts can be carried to the millions, art and industry inevitably interpenetrate. As automation releases man from his long bondage, industry returns him to his heritage of craftsmanship and a creative leisure like that which produced the arts and festivals of old. So by a long path man is returning to his heritage of playtime and individual creation, released at last by the very forces which once held him in their iron fingers. This is the exciting promise of technology, that by the very flood of its material benefits, it will release us to a life that is not material, but creative.

If by a great circle we return at last to the garden of Eden, who shall say that the journey was not worth while?

# CHAPTER SIXTEEN

---

## *Science and Man*

**B**orn in the age of reason, when science and the scientific method were beginning to promise a new life, the American republic has always rested its hopes in science as a social force. From the experiments of Ben Franklin and the inventions of Thomas Jefferson to the latest industrial product, science has been built into the American scheme—not as a thing abstruse or curious only, but as the servant of the common man, as a creative force which by increasing production and extending benefits to all is essential to the democratic process. By its many provisions of quick transportation and communication it has given us a wider world to live in, broadening both our interests and our responsibilities, bringing the performing arts into our homes, altering the roles of male and female, and with its speedy transformations remaking the world so fast that our children are always having to explain it to us.

It has prolonged life and lowered infant mortality, so that the proportions of young and old among us are changed. It has made childbirth a matter of choice and therefore a source of happiness rather than a burden. It has destroyed many diseases, found cures for others, and relieved suffering. It knows how to provide enough food for all, and it can wipe out humanity as casually as a foot destroys an anthill.

Science, used as a tool, has made our civilization what it is. Its most abstract theories, once tested in the laboratory, are soon turned to practical uses and the making of more consumer goods. Whole industries spring out of pure research which unexpectedly leads to such new products as nylon or plastics.

But science as an attitude, a habit of mind, is of equal importance, for it has gained common acceptance as the correct way to approach problems and to search for solutions, not only in the material world but in the human. Its method provides a substitute for prejudice and superstition. The scientific demonstration is so convincing that advertising has seized upon it as the clinching argument. "Four out of five doctors agree that. . . ." "Buy the car the engineers favor." And though nobody knows what torsion bar suspension is, it sounds so scientific that advertisers count on it to sell cars.

Recognizing the central role science plays in the modern world, Congress in 1950 established the National Science Foundation to "develop and encourage the pursuit of a national policy for the promotion of basic research and education in the sciences" and "to appraise the impact of research . . . upon the general welfare." Though criticized for its failure to assume active direction of its policy-making function, the Foundation has established a number of important principles, such as supporting basic rather than applied science wherever possible, improving secondary school science teaching as a means of producing more scientists, and preferring unclassified to secret work.

## Science and Social Reform

Like bright young mechanics in a back-yard garage, Americans are always tinkering with their society, hoping to make it better. One of the encouraging things about a culture which has many points of stress is the large amount and the generally high level of objective, scientifically based criticism its members bring to bear on it. Though selfish or narrow interests may win, yet it is recognized that scientific evidence is the weightiest and should prevail in decision making.

The nation itself arose out of protest with conditions as they were in seventeenth century Europe. Reform based on revolt was thus the characteristic tone of American society, but a reform based also on faith—first in God, then in human progress. The religious tone, the moral tone are characteristic of American reform to this day, which is one reason why observers whose ears are attuned to Marx and Lenin cannot recognize reform in its American pattern, or are suspicious of it if they do.

America's vast literature of protest and reform is too little known abroad. It goes back to the very beginnings, as one may see by reading the first great book written in English on these shores, William Bradford's *Of Plimoth Plantation*. It runs on through the colonial period to Jefferson, through the writings or the actions of William Lloyd Garrison, Susan B. Anthony, Demarest Lloyd and the other preachers of the social gospel, through all the reform movements of the 1840's—abolition, spiritualism, socialism, transcendentalism—and on through the century to the muckrakers.

From Bryan and Teddy Roosevelt to Wilson and LaFollette, to the New Deal and then, surprisingly, to Eisenhower, reform has tempered politics. Now it is apparent that the party of the conservatives has embraced the social gospel as its own, however some of its members may squirm at such close contact. Proposals advanced by reformist groups—Populists, Socialists, Progressives— sooner or later are enacted into law.

Two axioms undergirded the movement of protest and reform: that human reason and a growing body of scientific knowledge could provide an ever-rising standard of living, and that the output must be universally shared. That this has become standard American doctrine, the words and actions of both major parties attest. In recent years both the parties and the people have come to realize that their own wellbeing can be assured only by extending it throughout the world.

The Puritan protest combined with the Age of Reason, and the social message of Christianity with the development of scientific method, to make science in the United States an instrument for human betterment. From Jamestown and Plymouth to Brook Farm and the Oneida Community, from the Bible Commonwealth to the interracial housing development, the country had always been prolific of social experiment. The new settlements in the wilderness often undertook some special program, as John Jay Shipherd built his community at Oberlin, Ohio, around a school which would educate young people to carry the Gospel, and the Oberlin way of community sharing, throughout the wilderness.

These communities were social laboratories. Later, social scientists studied average communities to see why they succeeded and where they failed. Best known of many was the Middletown study of Robert and Helen Lynd. Their work had been preceded by that of the social settlements which explored the problems of poor neighborhoods and tried to meet their needs. It was followed by a flood of studies, the most extensive of which was the Yankee City project of W. Lloyd Warner and associates.

From massive evidence social scientists built up an impressive body of scientific knowledge about human behavior, communities, social institutions. They looked at human actions with the same detachment the biologist used in his microscopic examination of living cells, or the physicist in studying the structure of the atom. They learned how to predict social behavior and how to avoid or correct social ills.

Their principles began to seep into the public consciousness just as Darwin's and Freud's ideas had penetrated before them. Once the principles of sociology became for the common man a part of that science whose magic authority he honored even when he could not understand it, progress towards social justice was assured. Science had delivered the goods so often that all its proven successes came to the support of a new science struggling to establish itself. The sore spots sociology had probed must be cut out or cured. And as the medical doctor not only diagnosed the illness but cured it, so the social doctor would recommend programs for the cure of racial tension, juvenile delinquency, broken homes.

The work began with community surveys to determine needs. Greenville, South Carolina, for example, faced up to its biggest problem, the needs of its Negro residents. The Community Council, recognizing that this was everybody's problem, set up a committee of white and Negro leaders representing all points of view. Twelve fact-finding committees went to work on everything from housing to employment. Each committee was headed by co-chairmen, white and Negro. Two hundred people pitched in to make the survey, housewives calling on their neighbors, ministers riding the buses to see how people were treated.

When Greenville had taken a look at the facts, housing and slum clearance projects got under way. Negro doctors were for the first time invited to medical society meetings. Perhaps most significant of all, the act of working together on committees was itself a social advance. The survey—locating the problem, cooperating first to analyse and then to overcome it—was a realization of John Dewey's definition of democracy as the method which uses experimental methods to release the powers of human nature in the service of a freedom which is cooperative and a cooperation which is voluntary.

This idea of making a better community has fascinated Americans from the very beginning. To bring the dream to life, every sort of social service is used—recreation programs, family service centers, mental hygiene clinics, community nurses, well-baby clinics, pre-natal care, employment bureaus, Boy and Girl Scouts, care of the aged and of dependent children. To raise the money for all these services, more than two million men and women go out every year to ring doorbells and collect the nearly $300,000,000 needed to operate the programs of the Community Chests and Councils. They also contribute millions of hours in such voluntary work as helping in hospitals or serving as Scoutmasters. The upgrading of society is not a thing to be bought, or to be provided by government. It supposes a personal response, a willingness to give of one's own time and person.

The findings of the social sciences are being applied in all areas of society. The pastor uses them in ministering to his people. The schools use them in guidance programs and in their consideration of the student's personality and individual needs. Industry uses them in personnel work—in striving for better relations with its employees and with the public. Hollywood uses opinion polls to learn what the public wants, advertisers to find out what kind of product is desired.

Techniques of interpersonal relations are studied and methods devised which make for better group and committee work. Thus social sciences provide useful tools, whose value depends on the use that is made of them. Dynamite can clear the way for a new road or destroy an innocent victim. Money can be used either to ennoble or to corrupt. Even religion can be used to heighten discord and hatred. So the tools of social science in unscrupulous hands can be manipulated so as to make employees pliable to the will of an employer, to influence public opinion, to arouse and engage emotions for commercial or political purposes.

Conspicuous among all the projects applying scientific principles to human betterment is TVA, whose technical achievements have already been mentioned. Even more important is its social accomplishment. Instead of forcing its program upon hostile communities, it worked patiently to arouse community interest and understanding. Officials went out to meet the farmers in their homes, invited them in small groups to rural schools, and explained what they could achieve by cooperation. Gradually belief took hold. Farming methods changed. Crops improved. Community spirit developed. Better sanitation, housing, schooling, recreation followed. Government made its skills available to the people, but it did not impose them. It waited for voluntary cooperation, knowing that the only sure change is that which grows from within.

*New Frontiers*

Medical science can remove an appendix, set a leg or conquer polio. Agricultural science can produce low cost foods in quantities sufficient to wipe out hunger. But this is only half the battle. Men hurt each other more than they are hurt by disease, by the pressures they build into their institutions. Tension, conflict, competition and acquisitiveness have more victims than the viruses and the bacilli.

So now the natural and the social sciences converge on the problem. The doctor calls in the psychiatrist. The agricultural technician preparing to introduce new techniques to a village in India or Thailand makes use of anthropologists to be sure that he violates no tabus and presents his program in the way the local mores will be likely to approve. The industrialist who wants to introduce a new machine carefully prepares the ground by conferences first with human relations consultants, then with his managing staff, then with union representatives.

Social and natural sciences are not only converging upon problems which need a joint attack for their solution. They are also interpenetrating each other. Biophysics and biochemistry are filling in the gap which once separated the physical from the biological sciences. Similarly the gap between the biological and social sciences is being bridged. As the chemistry of biological functions is coming to be understood, so the biological basis of social behavior is growing clearer. Once the missing links draw the chain of being together, it may even become possible to control human temperament and social progress by chemical means. Already the day has come when, after brushing his teeth, a man may take from the medicine cabinet the pill needed to give him energy for skiing or mental drive for an important sales job.

The science of cybernetics concerns itself with the study of messages as a means of controlling machinery and society.* That casual addition of the words "and society" shows how far we have gone towards a mechanization of civilization, or a socialization of the machine. Norbert Wiener includes in the science of messages not only the study of language, communications media and devices like computing machines, but everything which contributes to the exchange of signals by which society is controlled. He believes that society can only be understood through a study of all the messages which serve it, and that the future development of these messages will be of increasing importance as machines take over functions once thought to be exclusively human.

They are already doing it. Computing machines—"electronic brains"—can already perform in a few minutes tasks that formerly occupied years, and even then involved greater chances of error. Systems are now being developed which will make the contents of a whole library on a given subject immediately available. A machine which can translate from one language to another has been produced. More and more, man is going to be freed by machinery not only from the physical drudgery but also from much of the mental drudgery on which he has spent his life. An era of freedom for the full exercise of his creative powers is at hand.

## The Science of Democracy

The philosophy of science and scientific method as applied to the needs of a democratic society is pragmatism. It asserts that only by examining the consequences of an act, rather than by adhering to a closed system of abstract principles, can the choice be made between good and evil, true and false. Most philosophy had been bemused by the notion that the world was part of a fixed system whose first principles, once discovered, would solve all problems. The pragmatist sees the world as a constantly changing thing, in

* Norbert Wiener: *The Human Use of Human Beings.*

which dogma and the pretense of finality in truth can do only harm.

William James, who defined pragmatism and gave it its name, cut through the philosophical disputes which had gone on for ages in a realm of hazy abstraction by insisting that the test of any proposition was its practical effect in the world of men. The pragmatic method settled interminable metaphysical disputes by confronting them with the test of usefulness. Said James: "The true is the name of whatever proves itself to be good in the way of belief, and good, too, for definite assignable reasons."

It was John Dewey with his instrumentalism who wed philosophy to scientific method and brought them to the service of the workaday world. He insisted the only way to evaluate ends is to see what would result from the use of the means designed to reach those ends. The means are a part of the ends. We do not know what we have chosen until we see what will happen as a result of that choice. Allegiance to ideals does not free us from judging them by their consequences.

While Dewey was building a useful philosophic base for the reconstruction of society through the application of scientific method, Oliver Wendell Holmes was leading a movement in the law known as realism. Law was to be regarded not as an abstract entity, but as an instrument which furthered the changing needs of man and was responsive to social change.

James Harvey Robinson taught that history was not merely a chronicle of the past, but an instrument by which the present could be understood and the future influenced. History thus became an ally of the social sciences. Both Dewey and Robinson and their followers believed that the time would come when the scientific outlook which the industrial revolution had fostered would be communicated to politics. By seizing upon the methods of science, industry had changed the world. But in contrast with technological virtuosity stood an appalling social lag. Instead of condemning the method which had made industrialism possible, Dewey wanted to apply its principles to society in an attack upon poverty, ignorance, inequality.

There were those who, ignoring Dewey's demonstration of the connection between means and ends, argued that science had no way of determining values. The fact was that scientists could demonstrate the advantages both to the individual and to society of the democratic process as opposed to other forms of social organization. Value, as determined by free men charting their own goals and designing their own methods of reaching them, was built into the pragmatic approach.

Even those who insisted upon deriving a system of values from some a priori, absolutist system would have to admit that science in choosing to undertake vast programs of medical, social, industrial and pure research had done more in a half century to make things better for man than abstract philosophy had achieved in nearly three thousand years of arguing over such matters as first cause, the unmoved mover, and pure reason.

As James Bryant Conant asserts, the scientific theories of the last century or so are monuments, as much as the Parthenon or the medieval cathedrals, of what the human spirit can accomplish, a demonstration of the flowering of man's creative powers. "To have constructed a great fabric of new concepts and conceptual schemes arising from experiment and observation and fruitful beyond measure of new experiments is no small achievement." *

Americans embraced science as their own, as the way of thought which best expressed their pluralistic, pioneering, optimistic, changing, anti-authoritarian society. It was their endless frontier—the road to continuous growth and improvement.

## The Foundations

Nowhere was the faith and the practice of this faith better seen than in the foundations which, based upon great fortunes made possible by technology, sprang up in the twentieth century to foster programs of research leading to human betterment.

Of the hundreds of foundations now operating, a few must serve as examples. The Carnegie Corporation of New York (one of several foundations established by the Scotch immigrant boy who became a great steel producer), established for the advancement or diffusion of knowledge, now concentrates on grants to institutions conducting programs of study which give promise of new knowledge leading to better conditions. The Russell Sage Foundation devotes most of its funds to increasing the application in social practice of

* *Modern Science and Modern Man,* p. 187.

the results of social science research. The Twentieth Century Fund, founded by the Boston merchant Edward Filene, carries out its own research and public education program in current economic and social problems.

The Rockefeller Foundation was designed "to promote the well being of mankind throughout the world." Supporting many fields of inquiry, the Foundation stresses the advancement of knowledge and the application of such knowledge to human interests and needs. Medicine, biology, agriculture, social sciences and the humanities are included in its scope.

The John Simon Guggenheim Memorial Foundation supports not only scientists and research workers but creative artists of all kinds—poets, composers, sculptors, painters. Unlike many of the foundations whose support is given through other institutions, it selects the individual worker who gives promise of unusual ability. Its grants have brought heartening encouragement to hundreds of creative people whose work is by nature solitary and who might otherwise get little recognition from a society which as a rule does not put a high monetary value upon creative effort of an original and pioneering nature.

Biggest of all the foundations is the Ford, "a large body of money completely surrounded by people who want some," as its unauthorized biographer put it.* Its stated assets in 1953 were over half a billion dollars, but in 1955 it gave that amount away in one swoop to more than four thousand privately endowed colleges, universities and hospitals, without distinction as to creed. The money, coming entirely from the profits of the motor industry, was a dramatic demonstration of private industry's sense of public obligation, and of its contribution to the nation's welfare.

The study made to determine the policy and program of the Ford Foundation concluded that five areas were most in need of support—the establishment of peace, the strengthening of democracy, the strengthening of the economy, education in a democratic society, and studies in individual behavior and human relations. It was ironic and yet fitting that none of the money was felt to be needed to develop the physical sciences and technology which had made the amassing of such a great fortune possible.

* Dwight Macdonald, *The Ford Foundation: The Men and the Millions.*

In the foundations—including those which get their support from millions of small contributors for such work as cancer research or the control of infantile paralysis—Americans reaffirm their belief in the moral obligation to be intelligent, in the power of science to solve human problems, in their responsibility to support such work, and most of all their faith that the future, intelligently and positively approached, is always bound to be better.

## CHAPTER SEVENTEEN

---

# *Where Are We Going?*

"I am willing to love all mankind except an American," croaked Doctor Samuel Johnson some two hundred years ago. Since that time there have been more than a few to agree with him, though they have often disagreed among themselves as to why they should not love us.

For quite some time the cry was materialism, and to some extent it still is. There is no doubt that in the exuberance of building the nation and harnessing its resources, Americans gave altogether too much attention to the material and ignored the arts. But that phase passed long ago. The material abundance which impresses visitors is taken for granted here. The billions the United States has spent abroad to relieve suffering, re-establish industry, render technical assistance and help others prepare their defenses against the demonstrable tyranny of communism, though based on enlightened self-interest, did not come from a people who value goods so highly that they cannot bear to part with them. Quite different motives were at work, not only in the government grants but in the many voluntary programs of aid freely given.

## Some American Paradoxes

Americans have the same amount of native talent as any other people, but it may be disguised. Europeans, for example, often conclude that we have no intelligentsia because they do not hear much conversation based upon ideologies and do not find Americans clustered in ideological groups and cliques. This does not mean that Americans lack intellect, but that their history has bred in them a suspicion of isms, closed systems and doctrines which explain all things according to a set of all-embracing assumptions. They have seen such schools come and go abroad, and it is their conclusion that none of them—no matter how firmly embraced—has demonstrated final truth.

They prefer to be instrumentalists and pluralists. They tend to think that knowledge must be good for something—for man, in fact, and for his adjustment to society. Experimentalists, they would agree that one idea might work here, another there. But they do not want to get committed to remodelling the whole world overnight on the basis of a new idea. They are reformers, but reformers of human ills and shortcomings, not of systems.

Perhaps this explains why the Japanese student complained to Clyde Kluckhohn that Americans lacked a specific ideology they could communicate, while Russians could give a very coherent account of theirs. The Russians have a system. The Americans have a set of principles about human rights, but the way they go about securing these rights varies all the way from the building up of industrial output to a Supreme Court decision on segregation.

"America is not only big and rich," writes David Riesman in *The Lonely Crowd* (p. 349), "it is mysterious; and its capacity for the humorous or ironical concealment of its interests matches that of the legendary inscrutable Chinese."

Only the two-week visitor sees the United States as a clear and logical pattern. To those who spend their lives studying it, a number of confusing paradoxes are pressed into the matrix. For here there is great personal freedom and great conformity, poverty amidst great plenty, great friendliness and shameful brutality, generosity and selfish corruption and graft, easygoing informality and burdensome tension, kindness to animals and unkindness to Negroes or other minorities, respect for education and tolerant scorn for the professor, permissive social customs and puritan restraint, fortunes made with great effort and easily given away, the strongest government in the world which yet is often at the mercy of its component parts, and capitalism calmly handing to workers the plums that socialism elsewhere has vainly demanded.

Born in the age of enlightenment, the United States has always kept its faith in man's ability to steer his course by reason and to devise a rational social order. Influenced in its youth by romanticism, it embraced the idea of man's diversity and the sacredness of the individual. Forced to build a civilization in the wilderness and then to fight for survival, its citizens have been guided by the raw test of results rather than by the refined rule of perfect doctrine.

The founders of the nation, we believe, gave us a political theory which contained both a set of values and a philosophy of government. These are things we have never had to fight over. Our revolution was primarily a political one, but it gave us the instruments with which to bring about gradual economic and social reform. As a result of this gradualism, no important reform has ever been undone, and each has in the end been accepted by the party which opposed it and has become a part of our civilization. From Jefferson to the Fair Deal, significant reforms have been constitutionally carried through and then maintained by the opposing party. The American Revolution did not set out, like the French or the Russian, to destroy a social system. Consequently the country has never been torn apart by class strife. The revolution has been digested socially. It has progressed step by step without creating a right and a left so antagonistic that they would rather destroy each other than unite to solve the problems which face them.

Karl Marx has never made much sense to a nation where everyone from the executive to the machine operator may wear a Hart, Schaffner and Marx suit, or enjoy the zany humor of Groucho Marx and his brothers.

The struggle to use the rights which the Constitution guaranteed to the common man was embodied in the conflict between Alexander Hamilton and Thomas Jefferson. The battle they engaged in has been fought in every generation since, but only in our time has it become clear that the final victory is Jefferson's and his interpretation of the American dream the one that is to prevail. By a curious paradox, Jefferson and Hamilton were both wrong and both right. The nation did not remain the land of small landed proprietors Jefferson envisioned. Yet the industrial strength Hamilton aimed at brought benefits which, together with the universal franchise Jefferson believed in, achieved the Jeffersonian ideal of a fair distribution.

The founders intended that American civilization should be

different from that of the old world, weighted down with its historic cruelties, its class divisions and old quarrels. Founded in the full light of a rational age, it could start with no burden of old customs, hatreds, superstitions. It would be a home for humanity, an asylum for the oppressed.

Through the exercise of political rights, the citizens could achieve those cultural and economic rights which the Declaration or the Constitution opened the way to. In time the right to life would be interpreted as the responsibility of government for the health, continuous employment or care of all its citizens.

## Basic Assumptions

What are the basic assumptions of American society?

Respect for human life and human worth. Equality of rights and opportunities. As much liberty as is compatible with the welfare of the whole society—that is, individual liberty which will not abuse the liberties and rights of others. The dignity of labor. A fair distribution both of work and benefits, in a society which no longer has the independence of the isolated frontier family, but is interwoven like a piece of cloth which will be destroyed if the strands are separated.

To such a society, the words of William Penn provide a ground rule: "Liberty without obedience is confusion, and obedience without liberty is slavery."

Robert Lynd, listing a number of basic American assumptions in his *Knowledge for What?* found that many of them were balanced by opposites. For example:

Individualism is the law of nature. But no man should live for himself alone.

Democracy is the best form of government. But you can't leave everything to the popular vote.

Everyone should strive for success. But the kind of person you are is more important than material success.

Religion and the finer things of life are important. But a man ought to earn as much as he can for his family's sake.

We should welcome progress and new things. But old ways are best.

Education is a good thing. But practical men are the ones who get things done.

Science has brought many benefits. But it has no right to interfere with business matters.

These balanced judgments can be taken as a philosophy of the timid, or as a demonstration of common sense, or as a confused response to a confusing world. But they do indicate a recognition of the contrarieties of life and the need to recognize conflicting claims. This is surely one of the pillars of wisdom.

The sociologist Robin Williams * has noted several other basic assumptions:

Active mastery of the environment rather than passive acceptance is the right response.

Interest in the external world of things is more important than inner experience, manipulation than contemplation.

Change is the only constant; therefore we must be adaptable.

The future is more important than the past.

Human reason can remake the world; this rather than what has been done in the past should be our guide.

There is one moral law for all; the rights of man are universal.

William H. Whyte, Jr. who has studied the new suburban areas remarks that although the new suburbanites obscure some harsh realities when they speak of their democratic ideals, "yet their unwillingness to concede class divisions is itself a very powerful factor in keeping the divisions from crystallizing." † He also notes that young couples on their way up socially, some of them the children of immigrants from ethnic enclaves, are accepted by college graduate couples and soon elevate their standards of taste or speech to conform with their neighbors.

Visitors from Europe are always surprised, and a little shocked, by the buoyant optimism they find here. To them it appears like the innocence of inexperience, as perhaps it is. Yet three hundred and fifty years of living on this continent, subduing its rawness and

* *American Sociology*, p. 441.
† *The Organization Man*, p. 312.

assimilating millions of newcomers from all cultures does, we feel, give us the right to be happy about it.

Problems do not dismay us, because we have licked them in the past. Juvenile delinquency and mental disorder at home, disease and hunger abroad—we view them with a girded insouciance, form some new associations, and go to work. Have we not disposed of robber barons, diphtheria, substandard food manufacturing, monopolies, witch trials, and property as a qualification for voting? If we are too prone to seek simple cures for complex problems, has it not often happened that the simple or even providential cure has solved the problem, as foreign markets once solved the farmer's problem, unionism the worker's, and voluntarism just about everything else?

Wrote the Polish journalist, Melchior Wankowicz, after observing American life: "The newcomer from the disillusioned, tired, skeptical Europe feels a heartwarming glow in the sincere optimism of a nation that is on the whole contented and satisfied with its present. That form of patriotism, free from any ideological complications and histrionics, simple and straightforward, constitutes a source of moral strength that can never be overestimated." *

*Democracy as Process*

De Tocqueville noted long ago that Americans paid little attention to philosophy, yet had a philosophical method which they all followed.

"To evade the bondage of system and habit, of family maxims, class opinions, and, in some degree, of national prejudices; to accept tradition only as a means of information, and existing facts only as a lesson to be used in doing otherwise and doing better; to seek the reasons of things for one's self, and in one's self alone; to tend to results without being bound to means, and to aim at the substance through the form;—such are the principal characteristics of what I shall call the philosophical method of the Americans." †

This is the pragmatic approach, the method of testing ideas by their results, of being guided by experience rather than by absolutes.

It was Kant, with his curious contempt for the living variety of

* *Polish Daily*, Detroit, Jan. 1, 1954.
† Page 143.

experience and his exaggeration of the value of system, order and regularity for their own sakes, who led the way to an absolutism which had disastrous consequences. Marx, following this tradition, anticipated some final social state. The resulting dogmas are so rigid that those who accept the Marxist teaching ignore any fact which will not fit into its mold. They ignore the socializing of capitalism in the United States just as they ignore the slaughter of millions in Russia in an effort to impose collectivization, or the continuing crime of slave labor, or the slaughter in Hungary with its demonstration of what political "cooperation" with Russia amounts to.

Democracy is based on no such iron fiction. It is a balanced system of rights and duties. More than a government, it is a mode of associated living, of what John Dewey calls "conjoint communicated experience." The moral and ideal meaning of democracy, says Dewey, is that social return is demanded from all, while an opportunity for the development of distinctive capacities is afforded to all. It is not an external institution, but a way of personal life.

The best illustration of this proposition is voluntarism—the means by which democratic process is employed while carrying out civic acts. The citizens who form an association in order to start a recreation program for the children of their community are not only working for a democratic end—the improvement of the social order by providing for the constructive and healthful use of their youngsters' spare time. They are making constructive use of their democratic rights by organizing freely, cooperating on a basis of equality to achieve together something they could not accomplish alone. Their children, furthermore, in organized play will be learning the same art of voluntary association. The thousands of instances in which such a pattern is repeated make American democracy what it is—not a government merely, but a way of life.

The democratic way assumes that society is not static but changing. It therefore tries to shape the experiences of the young so that instead of repeating the habits of their parents, they will form better ones. For this reason alone, since men tend to look to the past for guidance and to follow the ways of their parents even after their inadequacy is proven, democracy is a difficult ideal to follow.

The source of the American democratic tradition is therefore moral, not technical. It is based on faith in the ability of human nature to achieve freedom for the individual accompanied by a regard for others, and upon social stability produced by cohesion, not coercion.

Democracy is an intellectual ideal as well as a moral and religious one, for it demands hard thought based on real experience and translated into useful action. Its faith is in a shared life, a life enlarged and made meaningful by the many human contacts which are necessary to its functioning. And it is an aesthetic ideal because it aims at the communication of experience—not to a limited group through an aristocratic art, but to all, and through continuously rising standards.

Democracy offers the only way of life based on experience rather than dogma; that is why it is so hard to understand. It offers no complete and finished system such as socialism, communism or fascism. It addresses itself to concrete problems, firsthand experience, specific human needs, better community living. Because it does not pretend to have all the answers of a finished system, it does not pretend to avoid all mistakes. But it does promise to learn from them.

A closed system like communism cannot learn from its mistakes, for since it claims to have all the answers, the only thing it can do when things turn out badly is to blame more officials, conduct more secret trials, execute more people. Since by definition the system cannot be wrong, the fault must lie in the people.

Democracy looks at it the other way: the people and their needs are what matter. Therefore if the needs are not met, the method must have been wrong. One merely tries another. Hence the combination of socialist and capitalist practices which puzzle visitors but which Americans take for granted. We are not trying to build a perfect system; we are trying to meet human needs.

To the accusation that Americans are not reflective because they show so little interest in ideologies, we would answer: is it not a mark of reflectiveness to penetrate the limitations of ideology and to show an ability to think *beyond* a closed system? In philosophy we are not Newtonians, but Einsteinian relativists. Our system is not closed but open, not finished but ongoing.

To follow such a philosophy is no easy thing, because it frustrates our childish wish to be taken care of and demands that we do our own thinking, manage our own communities. Since social change and progress inevitably bring about disorganization, and since disorganization is unsettling, it takes a strong people to accept this philosophy rather than to give up and be ruled by a group who are willing to admit that they know all the answers.

## The Individual and the Group

Every culture must grapple with the question of the relative importance of the individual and society, and every age must reassess the balance between them. The United States has been through its individualist stage. It had independent artisans and craftsmen proud of their work. It also had its robber barons, its lords of great wealth and its sloughs of poverty, its spoils system and shameful political corruption. The United States has experienced both the merits and the defects of individualism. It has experimented in a thousand ways with the balance between individual and society.

American institutions were designed with the accent on individual liberty. We have enjoyed both the merits and the defects of this emphasis. But in recent years we have been revising our emphasis towards the group, the community. William H. Whyte, Jr. says in *The Organization Man* that we have gone too far. In the industrial organization he sees an accent on conformity, on group process at the expense of good hard individual thinking, on a cheerful acceptance of the status quo which he thinks stultifying. In the social life of the organization man he finds an emphasis on the group which destroys or seriously hampers privacy and individuality. Suburban communities organize in social groups where the sharing becomes practically communal. Men team up to buy one lawnmower for the unit, women form a baby sitter "bank," taking turns for each other. Silver, dishes, books, records are loaned back and forth.

Many of these new suburbanites have come out from cities where they had no community life. In rediscovering the warmth of the small neighborhood they are merely making a belated discovery of an older America, the one that has always existed in the small town and which has a tradition reaching back to the first settlements in the wilderness with their newness, their smallness, their independence of outside power and their need of mutual assistance. The new accent on the group is, like most things that are new, a rediscovery of the old. It is a recovery of something that Plymouth, the wagon trains and the ideal communities of the 1840's had—a balancing and fusing of man as individual and man in the group.

To fear that the present group work in research and administration will topple us over is to overlook the self-balancing strength of a society which is made up of millions of small primary groups and millions of secondary associations—civic, economic, social, political, cultural.

Such a pluralistic society, with its competition for attention and agreement, is full of zest. Not only are we solicited to buy this or that car, take a train rather than a plane, support private against public power, vote Republican or Democratic. We are appealed to both by management and labor, by grain farmers and dairy farmers, by conservationists and would-be exploiters, by progressive and traditional systems of education, by a wide variety of religions. Life that offers so many choices, that invites us to get involved at so many levels, is bound to be stimulating.

Wider choice is also open to us as our work load lessens. An industrial recruiter recently held three hundred interviews with college seniors, not one of whom asked what salary was being offered. As abundance becomes more widely distributed, there is no longer the impetus to succeed over others at great hazard of health and happiness. Striving is less necessary. Other values—peace of mind, family life, hobbies and recreations become more and more the important things, while work takes less and less time and thought.

Success will become a matter of how effectively one spends one's leisure time—who can win games, travel far and interestingly, talk about his accomplishments, make himself felt in his community, get satisfaction out of time rather than materials. In short, the skillful use of time for the benefits it can bring to the individual, the family, the community, will be the test of success.

### Achievement

While the world is in turmoil, the United States has somehow managed to create a livable society from diverse materials, and has demonstrated that government by discussion and distribution is the straightest road to a civilized life. Freedom is still ours—freedom to move about as we please, or to criticize the government, freedom from standing in line or fighting unreasonable regulations.

The European, writes Leslie A. Fiedler, "overwhelmed by a conviction of human impotence, regards with horrified admiration a people who, because they are too naive to understand theory, achieve what he can demonstrate to be theoretically impossible." *

Any final judgment of the American achievement will have to wait a while. But one can report the presence of great intellectual ferment, a high level of self-criticism, the burgeoning of the social sciences and of technology, a frontal assault on the remnants of class distinction, a determination to make the atomic age one of fulfillment of the democratic dream.

To describe the achievements of a society so varied and so large seems hopeless, but the feel of it can be conveyed by a capsule history of one man. From many possibilities Supreme Court Justice William O. Douglas is chosen because his name is known abroad. Born in Minnesota, the son of a circuit-riding preacher who died when he was six, William Douglas moved with the rest of his family to the state of Washington on the west coast. He worked his way through school, won a scholarship to Whitman College, washed windows and helped in a store for ten cents an hour, earned his meals by waiting on table, and for the last three of his four college years saved money by living in a tent on an empty lot. During summer vacations he picked fruit, logged the north woods, fought forest fires. After an interval out for the First World War, he finished college as president of the student body and graduated Phi Beta Kappa.

For two years he taught high school in his home town. Then he went east as a sheep herder on a freight train, rode the rods as far as Chicago and with his last money bought a ticket to New York, where he arrived with six cents. He entered Columbia Law School, tutored and wrote a book to pay his way, finished second in his class. He worked in one of the big corporation law firms, taught law at Columbia and Yale, and through his studies in bankruptcy was called to the Department of Commerce, then to the Securities and Exchange Commission of which he became chairman, working

* *Partisan Review,* XIX (1952), p. 295.

to bring about important reforms in the financial world. In 1939 he was appointed to the Supreme Court, the second youngest man in history to be so honored. Many of his summers since that time have been devoted to travels in distant parts of the world and to an understanding of the problems and contributions of other cultures.

The American faith says that among the youngsters who are peddling papers and mowing lawns throughout the country today there are other Douglases growing up. And they will know how to deal with the problems that confront their generation.

The problems that now confront the nation are serious and sometimes disheartening—delinquency, alcoholism, mental disorder, crime, prejudice, corruption. But we have learned to look at tendencies, for we know that evil will always be with us. And most of us are heartened by the tendency. The maze of voluntary and government agencies at work on every one of the problems is encouraging not only because of the work being done, but because of the democratic process involved.

By 1980 we expect an expanded economy which will guarantee year-round income for workers and a thirty-hour week. Within the next ten to fifteen years we must double the number of college teachers to take care of those who will qualify for a college education, and at the same time we must build as much physical plant to accommodate them as we have so far built in three hundred years.

We expect the economy of abundance which has been achieved here to become global, and we hope to have a hand in bringing it about, by cooperating with other nations who are interested in programs based on mutual aid and respect.

In the United States the gospel of work and the social gospel are merging, and the kind of culture they are building is new and exciting to those who are experiencing it. We are even learning at long last to use the special insights of women, and to benefit from the way male and female approaches to problems can complement each other. Thus the gifts of half of humanity, so long imprisoned within the household, are helping to develop a new vision of what society is and what it should be.

*The American Myth*

Every nation has a myth which reveals its hopes and aspirations and therefore its failures as well as its accomplishments. It has a symbolic picture of itself toward which it strives. The American myth (the principal one) is that of the liberty-loving wanderer from Europe who (like Aeneas) finds a new land which he conquers from the savages, establishing civilization and a rule of law in the place of wilderness and barbarism. All men are to be free and equal. The vast resources of the new land are opened to them. With courage and resourcefulness they hack their civilization out of the forest. Their works prove, says the myth, that they were a people destined, by virtues, religion and arts superior to those of the natives, to possess and develop the continent.

As tinkers, inventors, scientists, technologists and business men they have built a productive machine which is close to realizing their dream of abundance for all. Education and opportunity for all are also part of the dream, always increasingly fulfilled.

Having abandoned Europe, the land of his fathers, for the new world, the American always champions the little guy, the underdog. He suspects and resists authority. His delight is in the things a young man delights in—restraints overthrown, buxom young women, manly sports, crude and heady pleasures, exuberant conclaves such as the American Legion or the national political conventions, great optimism and sudden but brief depressions, joy in his strength, and a yearning for wisdom, beauty, and order like that of the young man who seeks to recapture the mystic longing and sensitive awareness of his adolescence.

America still sees itself in the image of the younger son; probably it always will, for history has conditioned it to be perpetually the frontiersman, throwing off the restraint of the father, of the past, of authority. So no one need fear that Americans will ever want to dominate; this simply is not their image. They are much more likely to want to withdraw, to rediscover their own wild lands, to reject the paternal image of the old world. They are doomed always to be in revolt, always to be reducing the world to order through cooperation rather than through authority. Hence the burgeoning of the social sciences, the techniques for wiping out class differences, putting the boss on a level with his employees and stressing the equality of the working group.

## The Sixfold Process

Nobody questions any more that in the United States we are shaping a social order which can no longer be described by the old words individualism, private enterprise, capitalism, or even democracy. Excellent and penetrating analyses of segments of our social order have been made, yet we lack a unified organic theory of our society.

American society can best be understood as a process involving six characteristic modes of action—individualism, voluntarism, federalism, counterbalance, interpenetration and fusion. This process constitutes a social order that is still evolving and one that by the logic of its adaptability will one day become widespread.

As an example, let us begin with an individual, say Governor William Bradford of Plymouth, who as a very young man decided of his own free will to join the group of dissenters we know as the Pilgrims. At that point the individual enlarged himself by joining a voluntary group of like-minded people, banded together for religious purposes and ultimately, when they came to North America, expanding their principle of voluntarism to establish the little commonwealth of Plymouth and a sort of business corporation to handle its commercial affairs. The principle of federalism was called to life in the New England Confederation, when a handful of weak little village republics joined together for military purposes.

For a while they balanced their small powers against each other, as Boston and Plymouth for example contested for the Connecticut Valley. The next stage, interpenetration, occurred when these little plantations—as for instance Hartford, Weathersfield, Saybrook and others—joined to form one provincial government. Within this limited frame of reference the stage of fusion was perhaps reached when Connecticut became a state.

The same process could be traced in the formation of the federal government.

Let us turn now to the principle as it operates in our society today, picking education as an example. Schooling is based on the individualist doctrine that every citizen is entitled to equal opportunities and that he can capture this opportunity only through education. The voluntarist nature of the school system is clear from its origins, since every town set up its own local school system, the citizens taxing themselves to cover the costs, hauling wood and boarding the teacher cooperatively.

But voluntarism enters the picture in two other ways, and in order to understand how our society functions we must introduce a distinction here. The teachers organize a voluntary association with mixed social and professional purposes, which is tied to regional and national organizations. We may call this system of association functional since the teachers have organized it to strengthen themselves professionally, to enhance their functioning as teachers.

Parents and teachers organize a Parent-Teacher Association, and this we may call societal, since it deals with the school's place in society, bringing together two basic institutions, the school and the family, for purposes which are assumed to have a value to the community and which constitute an accepted part of the community life.

The federal principle is demonstrated by both branches, functional and societal, in the national organizations to which they belong. Once federalized, all these weak little local organizations suddenly gain strength. They now act as a counterbalance in the intricate power network of the nation, throwing their weight in favor of better schools while other interest groups are plunking for lower tariffs, aid to farmers, more liberal labor laws, wildlife conservation and a thousand other things. For ours is a society made up of unnumbered local voluntary organizations, federalized through conventions and national headquarters, and thus powered to affect decisions in Washington.

So far, the system seems designed to breed conflict and not much else. But now comes the phase of interpenetration. Groups acting on each other arouse not only hostility but, often, imitation. Education, once regarded as the sole prerogative of schools and teachers, begins to penetrate other aspects of the society. Labor unions set up their own classes and schools. Industry begins programs of in-training, or pays the tuition of employees who elect to continue their studies. The farm organizations sponsor discussion groups, lectures, documentary films, essay contests.

The same organic process could be followed for any group in our society. The lawyer who belongs to his local bar association (functional), and who serves the Legal Aid Society and his Community Council (both societal) is one of a hundred examples of how Americans cooperate both professionally and civically to further goals which merge the individual with the social. Labor and industry, once thought to be basically antagonistic, are reaching the stage of interpenetration. Unions show an intelligent interest in problems of management; management has learned to get along with the unions. Shorter hours and higher wages resulting from automation will lead towards the stage of fusion, when the difference between the manager and the worker, as measured either by his material possessions, his leisure activities or his attitudes, will grow less and less and finally seem inconsiderable.

A hundred other illustrations rise to the mind to illustrate this organic sixfold process: the political and social activities of a church which once restricted itself pretty much to theology; the history of the political parties, so little distinguishable one from another, often interpenetrating to form new voting coalitions, inevitably mirror images of each other because they must fuse all major political powers within their own structure in order to keep or get power.

Let us take an example of something that is still evolving and, using the theory, predict its course.

Recently there have sprung up all over the land little groups of individuals who, as property-owners in a profit economy, want to put their savings to work. They form investment clubs, pool their funds, get someone to talk to them about stocks and bonds, discuss several likely securities, and every month invest their funds jointly.

Inevitably these groups will federalize. They will have state and national conventions. They will set up an office in Washington or New York—perhaps both. They will begin to bring pressure to bear which will counterbalance the pressures of the big investors, the banks, the large corporations. They will work for special tax privileges for the small investor. But in this very process they will be fusing their interests. As individuals they are workers and consumers, as an association they are investors, as members of the national organization they become a political influence. And contributing as they do to the whole process, they aid and hasten the state of fusion when all these various functions and interests grow less and less distinguishable.

By fusion I do not mean to imply a stable, changeless condition, but rather a tendency. Our society is a changing one; that is its strength. But its basic factors—abundance and full production, ever widening distribution of product and wiping out of differences in income, education and class—make it inevitable that points of view shall interpenetrate increasingly. The sons of the laborer, the minister and the factory owner go to high school together, and even to college. When all who are able to meet the requirements go on to college, education will cease to be a differentiating factor. Interpenetration of ethnic groups as immigrant stocks merge is another instance. Protestant sects federalize; ultimately, perhaps, they will fuse.

The gloom-sayers see in our mechanized society forces which are sterilizing mankind by making him only a cog in a great machine. Romantics masking as realists, they see in the pre-industrial era a satisfaction arising from craftsmanship which has been lost, a security in working for oneself which has evaporated.

Nonsense!

What security had the eighteenth century craftsman against competition, against diseases for which no cures were known, against tyrannous governments? Who wants to return to the twelve-hour day and child labor? The forty (soon the thirty) hour week, social security benefits, unemployment compensation, modern medicine and education have hedged men about with such security as they never dared hope for even fifty years ago. And not only security.

There has been a tendency to romanticize the older community where all functions are performed by the whole group working together, as if it possessed some innate virtue. Voluntary association is the appropriate response to a far more intricate social structure. It offers a means of trying out ideas which may later gain government sponsorship, and thus prevents little errors from becoming big ones.

As interests federalize, counterbalance and interpenetrate, there inevitably results a harmony of understanding even when dissonances of disagreement still sound. Harmonious diversity is the hallmark of American life—a harmony sharpened by dissonance, a diversity held together by counterbalancing powers.

To those who think of a society as a closed system it must appear incredible that American society with all its diverse groups and interests can function at all. The external conformity visitors complain of is the result, not of flat sameness, but of a continuing effort to harmonize conflicting interests, to find and strengthen areas of agreement, to "accentuate the positive." We have made our consensus out of cleavage, and we have built our agreement out of disagreement. No wonder we prize the conformity we have so hardly won! It is not, as observers assume, that we don't know how to be different. We have sunk our differences by great exercise of restraint, in order that we may live peaceably together. If the symbols of our unity appear vague, we can only answer that they have to be to gather us all in. The things in which we conform— as for example our equalitarian manners, our commitment to the economic system—are symbols of a hard-won consensus.

"E pluribus unum" turns out to be more than a phrase on a coin. For in our culture religious and political thought begin to flow together, the private and public become one, national and international interests become indistinguishable, political theory under John Dewey's hands becomes a unique philosophy of education, and idealists find that in a world of abundance and equality their goals are merging with those of the realists.

Equality itself becomes a unifying principle, both a fact and an ideal, a moral imperative and a social reality. From physiology to theology, as Daniel Boorstin remarks in *The Genius of American Politics*, equality is the unifying continuum.

As all these interpenetrations develop, it begins to appear that a new synthesis, a new fusion may be in the making. For as interests overlap more and more, so will motives.

John Dewey phrased the hope this way:

"When philosophy shall have cooperated with the course of events and made clear and coherent the meaning of the daily detail, science and emotion will interpenetrate, practice and imagination will embrace. Poetry and religious feeling will be the unforced flowers of life. To further this articulation and revelation of the meanings of the current course of events is the task and problem of philosophy in days of transition." *

A premise of equality, an instinct for voluntary action strengthened by federalism to provide a needed counterweight in the dynamics of social balance and evolution, a growing interpenetration of interests, standards and attitudes, and a goal never to be reached, like the meeting point of railroad tracks—this is the portrait of a dynamic society. It is also a blueprint for the future, perhaps for other men's futures too, because it solves the dilemma of those who would fuse the social justice of the socialist with the incentive and drive of the democratic capitalist. Already we are riding these two tracks in a train that sways with counterbalancing forces and shudders with the drive of its great motors. Only the reactionaries on both sides believe the ride would be improved by removing one of the rails.

## The Cultural Heritage

This American civilization is a thing of long heredity, for though civilizations falter or mark time, the flow of life goes on. America as much as Europe is heir to Greek democracy, rationalism, love of the beautiful, and the cult of the body. Even in its frankness towards sex, its religious frenzies and its bacchanalia it shows its ancient roots. We are heirs to the Jewish insistence on moral law, the belief in an ordered, God-controlled universe and the sense of being a chosen people. The law of love, of helping one's neighbor and sharing with those in need, and the divine nature of each individual are a precious Christian heritage which we accept as the chief motivating force of our history and the reason of our being.

The Roman love of law and order, the feeling for that mystic unity of all nature which came to us from India through the Transcendentalists, the music and rhythm from Africa, and a sturdiness and enterprise brought to us by immigrants from all parts of the earth where men hungered for justice and a chance to make use of their latent powers—these have all gone into the trough to be kneaded with that yeast of hope and energy which the new world seems to breed.

The men who built the first settlements along the Atlantic coast

* *Reconstruction in Philosophy*, p. 212.

knew what they were doing. Theirs was an experiment consciously undertaken, for as William Bradford expressed it, "as one small candle may light a thousand, so the light here kindled hath shone to many, yea in some sort to our whole nation." Americans still look at their nation as an experiment, just as Lincoln in the Gettysburg address expressed the meaning of the Civil War as a test to see whether government of the people, by the people, for the people could endure.

Industrialism, which separated man from the soil, from a permanent home, from an employment which permitted him a sense of completing what he made, has destroyed or frayed the chains which anchor man to life. It has drained meaning out of the symbols through which the significance of life was apprehended—home, nature, the seasons, the fertile earth.

But in recent years we have been putting that meaning back again. Through the development of the social sciences, the work of John Dewey, the growing social awareness of industry, the consciousness of community needs in the building of new housing developments, the guidance services of the schools and a hundred other ways our culture has been searching for the meaning of human activity, and developing ways to recapture the cooperation of an earlier day.

Americans seem always to have loved teamwork. In its origin team means family, and in our teams, clubs, associations, political parties and all the other group activities of a live community we extend the family pattern outward. Every society rests upon an emotional culture, and since emotions are formed upon childhood associations, a society must base its culture upon family relationships. A community is a social unit to which the family emotional culture has been extended. It is no accident that we call our college alma mater, the church a mother, the nation a fatherland, the secret order a brotherhood. To extend family feeling and symbol to the community, the nation and the world is the logical outcome of democracy, which expects its citizens to become actively engaged in the social process. For democracy, as we have said before, is not simply a form of government; it is a way of life.

"America," said Scott Fitzgerald, "is a willingness of the heart." If this seems sentimental, let us acknowledge that America is that too.

## CHAPTER EIGHTEEN

---

# *The World Community and the United States*

Ever since it burst upon the consciousness of Europe nearly five hundred years ago, America has been thought of as a kind of child wonder—or better, perhaps, as a damsel from the days when knighthood was in flower. Men have dreamed of her, wooed her, fought over her, risked their lives for her, joyed themselves in the possession of her or died in her dangerous embrace. For four hundred years the history of Europe has been troubled, by the passion first to possess her exclusively, and then, at least, to share her favors.

When Spain, with the loss of the Armada in 1588, failed to maintain monogamous control over the new world, it had to share the prize reluctantly with other suitors. But the dream of monogamy, persisting, led to a succession of wars in which France, Spain, England, Holland and several lesser powers stubbornly fought to make an honest lady of this bewitching companion by having her to themselves.

In the end, when Britain had got control of North America and saw no likelihood of capturing the southern continent, it was conveniently discovered that the lady was twins. The one with the colder disposition naturally fell to the British, the warmer to the Latin Spaniards. In time the children born of these unions (Canada excepted) threw over the parents and set up housekeeping for themselves, but they still clearly show their heritage.

The English suitor, who had dreamed of gold and found—in Virginia and New England—little but sand, codfish and a noxious weed known as tobacco, thought he had got the worst of the bargain and for a century or two continued to cast a jealous eye toward the southern twin. But with the new generation it was different. The sternness of this northern land was a challenge to them, its vast empty spaces an inspiration. The tobacco on the great Southern plantations turned out to be worth more than gold. On the little eastern streams rose mills and factories. Westward the little settlements pushed until they at last reached the Pacific. Centuries passed before the body of the land could be occupied and had in possession.

Floods of Europeans, at a risk in many ways as great as that of the early explorers and settlers, poured across the Atlantic, swarmed up the beaches and spread out into the cities and the countryside. The hunger to be nurtured by this provident mother—it was as a mother rather than as a mistress that she appeared in her latter-day respectability—was unabated.

Though this parable of America as the dreamed-of perfect woman —mistress, wife and mother—may seem fanciful, it is precisely the way the early dreamers conceived her. When John Donne, that great Elizabethan, looked for words of highest praise for his mistress, he sang at a moment too intimate to permit any intent of ridicule:

> Oh, my America, my Newfoundland,
> My kingdom, safest when with one man mann'd,
> My mine of precious stones, my empery:
> How am I blest in thus discovering thee!

When Sir Walter Raleigh sought words to describe Guiana, where he hoped to found an English colony, he exclaimed: "Guiana is a country that hath yet her maidenhead, never sacked, turned, nor wrought, the face of the earth hath not been torn, nor the virtue and salt of the soil spent. . . ."

It is Liberty personified as a woman in the harbor of New York which has symbolized America to millions "yearning to breathe free" as Emma Lazarus' poem, in the entrance to the statue, puts it. America is "mother of exiles."

America, then, has been for centuries a source of maidenly charm and motherly nourishment to Europe. America was more than the land of promise—she was the impossible ideal realized, the perfect woman, Goethe's *Ewig-Weibliche*.

In the twentieth century America has continued in her role of nourishing mother, for her body continues to pour out such bounty that it can be shared with the peoples of the earth. But recently—especially since the end of what we hope we may call the last World War—a change has come over the mother image.

America, as the United States of America, has turned masculine. His is now the mailed fist and he now does the wooing. The American—after resisting for centuries any alliance with Europe—suddenly turns up as a suitor for Europe's hand, insisting on his right to marry her in order that he may protect her. The larger the dowry, naturally, the more the wooed one tends to hold back. Does the suitor harbor some evil design, or will he, like one of those medieval knights, turn out to be some horrible dragon in disguise?

To the richly cultured people of Europe, accustomed to thinking of America in its feminine role, the shift is unsettling. They do not relish being thrust into skirts after wearing the pants so long—a shift which might be equated with that from creditor to debtor status. They do not like to see their ideal woman appear suddenly with beard, muscles and armor.

If this account of the love affair between Europe and America seems trivial, it should be remembered that the strongest thoughts men have are those which come most forcefully home to them in human, symbolic terms.

## The Quest for Peace

So long as the American image was maternal, the world was willing to accept the moral role we played. We stood for revolution against tyranny, self-determination of all peoples, the rights of the individual, a democratic form of government, justice and equality for all. For many years we were the world's conscience, condemning aggression, inspiring the struggle for freedom everywhere, offering asylum to patriots who had to flee into exile, supporting independence movements with American dollars. At the same time we tried to stay aloof from the world's quarrels, following the advice of Washington and the principle of the Monroe Doctrine.

Although we did leap thoughtlessly into war with Spain and found ourselves suddenly stretched out across the Pacific to the Philippines, we took a rather shamefaced attitude towards our deviation into imperialism, never called our acquisitions colonies, and soon began talking about preparing the Philippines for independence. When we became tangled with the European brand of imperialism, as in the Boxer Rebellion in China, we returned our share of the indemnity for the education of Chinese students in the United States.

The Good Neighbor policy towards the other Americas, carried forward in the many treaties and conventions with other American countries, the carrying out of our plan for making the Philippines independent, our sympathy with colonial peoples because we had once been colonial, our virtually divesting ourselves of naval power in 1920 and 1921 as proof of our peaceful intentions, our forswearing the use of force even for the protection of our own interests (at the Montevideo conference of 1933 and the Buenos Aires conference of 1936), our agreeing not to fortify Guam or the Philippines (1922 and 1930)—these and many other acts demonstrated a desire for peace and the independence of small nations so strong that we would willingly surrender sizable parts of our own strength, and security to make them possible.

In the thirties we tried by reciprocal trade treaties to foster a healthy world economy. By 1939 Cordell Hull could report that nineteen countries, representing three-fifths of all world trade, had entered into agreements with us. Though this failed to breach the high tariff wall, it did reverse its upward trend.

Meanwhile we had entered into one scheme after another designed to guarantee peace. Futile and even tragically wrong-headed as these actions may now appear, they demonstrated a deep-seated feeling among Americans that war was a crime, to be avoided at any cost except the loss of our basic freedoms and our form of government. "There never was a good war or a bad peace" became an American axiom.

In 1928 we signed the Kellogg-Briand pact which, developing out of the American peace movement, pledged us and fifty-nine other nations to the outlawing of war. While aggressors were arming again, we blamed our munitions makers for World War I, limiting our own freedom of action by the Neutrality Act which actually encouraged Hitler and Japan by assuring them we would not arm their intended victims. From the seizure of Manchuria to the invasion of Poland, American determination to stay out of war, by emboldening the aggressors led straight to world conflict.

Throughout the period between world wars we tried to substitute a moralistic-legalistic approach for the realities of world power. We refused to recognize the important role played by economic factors, raising tariffs and thus preventing our former allies from paying their debts. We encouraged Japanese aggression by excluding her emigrants and refusing to buy her goods, thus forcing her to find other markets and other sources of raw materials.

Embarrassed by our power, we avoided our international responsibilities. Our attempt to end drunkenness by outlawing alcohol and to end war by outlawing arms came from that same Calvinist instinct which hoped to conquer sin by enunciating the moral law. Those who criticize the moral approach, however, should recognize that without this hatred of aggression, public opinion would hardly have supported the build-up against the aggressors which finally took place.

To an extent seen in no other country, diplomacy depends upon popular support. There is no governing class, no diplomatic elite. Since the people cannot be expected to know all the complications of our tremendously extended international relations, issues must be presented to them in an idiom they can readily grasp. Hence the lofty, moralistic tone so irritating to our friends overseas. But hence also the necessity that our diplomacy remain on the side of the weak, the small nation, the people seeking independence, peace, and a developing economy which will give them a fairer share of the product.

## Second World War and After

After war broke out again in Europe and France had fallen, we joined with our natural ally, Great Britain, to assert in the Atlantic Charter the same principles of freedom, independence and economic and social rights which had always been our guide, no matter how far short we might have fallen in attaining them.

By war's end, we had contributed $90 billion in Lend Lease aid, in addition to supplying our own troops. In an effort to befriend Russia and make her welcome in the family of nations, we even violated the Atlantic Charter and our own ideals, giving in on such

items as the Baltic states, Poland's eastern frontier, and Russian influence in the Balkans and Manchuria. When Russia was being
driven far into her own borders by Hitler's armies, we might have
withheld aid until it was asked for and then given it on our own
terms. But we chose the more generous, and as we believed the
more honorable course.

When the war ended we hastily dismantled our army, abolished
controls, closed our wartime agencies and turned with relief to
what we supposed would be an era of well-merited tranquility. We
offered to share atomic energy with the world, and in the Acheson-
Lilienthal proposal for outlawing atomic war made an immense con-
cession in the hope of establishing peace. But the Russian government rejected our offer, proposing a mere joke in its place.

Meanwhile the Russians went busily to work to extend their
empire. They absorbed the Baltic States, sovietized East Germany,
seized control of Poland, Czechoslovakia, Hungary, Bulgaria, Ru-
mania and Albania, adding 392,000 square miles to their domain and
ninety million people to their subject population. At the same time
the United States was completing its pledge to give full independence to the Philippines and Great Britain consented to the independence of India, Pakistan, Ceylon and Burma. Indonesia gained
independence from the Netherlands. These changes gave freedom
to 555,000,000 people and 2,894,000 square miles of territory.

The United States had previously initiated conferences which led
to the establishment of the United Nations. Americans hoped that
this body would succeed where the League of Nations had failed
in maintaining international peace and security. But Russia's determination to swallow up her neighbors and subvert governments
in distant places made this impossible. It also became clear that she
had no more desire to cooperate in the economic sphere (through
the various UN agencies) than in the political.

In 1947 when Great Britain announced that she could no longer
continue financial and military assistance to Turkey and Greece,
we had to face the fact that our power imposed upon us a responsibility we could no longer evade. With the Truman Doctrine,
American foreign policy finally made its great shift. No longer
could we delude ourselves with the dream of withdrawing into our
own comfortable borders. No longer could be expect Britain to

patrol the seas and maintain a balance of power, or the United Nations to deal with every emergency. As long as Russian power was committed to a policy of imperialist expansion and the creation of unrest and revolt, ours was the only power which could counterbalance it.

"It must be the policy of the United States to support free peoples who are resisting attempted subjugation by armed minorities or by outside pressures." That was the essence of the Truman Doctrine.

To deal with the economic crises in Europe we came up with the Marshall Plan, the most extensive offer of economic aid ever made by one country to others. Its aim was not to make the beneficiary countries feel obligated, but to make it possible for them to pursue their own best interests. Our own self-interest was also involved, since we now recognized that a healthy economy throughout the free world was essential to our own safety.

Also in 1947 we joined ourselves with the other countries of the Western Hemisphere in a defensive alliance, and strengthened our armed services by creating the Department of Defense. In the following years we extended our alliances to include Europe and the Pacific.

After the communist coup in Czechoslovakia in 1948, made possible by a powerful Russian force close to the border, we realized that we could no longer avoid building up our defenses. Russia, on the basis of population, had a military force three and a half times greater than ours.

Then came the attack on Korea. Now it was clear that communist leaders were ready to risk war anywhere around the world in their plan for control. By prompt American action, immediately backed up by the United Nations, that threat was met.

Although the United States was born in a war to end its own colonial status, and in South America, the Philippines, and elsewhere has been the champion of those who seek independence, the communist rulers of Russia while busily gobbling up independent nations all around them have tried to make it appear that the United States favors colonialism. It is true that where we were trying to build up our allies in Europe, we stepped lightly with regard to colonial areas like Algeria where the interests of Algerian-born

Europeans had to be considered. Yet any impartial review of the last ten years will show that while the Western powers have been aiding the independence of peoples, Russia has been enslaving them, or where they proved resistant, wiping them out.

Having at last learned the hard way that aggressors are not deterred by seeing their opponents disarm, the American people have finally committed themselves to a policy of curbing aggression by maintaining sufficient military power of their own and sharing economic power with their friends, in order to guarantee the independence of all those opposed to the Soviet design for world control. Yet to their surprise, once they had made this difficult and expensive decision, they found that their motives were mistrusted. Having learned at last that they had an obligation to prevent war by maintaining their power—a thing they had been accused of failing to do before both World Wars—they now found themselves branded as warmongers for doing it!

Still attached to their old dream of a world in which war should be no more, they had tried repeatedly for disarmament agreements —first to outlaw atomic warfare, then to establish an inspection program of military installations without which disarmament would be folly. Years of patient negotiation brought only one result: evidence that Russia would not agree to any bona fide inspection plan.

The United States could stand on its record, for it had never plotted aggression as the Soviet had designed its attack on Finland and Poland, and it was remarkably free of those deals at the expense of a third power which had been so frequent in old-style diplomacy. (Even in the Yalta agreement on Russia's influence in Manchuria, which shamed most Americans, China eventually gave more than the United States had undertaken to recommend to her.)

War brings the kind of regimentation, debt, high taxes and destruction of material wealth which seem criminal to a culture valuing high productivity. As for the argument that industry is warminded because of the fat profits that result, it could be pointed out that under the American system of renegotiation of war contracts, $10,431,637,000 had been returned to the government during and after the Second World War. Remaining profits were still subject to taxes as high as ninety-five per cent of the excess over normal peacetime profits. Then the profits which went to individuals were taxed again under an income tax that rose steeply in the higher brackets.

Dealing with an opponent who regards armed aggression as a political tool, the American people are at a disadvantage, since they will never be able to think in that fashion. They must always wait for the opponent to make the first move, because they do not believe in war as an instrument of policy and no American government could keep the support of the people if it followed such a policy.

Since we have always (for reasons explained) seen our position in the world as a moral one, it comes very hard to us to accept as allies governments whose internal policies are opposed to the freedoms we believe in. Yet there is no alternative if Soviet power is to be contained, just as there was no alternative to accepting Russia as an ally while Hitler and Mussolini were riding high.

At the same time we have to follow a foreign policy which will have the support at home of a people drawn from all parts of the earth. Foreign language groups may make special demands, as the Co-ordinating Committee of American Polish Associations did when it asked that we withdraw our recognition of all the Soviet satellite governments and recognize the governments in exile. Labor, business, agriculture, veterans, women and religious groups all have an interest in foreign affairs and continuously make themselves heard in Washington.

Contending forces are also at work on our immigration policy. Alarmed by the flood of immigrants coming into the country in the first two decades of the century, apparently faster than they could be assimilated, Congress passed a number of restrictive laws. The latest of these, the McCarran-Walter Act of 1952, has tended to shut out unfortunate and deserving people who in the past had looked to the United States as their only refuge from poverty and oppression. It has also considerably dimmed the world image of the United States as a champion of the oppressed.

Bills to revise the present act have frequently been introduced with the support of the Administration and of many religious, civic, educational and labor groups which have testified in favor of a more liberal immigration policy. Special arrangements were made to admit refugees from the communist terror in Hungary. But immigration policy, in view of world conditions, will probably be a live issue for years to come.

All these difficulties are to be expected in a nation which was able to live happily without a foreign policy for over a hundred years, and which is being forced to learn overnight lessons that in older countries have been studied for centuries. We have achieved a considerable degree of bipartisanship in foreign policy, and our people have committed their moral and material resources to a continuing struggle to raise the standards of living and of liberty throughout the world.

Until 1946 neutralism was our prevailing fault. Finally awakened, we see the same attitude in countries like India and are shocked by it. Yet India is merely living through the same stage we remained in after our struggle for independence was ended, and our only thought was to build the land we had won.

Because we have assumed great risks and tensions at great cost to ourselves, we have supposed that such effort would bring at least the reward of affection or respect. It therefore comes as a shock to find that even our allies harshly criticize our way of life, doubt our abilities and resent our strength. We find Europe demanding of us an exceptionally high standard of behavior and yet apparently delighted when we fall from grace. As P. G. Worsthorne * points out, Europe expects the United States to be both shield and conscience at the same time, or to be whichever European convenience dictates. So Great Britain wanted us to assert our anti-colonial principles in Indo-China, but in Iran to forget idealism and support British policy.

Another difficulty American diplomacy has to contend with is the necessity (which our government approves in principle) of conducting all its negotiations on a fully lighted stage, before a press which naturally stresses conflict and disagreement, viewing each situation as a victory or defeat for the United States. Yet diplomacy of necessity means compromise. Fuller reporting of the impressive accomplishments of all the UN agencies would help to foster faith in negotiation.

* In *Encounter*, III (Nov. 1954), pp. 15-22.

*Bold New Program*

The threat of aggression, first in one spot and then in another, has made the United States stress military alliances and expenditures instead of economic aid. Even so, economic aid since the war comes to more than $56 billion, a sum so huge that one can hardly conceive its meaning. Private investments abroad add another $10 billion. Too often the money has been siphoned off by profiteers in the country which was to be benefited. Too often it has been given to nations having alliances with us instead of to other underdeveloped countries equally in need of aid. Yet nothing else like it can be found in human history.

The stimulus given to European industry has resulted in an output seventy per cent greater than before the war. American tourists and soldiers add another $3.2 billion a year, and the results are felt in every European home. Britain's noted economist Barbara Ward asserts that the aid programs established the American claim to world leadership "and hence held together the unity of free men."

As a report to Harold E. Stassen, then Director of the Foreign Operations Administration, points out, technical cooperation is only a fancy name for a habit developed on the American frontier, where the knowledge accumulated in the settled areas was adapted to new conditions through voluntary cooperation. Then this frontier too became settled, passing on its knowledge to the next. It is in this spirit that the Point Four projects bring together American technical experts with those in other countries on a basis of voluntary cooperation.

The results are seen in a lake of lush green grass on a barren, sun-baked desert in the Hashemite Kingdom of the Jordan, in the fivefold increase of a wheat harvest in India, in farm demonstration programs in Iran, in village improvement projects which have taught cooperative methods, raised production, and brought health services and safe drinking water to farming communities all the way from Bolivia to Lebanon, Pakistan and Thailand.

"Point Four," says the description of the program in Lebanon, "is the vehicle on which scientific knowledge, technical invention and material progress become traveling companions with American ideals, American hopes and American aspirations for achieving real brotherhood among men."

Though smaller in scope, the many voluntary projects, sponsored by churches and by such associations as CARE and World Neighbors, are impressive because they are an expression of the instinctive desire of the American people to share their good fortune and their technical skills.

Paul Rusch, an American who before the war taught in an Episcopal university in Tokyo, is a good example. Returning to Japan after the war, he was impressed with the apparently hopeless problem of a rising population and a limited food supply. After raising funds himself, he began a very modest rural experiment at the little mountain village of Kiyosato. His idea was to see what could be done with mountain land hitherto unproductive. Today KEEP (Kiyosato Educational Experiment Project) grows nineteen kinds of vegetables and seven grains, has herds of Hereford and Jersey cattle and a modern dairy, as well as thousands of chickens. American friends donated the first cows and chickens. Each farmer who got ten chickens promised to hatch ten eggs and to pass ten healthy chicks on to another farmer.

A church, a lending library and a well equipped hospital now serve a people who a few years ago lived on the narrow edge of subsistence. Best of all, the people of Kiyosato have learned how to help themselves by helping each other. Gangs of 200 cooperate to open new roads. A vigorous 4-H movement is under way. When a home for infirm men ran short of food, four hundred farm children each bearing a single potato, came and filled four bushel baskets as their gift. In five years the community advanced further than in the previous five centuries. Thousands of visitors came to see what was happening, and similar projects have now sprung up in other parts of mountainous Japan.

Another man with an idea was Clifford Clinton, whose Meals for Millions markets a cheap multi-purpose food in needy areas without profit.

In Flagstaff, Arizona—a small city of eight thousand in the vast arid area of the West—the newspaper announces that a local citizen will add a dollar to every dollar contributed to CARE during the month of November. And each of these dollars will send twenty-two pounds of American farm products—milk powder, cheese, rice, beans, flour, and corn meal—to a refugee or jobless family in one of nineteen critical areas overseas.

"Here's an opportunity to feed hungry people and prove our friendship to those overseas," the editor comments. The people of Flagstaff will never see the people who get those packages. Yet they will feel good about contributing. More than fifty other voluntary relief agencies are sending aid abroad. The ten largest spent over $162,000,000 during the first six months of 1956.

World Neighbors, born out of the sermon of a minister who told his people that a program of Christian action based on individual contributions was the only answer to communism, is operating pilot programs of health, education and agriculture in Asia and Africa. It goes only where it is wanted, and it specializes in helping rural villagers to help themselves, by demonstrating better methods of farming, crafts, hygiene, child care.

World Literacy, Inc. offers the special techniques of Dr. Frank Laubach to teach adults how to read and thus to master a tool which will help them improve their farming and health practices. The Foster Parents Plan for War Children, Save the Children Federation, the National Committee for a Free Europe, the Crusade for Freedom, the International Rescue Committee and many other organizations are collecting huge sums in voluntary contributions to be used overseas.

Much might be achieved if more American voluntary associations would follow the lead of the labor unions, the learned societies, and service clubs like Rotary, combining with their opposite numbers in other countries to form world associations. Diplomatic relations among governments can never provide the intimacy of contact which is needed for world understanding, and there will never be a true world community until millions of people, meeting and exchanging ideas, form the human, emotional ties which alone can provide it.

Let us imagine that such exchanges, more and more of them, go on for twenty, thirty, fifty years. Is it not likely that the prejudices and hostilities which now keep people apart may dissolve as did the prejudices which kept the American people apart during the period of the Confederation? And is it not imaginable that this voluntary working together of peoples may produce associations capable of controlling and influencing the United Nations as our national associations now control and influence the government of the United States?

## A New World Culture?

In a world where crisis has become a constant, what can the United States do to foster a true sense of community?

The Chinese character for crisis combines two other characters— danger and opportunity. Never in human history have the two been more poignantly combined. Now, with the means of grace and the hope of glory in our grasp, we find the way stopped by a conflict which is made by man, not any longer by insuperable barriers of hunger and disease.

As Chester Bowles has pointed out, "The four revolutionary principles which so largely motivate the people of the Middle World" are "national independence, human dignity, economic advancement and peace." It is hard to see how any impartial student would have any difficulty deciding on which side of the iron curtain these motives have the best chance of survival.

We, unlike Marxists, have no patent medicine of social reform guaranteed to cure all ills. But in this very fact the strength of democracy lies, for since we do not seek to impose our particular system upon others, but only to create the conditions of health and economic prosperity which will allow a people to seek their own goals, we are able to offer help without slipping handcuffs onto the hand we grasp. We cannot foment revolution from without as Russia can, because our history has convinced us that social and economic improvement come only from within, through political action based upon a constitution which guarantees human rights. Our history does afford, however, a blueprint for a permanent revolution of constantly rising standards for more and more people —more and better food, health, leisure, education, equality and opportunity.

Respect for the United States abroad depends very heavily upon how we meet our own problems at home—how we handle delinquency and crime, slums and the ugly slag that boils up to the surface of our industrial civilization, whether we give equal protection and benefit to all our citizens, whether we have the maturity and responsibility which our position in the world demands. Nothing we say about international friendship will equal in its impact what we do here at home.

Americans, in their eagerness to share with others, too often make the embarrassing assumption that our role is to "teach democracy" to the world. Those who have fought for their freedom in France and Indonesia, in Greece and Finland do not need to be "taught." Nor should we insist that everyone must choose between the United States and Russia. We had our century and more of isolation, and even if a more horrible threat looms over the world now than in those days, we must sympathize with those who want to be excused from the power struggle in order to work out their own destinies. We cannot expect to see our institutions transplanted to foreign soil. We can hope to exchange methods and attitudes.

The whole world gladly embraces the scientific method of the West, as well as its standards of universal education, government by law, public health, social security, and individual rights combined with governmental responsibility for the welfare of the people. But Western civilization has much to learn from other cultures.

The concentration on an all-embracing, immediately apprehended esthetic continuum characterizes the East. It sees time as a still pool rather than as a moving river. Where the West tries to analyse all experience, the East sees all things as in part indeterminate. Therefore the wise man does not commit himself, for in committing himself to a specific course he closes off a line of retreat if events change. This point of view has an important bearing on world politics.

The great task of our time is to achieve an outlook which will harmonize the higher standard of living of the most scientifically advanced and theoretically guided Western nations with the universal sensitivity to the beautiful, the abiding equanimity and sense of spirituality and identity of the East.

Ever since the American Transcendentalists attacked materialism and drew upon the spiritual resources of the East, there has been a quiet but continuing interest in Oriental thought and art among us. Oriental motifs have appeared in American art ever since the days when clipper ships brought treasures back from China. The Japanese influence on painting and particularly on architecture is widespread and growing. Religions of the Orient are the basis for a number of sects. Oriental studies have advanced rapidly in all the large universities. The increasing numbers of soldiers and travelers who have seen the East bring back at least a partial understanding of civilizations which were once known to the general public only through books or pictures. In Hawaii East and West have met and merged on many levels. There, on American soil, the two approaches to life are being blended.

Through travel and a continuing flow of information made available to all through the mass media, Americans are more closely in touch with the world than ever before. Labor, farm, youth, women's and service organizations devote a good deal of time to bringing the facts about foreign affairs to their members. Pick up any magazine of a service club or union nowadays and you will find at least one, and perhaps several, articles on world affairs. These organizations provide a basis for a broad consensus on foreign affairs which will influence Congress and support the administration. There is solid evidence that the great fluctuations in American public opinion are a thing of the past.

The American pattern of individualism, voluntarism and federalism is clearly moving forward with the American sense of responsibility and involvement in the world community. Individual concerns such as those of Paul Rusch and Clifford Clinton, realized through voluntary group action, and the federalist principle seen in the UN and its allied organizations are signs of the times. Ours is a world in which the balance of power is in the long view less important than the interpenetration of cultures which is leading towards a new world civilization, towards a balance between the analysis of science and the synthesis of art, towards the raising of material standards so that all men may have the fullest enjoyment of their intellectual and spiritual heritage.

In the 1920s security in the United States meant a bond or a stock, as George Soule has noted. In the thirties it meant protection against poverty in old age. In the forties it meant a world made safe from dictators. In the fifties it has often come to mean the protection of state secrets from a potential enemy. In the sixties it can mean, if we make the most of our capabilities, a life made secure by creative and purposeful activity.

The seeds of that life are already sown. We have created an open society, always tinkering with its institutions in the hope of improvement, tense with the pressure of its onward movement yet informal and friendly, sustained by its conflicts and contradictions as much as by its agreements, driven by faith in the future, angered at present injustices, yet ever renewed with a strength which is spiritual and mental as well as physical and material. Its vitality is in part a product of its youth, its optimism a product of its abundance.

Perhaps the best that may be said of it is that its tone is positive rather than negative, hopeful rather than despairing, loving rather than hating. It does not seek to destroy, but to build. It does not seek to set class against class but to wipe out class distinctions. It does not seek to adjust differences by redistributing the insufficient goods of the world, but by raising production to heights that will provide for all a plenty only the few once had. Accustomed through the centuries of its growth to a life which was sustained only by neighborly cooperation, it has now accepted the fact that the new neighborhood is the world.

# Select Bibliography

Allen, Frederick Lewis. *The Big Change*. New York, 1952.

Almond, Gabriel A. *The American People and Foreign Policy*. New York, 1950.

American Assembly. *United States Agriculture: Perspectives and Prospects*. New York, 1955.

Antin, Mary. *They Who Knock at Our Gates*. Boston, 1914.

Bailey, Stephen K. and Samuel, Howard D. *Congress at Work*. New York, 1952.

Barnes, Harry Elmer and Ruedi, Oreen M. *The American Way of Life*. New York, 1949.

Barnouw, Erik. *Mass Communication*. New York, 1956.

Barzun, Jacques. *God's Country and Mine*. Boston, 1954.

———. *Music in American Life*. New York, 1956.

———. *Teacher in America*. Boston, 1945.

Beard, Charles A. and Mary R. *The American Spirit*. New York, 1942.

Binkley, Wilfred E. *American Political Parties*. New York, 1943.

Blegen, Theodore C., ed. *Land of Their Choice*. Minneapolis, 1955.

Blesh, Rudi. *Modern Art USA*. New York, 1956.

Boorstin, Daniel J. *The Genius of American Politics*. Chicago, 1953.

Boulding, Kenneth E. *The Organizational Revolution*. New York, 1953.

Bowers, Claude. *Jefferson and Hamilton*. Boston, 1925.

Brogan, D. W. *The American Character*. New York, 1944.

Brownell, Baker. *The Human Community*. New York, 1950.

Bryce, James. *The American Commonwealth*. New York, 1900 (abridged).

Bush, Vannevar. *Science the Endless Frontier*. Washington, 1945.

Chafee, Zechariah, Jr. *The Blessings of Liberty*. Philadelphia, 1956.

Chapin, F. Stuart. *Contemporary American Institutions*. New York, 1935.

Chase, Stuart. *The Proper Study of Mankind*. New York, 1948.

———. *Roads to Agreement*. New York, 1951.

Childs, Marquis W. and Cater, Douglas. *Ethics in a Business Society*. New York, 1954.

Commager, Henry Steele, ed. *America in Perspective*. New York, 1947.

———. *The American Mind*. New Haven, 1950.

Conant, James B. *Modern Science and Modern Man*. New York, 1952.

Cooke, Alistair. *One Man's America*. New York, 1952.

Cowley, Malcolm. *The Literary Situation*. New York, 1954.

Coyle, David Cushman. *The United States Political System*. New York, 1954.

Curti, Merle. *The Growth of American Thought*. New York, 1943.

Denison, J. H. *Emotion as the Basis of Civilization*. New York, 1928.

Dewey, John. *Reconstruction in Philosophy*. New York, 1920.

Dewhurst, J. Frederic and associates. *America's Needs and Resources— A New Survey*. New York, 1955.

Douglas, William O. *Being an American*. New York, 1948.

Edman, Irwin, ed. *John Dewey*. New York, 1955.

Elliott, Mabel A. and Merrill, Francis E. *Social Disorganization*. New York, 1941.

Ewen, David. *Twentieth Century Music*. New York, 1952.

Ferguson, Charles W. *Fifty Million Brothers*. New York, 1937.

Fitch, James Marston. *American Building*. Boston, 1948.

Flanders, Ralph E. *Letter to a Generation*. Boston, 1956.

Ford Foundation. *Report of the Study for the Ford Foundation on Policy and Program*. 1949.

*Fortune*, Editors of. *The Art of Success*. Philadelphia, 1956.

———. *The Fabulous Future*. New York, 1956.

———. *U. S. A. the Permanent Revolution*. New York, 1951.

Galbraith, John Kenneth. *American Capitalism*. Boston, 1952.

Gardiner, Harold C. *Fifty Years of the American Novel*. New York, 1952.

Goldman, Eric F. *Rendezvous with Destiny. A History of Modern American Reform*. New York, 1952.

Gorer, Geoffrey. *The American People*. New York, 1948.

Gunther, John. *Inside U. S. A.* New York, 1947.

Handlin, Oscar. *The Uprooted*. Boston, 1951.

Hansen, Marcus Lee. *The Immigrant in American History*. Cambridge, Mass., 1940.

Hart, James D. *The Popular Book*. New York, 1950.

Hartz, Louis. *The Liberal Tradition in America*. New York, 1955.

*Higher Education for American Democracy. A Report of the President's Commission on Higher Education*. New York, 1948.

Hoffman, Frederick J. *The Modern Novel in America 1900–1950*. Chicago, 1951.

Hofstadter, Richard. *The Age of Reform*. New York, 1955.

Hollingshead, August B. *Elmtown's Youth*. New York, 1949.

Howard, John Tasker. *Our American Music*. New York, 1946.

Johnson, Gerald W. *Our English Heritage*. Philadelphia, 1949.

Kennan, George F. *American Diplomacy 1900–1950*. Chicago, 1951.

Kluckhohn, Clyde. *Mirror for Man*. New York, 1949.

Langer, Susanne K. *Philosophy in a New Key*. Cambridge, Mass., 1942.
Laski, Harold J. *The American Democracy*. New York, 1948.
Lazarsfeld, Paul F. *The People's Choice*. New York, 1948.
Linton, Ralph. *The Study of Man*. New York, 1936.
Lippmann, Walter. *The Good Society*. Boston, 1937.
———. *U. S. Foreign Policy: Shield of the Republic*. Boston, 1943.
Lubell, Samuel. *The Future of American Politics*. New York, 1952.
———. *Revolt of the Moderates*. New York, 1956.
Lynd, Robert S. *Knowledge for What?* Princeton, 1939.
Lynd, Robert S. and Helen. *Middletown*. New York, 1929.
———. *Middletown in Transition*. New York, 1937.
Macdonald, Dwight. *The Ford Foundation: The Men and the Millions*. New York, 1956.
McNickle, D'Arcy. *They Came Here First*. Philadelphia, 1949.
Maurer, Herrymon. *Great Enterprise: Growth and Behavior of the Big Corporation*. New York, 1955.
Mead, Margaret. *And Keep your Powder Dry*. New York, 1942.
———. *Male and Female*. New York, 1949.
Mencken, H. L. *The American Language*. New York, 1921.
Mills, C. Wright. *White Collar*. New York, 1951.
Mowrer, Edgar Ansel. *The Nightmare of American Foreign Policy*. New York, 1948.
Mumford, Lewis. *The Culture of Cities*. New York, 1938.
Muntz, Earl E. *Urban Sociology*. New York, 1938.
Myrdal, Gunnar. *An American Dilemma*. New York, 1944.
Newcomer, Mabel. *The Big Business Executive*. New York, 1955.
Nisbet, Robert A. *The Quest for Community*. New York, 1953.
Northrop, F. S. C. *The Meeting of East and West*. New York, 1946.
Perkins, Dexter. *The American Approach to Foreign Policy*. Cambridge, Mass., 1952.
Peterson, Florence. *American Labor Unions*. New York, 1952.
Potter, David M. *People of Plenty*. Chicago, 1952.
Powdermaker, Hortense. *Hollywood the Dream Factory*. Boston, 1950.
Rappard, W. E. *The Secret of American Prosperity*. New York, 1955.
Redding, J. Saunders. *They Came in Chains*. Philadelphia, 1950.
Riesman, David. *Individualism Reconsidered*. New York, 1954 and 1955.
——— with Nathan Glazer and Reuel Denney. *The Lonely Crowd*. New Haven, 1950, and Garden City, 1955.
Rossiter, Clinton. *The American Presidency*. New York, 1956.
Rosten, Leo C. *Hollywood*. New York, 1941.
———. *Religions of America*. New York, 1955.
Santayana, George. *Character and Opinion in the United States*. New York, 1921.
Seldes, Gilbert. *Writing for Television*. New York, 1953.
Slichter, Sumner H. *The American Economy*. New York, 1950.

Sly, John Fairfield. *Town Government in Massachusetts*. Cambridge, Mass., 1930.
Smith, Bradford. *Bradford of Plymouth*. Philadelphia, 1951.
————. *A Dangerous Freedom*. Philadelphia, 1954.
Smith, Henry Nash. *Virgin Land. The American West as Symbol and Myth*. Cambridge, Mass., 1950.
Smith, Lillian. *Killers of the Dream*. New York, 1949.
Soule, George. *Economic Forces in American History*. New York, 1952.
————. *Men, Wages and Employment*. New York, 1954.
————. *Time for Living*. New York, 1955.
Spectorsky, A. C. *The Exurbanites*. Philadelphia, 1955.
Stearns, Marshall. *The Story of Jazz*. New York, 1956.
Stern, Frederick Martin. *Capitalism in America*. New York, 1951.
Sward, Keith. *The Legend of Henry Ford*. New York, 1948.
Terry, Walter. *The Dance in America*. New York, 1956.
Thorp, Willard, Curti, Merle and Baker, Carlos. *American Issues. Volume One: the Social Background*. Philadelphia, 1955.
Tocqueville, Alexis de. *Democracy in America*. (Page references are to 1-volume abridged Mentor Edition, New York, 1956.)
Truman, David B. *The Governmental Process*. New York, 1951.
Turner, Frederick Jackson. *The Frontier in American History*. New York, 1920.
Veblen, Thorstein. *The Higher Learning*. New York, 1919.
Ware, Caroline F., ed. *The Cultural Approach to History*. New York, 1940.
Warfel, Harry R. *American Novelists of Today*. New York, 1951.
Warner, W. Lloyd. *American Life*. Chicago, 1953.
———— and Abegglen, James. *Big Business Leaders in America*. New York, 1955.
Warner, W. Lloyd and Lunt, Paul S. *The Social Life of a Modern Community* (Yankee City Series). New Haven, 1941.
————. *The Status System of a Modern Community*. New Haven, 1942.
White, Morton G. *Social Thought in America*. New York, 1949.
Whyte, William H., Jr. *The Organization Man*. New York, 1956.
Wiener, Norbert. *The Human Use of Human Beings*. Boston, 1950.
Williams, Robin M., Jr. *American Society*. New York, 1952.
Wish, Harvey. *Contemporary America*. New York, 1945.
Wolfenstein, Martha and Leites, Nathan. *Movies A Psychological Study*. Glencoe, Ill., 1950.
Woodward, C. Vann. *The Strange Career of Jim Crow*. New York, 1955.
Young, Roland. *This is Congress*. New York, 1946.

For general reference the following were frequently consulted:
    *The Book of the States*. Chicago, 1956.
    *The Columbia Encyclopedia*, New York, 1950.

*Economic Almanac 1956.* New York, 1956.
*Economic Forces in the U. S. A. in Facts and Figures.* Washington, 1955.
*Encyclopedia of American History* (ed. Richard B. Morris). New York, 1953.
*Historical Statistics of the United States.* Washington, 1949.
*Statistical Abstract of the United States 1956.* Washington, 1956.
*The World Almanac.* New York, 1956.

# Index